The Industrialization of Intelligence

The Industrialization of Intelligence

Mind and Machine in the Modern Age

Noah Kennedy

UNWIN

HYMAN

LONDON   SYDNEY   WELLINGTON

First published in Great Britain by the Trade Division
of Unwin Hyman Limited, 1989

UNWIN HYMAN LIMITED
15–17 Broadwick Street, London W1V 1FP, UK

Allen & Unwin (Australia) Pty Ltd,
8 Napier Street, North Sydney, NSW 2060, Australia

Allen & Unwin (New Zealand) Ltd in association with the
Port Nicholson Press Ltd,
Compusales Building, 75 Ghuznee Street, Wellington 1, New Zealand

British Library Cataloguing in Publication Data

Kennedy, Noah
   The industrialization of intelligence
1. Society. Role of computer system
I. Title
303.4'834
ISBN 0-04-440345-3

Typeset in 10 on 12 point Garamond and printed in Great Britain
at The University Press, Cambridge

Dei gratia

Contents

Acknowledgements

Among the pleasures I have encountered in writing this book is this opportunity to pause and thank those individuals who were so selfless and helpful to me.

Richard Osborne, Patricia Motzkin and Richard Feldman studiously read and commented on large segments of the book in draft, and their comments on presentation and content alike were invaluable. Bill Kennedy and Rod Glasgow also read draft chapters and offered searching comments and creative suggestions relating to mathematical and logical theory that greatly contributed to the finished product, and gave me some modicum of confidence that I had handled these concepts correctly.

In addition to being an opportunity to deal with these old friends, the book served as a wonderful excuse to contact complete strangers to solicit their opinions and insights. This is a task that predictably confronts one with folks who for various reasons simply cannot be bothered, but the distress caused by the occasional rebuff was more than mitigated by the more frequent response one received from researchers who were most generous with their time and were admirably patient in communicating a bit of their understanding to a neophyte. My particular thanks to Professors Daniel Matt of the Graduate Theological Union; John Searle, Richard M. Karp and John L. Rhodes of the University of California, Berkeley; George Sheridan of the University of Oregon; Paul Bezucha of Amherst, and to Rita Adrosko of the Smithsonian Institution, Dennis Hehrer of Ford Aerospace, William Inmon of Data Dialogs and Jean Huchard, an independent scholar of weaving technique in Lyons. I regret that much of what we discussed could not be made to fit into this single book, and hope that these fine minds and generous spirits will not be too shocked at the way their thoughts have found their way into the text.

Dr Louis Mosnier's thoughtful and exceedingly patient translations of French and German texts were critical to my avoiding some rather frightening misconceptions on some points of fact and to broadening my perspective on other critical issues. Ken Caldwell, who assisted me in research, was an astonishing fount of information who, fortunately for this author, has thoroughly mastered the art of 'just in time'. Brad Bunnin served me as legal counsel in the finest sense of the phrase and in addition was most generous in helping me get my project off the ground. Michael Pountney, my editor at Unwin Hyman, displayed admirable patience and calm as the work was being produced and his comments were a model of economy and pith.

Acknowledgments

Connie Griffiths took in a lonely and somewhat stressed writer while he completed his research in London and kept his body and soul together for the duration. Many thanks to her and her family.

My literary agent, Teresa Chris, deserves special thanks for the faith she has shown in this project from the moment she picked it out of the pile in her office, a faith that at times far exceeded the author's. Teresa's guidance and indefatigable efforts are warmly appreciated by Anne and me.

To my sister Luci Woodard I owe a particular debt, because it was she who from the very beginning intuited the true spirit of what I was trying to do, even as I was frustrated in attempting to express it myself. Luci read and re-read the entire manuscript with conviction and cheer. Her comments were especially helpful and her enthusiasm seldom failed to boost my spirits when they flagged. Her influence on the final product was both welcome and profound.

All who have been with me as I wrote this book know of the role my wife Anne played in its realization. Of all the individuals to whom I owe thanks, it is only of her that it can be said that this book would not have been written but for her efforts. Anne married a man who had left a secure job with only a vague plan for writing a book, and she supported me financially and emotionally as I set out in a truly frightening new world. In almost four years of uncertainty, she saw me through my work without once complaining of the path we had chosen, and in fact brought out the joy in it. Her paramount concern was that I be satisfied with what I do, and she has sacrificed much to that end and succeeded. There is nothing more that anyone can ask of anyone else.

Introduction:
Capital Lost

Twenty-two centuries ago, the intellectual capital of the Western world lay on a low limestone hill at a mouth of the Nile, nestled between ancient Egypt and the Mediterranean Sea. This was the city of Alexandria, domicile of the enlightened Macedonian dynasty that ruled Egypt, irresistible siren to the scholars of the civilized world, renowned oracle of scientific discovery.

Though the administrative seat for a large inland kingdom, Alexandria was a creature of the sea and of the labyrinth of the Nile delta, and it was the waters that surrounded the city that nourished it to opulence and renown. The city straddled a slender isthmus separating the Mediterranean from an inland freshwater lake to its south, which in turn communicated with the Canopic branch of the Nile a few miles to the east. Maritime access to the Nile not only allowed Alexandria to dominate trade with the Egyptian hinterland, but also to control trade between the kingdoms of the East and those of the Mediterranean, since in those days a channel dredged by the Pharaohs from the Nile to the Red Sea was still passable. Canals criss-crossed the city within its walls, running along wharfs and underneath city blocks, linking the sea harbours, lake and river. A great trading centre at the crossroads of commerce, Alexandria became wealthy and worldly, tolerant and diverse.

The city itself was an architectural and engineering spectacle, having been fashioned by its foreign rulers in a consciously grand and sumptuous style. Paralleling its seaward shore at a distance of a half mile was the slender island of Pharos, to which a four thousand-foot causeway, the Heptastadium, had been constructed, creating twin man-made harbours open to the sea. The eastern of the two harbours was the Great Harbour, within which were the most exotic floating villas and pleasure craft, and whose one and a half-mile mainland shore was walled by the exquisite palaces, temples, theatre and other civic monuments that comprised the royal quarter of the city. Across the harbour from these splendid buildings, rising from a jetty that extended from the island, was the Tower of Pharos, a soaring lighthouse as tall as a modern 30-storey building, whose beacon was said to be visible from thirty-five miles away. A main processional street ran from the Great Harbour to the wharfs of the inland lake, bisecting the city on a north–south axis and perpendicularly

1

intersecting the other main street that ran the length of the city along the isthmus and emerged at huge fortified gates at the eastern and western land bridges. Both boulevards were more than 100 feet wide and bounded by ornate marble colonnades for their entire length, which in the case of the longer street was three miles. The other streets in the city were wide and straight, following the Greek plan, and were illuminated at night.

At the intersection of these two grand avenues stood a massive mausoleum that held the body of the city's founder, Alexander the Great. Alexander himself had selected the site for the city that would bear his name when he passed through Egypt in his frenzied campaign of world conquest. His death in Babylon at the age of 33 sparked an immediate struggle among his generals for control of his huge, but insecure, conquest. The most subtle of the generals, Ptolemy, son of Lagos, selected Egypt as his domain, which at that time already boasted an ancient and orderly society and offered the additional advantage of being at the crossroads of trade but isolated from the constant warfare that burdened his rivals in Greece, Persia and Babylon. Ptolemy cleverly spirited Alexander's body to the new city rising on the narrow strip of land between lake and sea, where he established the Ptolemaic capital of Egypt. Through selective warfare and comprehensive exploitation of the native Egyptian economy, the Ptolemaic dynasty flourished in their new kingdom. Astoundingly, its capital city of splendour, wealth and scholarship – the wide avenues and ornate palaces, temples, and gymnasia; the cavernous hippodrome and spacious theatres; the causeway and canals; the towering lighthouse – all had been built within a century of Alexander's original order to build a new city on what had been a barren site.

Near the mausoleum in the heart of the city was the Museum, literally 'the sanctuary of the Muses', symbol and locus of the intellectual prowess of Alexandria. The Museum had been modelled after the museum in the golden age of Athens four centuries before. It was calculated to lend prestige and attract Greek settlers to the fledgling kingdom, and at this it was remarkably successful, so that within decades of its founding it had grown from an outpost of culture into an institution that dominated the intellect of the world. The Museum was an immense complex of buildings, somewhat in the style of a modern university, encompassing lecture rooms, debating chambers, astronomical observatories, laboratories, dormitories, dining areas and even an exotic zoo.

But by far the most celebrated component of the Museum complex was the Library. The Ptolemaic dynasty established a zealous programme for collecting within its walls the most astounding collection of written treasures the world had ever seen, and their zeal soon devolved into ruthlessness. A regimen was established whereby all visiting ships would be inspected for books, and the ones deemed valuable would be confiscated and taken to the Library to be copied. The Library would keep the books, and ignobly return

2

only the copies of the originals to the former owners. This ongoing petty thievery was tremendously productive, but did not even hint at the extremes to which the Ptolemies would go to procure the world's knowledge. Ptolemy III went so far as to negotiate with the authorities of Athens to allow him to transcribe the official copies of the tragedies of Aeschylus, Sophocles and Euripides, and according to this agreement paid the modern equivalent of millions of pounds as security for the safe return of the precious legacy of Greek theatre. Once the books were in his hands, he had them copied and returned the copies to the Athenians, gleefully forfeiting his deposit.[1] By the end of this determined and devious king's reign the Library already contained 500,000 scrolls – the catalogue alone numbered 120 volumes – and with vigorous acquisitions and expansion its collection was to become even more immense. Among its works were virtually all the writings of classical Greek literature as well as the best tracts the learned world had to offer on engineering, mathematics and the sciences. The intellectual treasures of the Museum and Library drew the learned from the far reaches of civilization, many of whom lingered to seek the patronage of the generous Ptolemaic kings.

Alexandria became an unprecedented hotbed of invention. Out of the Museum sprang the era's lasting achievements in engineering, mathematics and astronomy. Euclid developed his geometry here, rendering mathematics as a system of logical inferences that could be developed one on top of another, and his textbook on geometry would be widely used in the West until well into the modern age. The first notion of latitude and longitude were invented in the Museum, as was an accurate measure of the circumference of the earth. Archimedes visited here often, and made many of his significant discoveries of buoyancy and physics in the company of Museum scholars. It was even the wise men of Alexandria who first invented 'machines' in the modern sense: complex systems of mechanical components for performing a specialized function as opposed to the simple levers and screws with which the rest of the world was facile, machines for telling time, for moving heavy objects, for capturing the force of the wind.

But despite its lasting intellectual achievements, much of the knowledge for which Alexandria was renowned had a strange and fragile quality to it, an intrinsic nature that seems foreign to the modern world. Scientific discovery and technological innovation did not have the durability that we expect today, and it is curious the number of promising inventions that lay fallow, of innovations that were simply forgotten. In Ptolemaic Egypt, science and technology were irrelevant to economic enterprise, so that there was not the imperative for practical application that spurs and disciplines modern research. Scientific inquiry was subsidized by royalty and dedicated to royalty's interests and amusement. A literary scholar might find himself commenting on Homer one day and writing jokes for a royal soirée the next. A learned mathematician might alternately develop Euclidian proofs or devise puzzles for the king, while a skilled engineer might design war engines for the army or toys for the court's children. Though the Museum boasted one of the world's first engineering schools, its inventions were predominantly of the nature of frivolous toys rather than tools.

In no arena was the fragility of Alexandria's knowledge more apparent than in what was to become of many of its machines. The most sophisticated machines in Alexandria, though impressive for the creativity and skill they evidenced, were generally employed as agents of spectacle rather than as means of production. There are accounts of coin-operated holy-water dispensers in the temples and of steam engines that could move massive temple doors from a great distance. Windmill-like devices were used to power booming pipe organs. There were even mechanical man-like robots fashioned as intriguing extras in theatrical productions. (In one production, robots were used to build ships, an obvious dramatic swipe at the sensibilities of the workers in the maritime metropolis, though there never seems to have been any serious thought to employ robots in this way.) The magical machines that came out of Alexandria doubtless served their primary purpose in impressing the masses and in enhancing Alexandria's reputation, and in many cases were the first examples of technologies that would play key roles in reshaping the modern world, but they were not precursors to their modern analogues in a strict sense because for the most part each of these technologies was forgotten and had to be rediscovered many centuries later.

Theoretical knowledge had a similar propensity. The Greek notion of science held it above vulgar pragmatics, leading to a pedantic tendency that tolerated intellectual laxity, sometimes with tragic consequences. One of the more weighty examples of pedantry obscuring rigorous analysis is the story of Aristarchus, a Greek astronomer who studied in Alexandria in the third century BC. Aristarchus employed a series of logical arguments to postulate that the sun must lie at the centre of the observable universe, that the earth and planets must orbit around the sun, and that other stars must be stationary and at such an immense distance that no change could ever be detected in their relative positions as seen from the earth. He was of course fundamentally correct, but Claudius Ptolemy,[2] considering the same problem 250 years later, simply ignored Aristarchus' arguments and constructed his own model that the earth was the centre of the universe and that all the heavens revolved around it. The Ptolemaic system prevailed in Alexandria and was adopted by medieval Europe as truth, since it carried the authority of the wisdom of the ancients, and thus was Western astronomy retarded for 1500 years.

To the modern reader accustomed to a world in which the march of technology is singularly directed, this regime of frivolous innovation and the associated spasmodic course of invention, mental lapse and rediscovery

4

seems bizarre. Today it is incredible to consider that knowledge, once apprehended, would ever simply be forgotten, or that technological breakthroughs
would lie unexploited through sheer lack of interest. In Ptolemaic Egypt the
pursuit of knowledge was considered an unquestioned virtue and its pos-
session a noble mark of prestige, but the notion that one might systematically
employ knowledge in the pursuit of wealth as one might employ a horse or
a hammer was not apparent. For all of its glory, the limited role science and
technology played in the Ptolemaic economy denied it the vitality it exhibits
in the industrialized world today, and doomed it to irrelevance and error.

In the modern era, knowledge has come to be seen as a tool, a thing
whose value is derived from its potential productive capacity rather than
from any intrinsic quality. In the parlance of the modern industrial world, the
intellectual potential to produce knowledge has assumed the economic role
of capital, a good not desired for its own sake, but employed instead in the production of other commodities or services. With the emergence of industrial
capitalism during the Industrial Revolution, capital goods of all kinds were
drawn into a pervasive capitalist system of production. Intellectual capital
became key to this process, and technical innovation, previously sluggish
and haphazard, became remarkably animated. Innovation in modern times
has constructed a vast system of intellectual capital, a complex structure of
technique and knowledge that is technology. In many areas of this structure
the pecuniary opportunities for innovation are apparent to at least some, and
it is in these areas and for this reason that the structure continues to expand.
There is no fear that any strut or girder will be lost or forgotten, as there is
no pretence that a king exists who can command that construction cease, or
even significantly alter its plan.

As human intelligence assumed the role of a tool in modern economies,
it enjoyed a new power while encountering a new threat. As a necessary tool
to production, its existence and influence were not subject to the whims of
the powerful: it had a critical social role to perform that was beyond the
ability of capricious individuals to subvert. But as its valuation became more
exclusively a calculus of its effectiveness as a tool, its value became subject to
erosion in the presence of alternative tools or methods. The capitalist system
of production cannot avoid considering the costs of cultivating intelligence or
examining the speed and efficiency with which intellectual judgements are
made and communicated. The social ethic of capitalism is one of self-interest,
and whenever capitalists find the opportunity to replace human intelligence
with more efficient machinery, they are guided by their ethic to do so.

Computers, more than any other technology, evidence the trend toward
augmenting or displacing human intelligence with machinery. Today the
world's computer population represents the capacity to make untold bil-
lions of mechanical decisions every second, decisions that, individually,
are incredibly specialized and stupid, but in concert are changing the

way we think and work. Of this capacity, the predominant share resides in the Western industrialized countries, industrial capitalism's domain, and capitalism's share would be even larger if not for the pitched economic and political rivalry between capitalist and centrally planned economies. The industrial capitalism that demands mechanical intelligence is today its pre-eminent employer.

In a sense, the mechanical intelligence provided by computers is the quintessential phenomenon of capitalism. To replace human judgement with mechanical judgement – to record and codify the logic by which rational, profit-maximizing decisions are made – manifests the process that distinguishes capitalism: the rationalization and mechanization of productive processes in the pursuit of profit. All productive functions throughout history have been subject to the human impulse to rationalize labour, to make it systematic and repetitive, but when rationalization and mechanization pervade any social function, when the domain of machinery and routine is bound only by considerations of cost-effectiveness, and when this boundary retreats under systematic assault, then that function has become 'industrialized'. The modern world has reached the point where industrialisation is being directed squarely at the human intellect.

Historically, industrialization has been accompanied by a precipitous cultural transformation, a reordering of the social classes and their relation. The human agony of the Industrial Revolution was the birth pains of a new social order arising from a newly industrialized society. Those who survived it witnessed a violent modification of the physical and social means of production that transformed the old order into something fundamentally new and unimagined. When we are awed and confused by a future obscured by rapid technological advance, we are anticipating a similar fate. But even with the social strain that has accompanied industrialization in the past and should be anticipated in the future, it is intellectually dishonest to characterize industrialization as an unmitigated evil, or even on the whole detrimental to mankind's interest. There is no doubt that the common inhabitant of any of the advanced industrialized countries is far more comfortable, better fed, more healthy, and more literate than her pre-industrial ancestors. Industry has for the past 150 years been driven by humanity's demand for physical, manufactured 'things' and has dumbly responded to the point that the industrialized world today is awash with commodities, while the most blatant evils industrial capitalism inflicted on the working class have largely disappeared in the West. Some of the more admirable liberal traditions of the Western democracies were born and nourished in the spirit of capitalism and are still propagated today largely through the perceived desirability of industrial capitalism's results. This being industrialization's legacy, the common man in technologically advanced societies seems justified in welcoming the next wave.

But history teaches a very different lesson to non-industrialized countries and to the poor in the industrialized countries. Capital's insistence on private profit, if unchecked, tends to perpetuate the poverty of the poorest, and technology transported to an undeveloped country is frequently more an agent of exploitation than of social betterment. There have always been prerequisites for participating in the industrial miracle, and as the nature and targets of industrialization shift, so will the prerequisites for benefiting from industrialization. Those who suffer at the expense of others will not be silent: an informed citizenry will be sensitive to their plight, if not due to moral compassion then at least through rational self-interest.

One cannot visit the Ptolemies' library in Alexandria today. By the eighth century it had disappeared, and characteristically the knowledge of how it was destroyed – or even precisely where it stood – was forgotten long ago. A Christian legend from the Crusades claimed fanatical Muslim conquerors ordered its scrolls burned, while a competing theory ascribes the same crime to fanatical Christians centuries before. Others suggest that the wisdom of the ancients perished even earlier in a fire growing outward from the harbour as Julius Caesar fought for his life from the isle of Pharos. But in reviewing the fantastic and conflicting accounts of the supposed crime that befell Alexandria, one gets the eerie sense that the intellectual capital of the Western world was not so much stolen as lost, as a child might lose a precision tool, unable to comprehend it having any function other than that of a toy, and inconsiderate of its potential for good or evil.

1

The Machinery of
Self-Love

Between the vast expanse of Western history that was characterized by the most slowly evolving precepts of traditional social order and the current age that is characterized by dynamic social change was a brief era when thoughtful men held that right human reason should reign over the earth. The Enlightenment lasted scarcely more than a lifetime, being neatly framed by the beginning and end of the eighteenth century, but in that brief time the fundamental philosophical revolution that heralded the modern age was conceived through the very forces of reason the movement championed and tempered in the experiences of a changing world it could not ultimately apprehend. Thought at the time to represent the dawn of a new age of rationality and virtue, the historical role the Enlightenment has been forced to accept is that of a curious philosophical bridge between an antique world we would only dimly recognize and the modern world in which we move.

Though its reign was fleeting, the social philosophy that was developed during this period contains premises that we retain as unspoken truths today. Running through the Enlightenment was an attitude that man should judiciously employ his rational skills to define and address the issues of individuals in contemporary society, and that conversely all aspects of nature that were not immediately reducible to rational reflection were outside the bounds of productive human conduct. A secular code of virtuous rationality was invoked in the consideration of all things of any social importance: of governments and laws, of metaphysics and morality.

Those who were aligned with the ancient institutions that relied on traditional authority – particularly kings and clergy – though not exactly in full retreat, generally were forced to accommodate the new age of reason on its own terms and cede to rational reflection some domain of their discretion. In no social sphere was this more obvious than the rise during the Enlightenment of several related notions regarding moral behaviour, new concepts that regarded morality as the domain of secular philosophy rather than the exclusive realm of Christian dogma. According to the adherents of natural religion and the so-called Deists who flourished during the Enlightenment among the well educated in England and France, God did indeed exist but it was irrational to believe that he would reveal himself in any way except through the mechanism of his works, which were assumed to be reflections of divine intentions. Since God himself must conform to the dictates of reason, his characteristics must be discoverable to anyone who could shrewdly observe and reflect upon his works as they were manifest in nature. Thus the traditional concept and authority of God was captured by rationality, as was the responsibility for prescribing the activities that characterized a moral life. Rather than surrendering to faith in scripture and traditional dogma, philosophers spoke of natural laws that were discernible only through reason, laws to which even the Almighty must be subject. A sort of umbrella science termed 'moral philosophy' became a part of the core curriculum in many European universities, which corresponded roughly to today's social sciences. This was predictably a very fractious turn of events to traditional Christians and their clergy, but it also bore the unmistakable stamp of reason and as a practical matter moderate-minded clerics and politically sensible secular philosophers learned to live with one another and to ignore the ramifications of each other's dogma.

The authority of secular philosophers to pass judgement on issues of morality expanded as the outlines of a future era of industrial capitalism became dimly discernible and the traditional oracles of morality seemed unable to speak to the moral issues of a new world. One of the most pressing ethical issues offered for philosophers' consideration was defining virtuous conduct among individuals in society and the obverse issue of to what extent selfish conduct should be tolerated or condoned. As if the high-minded reflections of Enlightenment philosophers were tardy in attending to the problem, the issue was forced on to the philosophical agenda by an impudent pamphleteer who threatened to topple not only traditional Christian notions of morality but also the secular moral philosophers' claim that they had anything of value to contribute to the question. The writer's name was Bernard de Mandeville, a well-travelled Dutchman who had studied philosophy and medicine in his native country before settling in England at the end of the seventeenth century. If he had writing in mind when he selected his new home, it was a propitious choice, for this was the time and place for popular polemics due to the recent expiration of the Licensing Act through which the state had previously censored the press. Soon after settling in his new country, Mandeville took to writing an incendiary treatise on the relationship between individual virtue and social prosperity, a treatise that was to enjoy the distinction of being roundly condemned both from the pulpit and from the highest echelons of secular philosophy.

The treatise that caused such a stir was a collection of writings that was eventually published as a book entitled *The Fable of the Bees: or, Private Vices, Publick Benefits* that appeared in its final form in 1729, though Mandeville had actually commenced the work in 1705 with the publication of a popular tract that contained the rough-hewn essence of his argument. A thoughtful and deliberate stylist, Mandeville apparently resolved to demonstrate that the deceptively simple thesis of his initial work would stand up to the most rigorous rational criticism, and so the twenty-four years between the first and the final version of his treatise were consumed in painstakingly expanding the original pamphlet to accommodate all conceivable assaults on his logic. At the heart of the final book was the original work, an allegorical poem entitled *The Grumbling Hive: or, Knaves turn'd Honest*, followed by the extensive exegesis he had developed over the intervening years in the form of dialogues and essays. The consistent theme of this ongoing intellectual exercise was that intuitive notions of virtue do not stand up to rigorous analysis, and that philosophical systems that rely on these concepts of virtue are fatally flawed.

The Grumbling Hive tells the story of individuals in society, who are thinly disguised as bees in a massive beehive. The hive is generally a thriving community, respected for its military prowess by rival beehives, but populated by bees that uniformly display the same petty vices as commonly pervade human society. Just like their human counterparts, the bees are skilled in disguising their vices as virtues. As was common in populist tracts, there are entertaining jabs taken at stereotypical objects of popular abuse: bee doctors that pay more attention to their grave demeanour than to curing illness, bee lawyers who trade in specious lawsuits, lecherous bee clergy who prey upon the public, bee bureaucrats who swindle the bee sovereign, and so on. But all in all the state of commerce and living conditions in the hive are adequate, making it on balance a good, if somewhat irritating, place for a bee to live.

One day, through divine intervention, all the bees in the hive suddenly see through their pretensions to virtue, and the vice that pervades their behaviour becomes glaringly apparent. The entire colony suffers through intense introspection on the motives and ramifications of each of their selfish acts and virtuously embarks on a new age in which every action is scrupulously examined to ascertain its basis in vicious motives. The colony becomes a resolutely moral place: quacks and shysters repent, people lose all sense of vanity and selfishness, and workers who are not performing socially responsible and competent work voluntarily gravitate to more virtuous endeavours.

The ironical conclusion of the allegory is that the elimination of vice from the beehive does not make it a Utopia by any standard, but rather a dull and listless place that contrasts unfavourably with the way things were when viciousness was allowed to rule individuals' behaviour. Without vicious motives, the instinct to harbour the luxuries and trappings of vanity disappear, and as the demand for these things declines the economy of the hive stagnates. Mandeville's immediate point was that a thriving hive is in fact highly dependent on the system of selfishness that characterized it before its moral redemption, and in the process he challenged intuitive notions of the nature of vice and virtue. His thesis was that the amalgam of the selfish behaviour of individuals in society was necessary to what was generally considered to be the progress of mankind, and that conversely if individuals acted according to the finest Christian values the material progress of society was bound to collapse.

Mandeville refused to accept cosy notions about human virtue. To him, it was hypocritical to suppose that there was some transcendent good behind apparently virtuous activity, as all human action is ultimately based on assessments of selfish gain. If one accepted the traditional definition of virtue as action that in some way acted contrary to the selfish animal passions of man, Mandeville could reply that actions that fit this description did not really exist, since all actions could in one way or another be seen as being motivated by some selfish desire, whether it was making more money or assuring oneself a better place in the hereafter. Conversely, the only real human motives were vicious – some subtle, some brazen, but all vicious none the less, and it was this viciousness that fuelled the material wealth of society. Animal passions and wants forced humanity towards opulence just as hunger forces animals to obtain food. Contentment with one's social position and moral rectitude in one's actions were actually the bane of industry and commerce and the enemies to what most people hold dear.

As if such a polemic were not provocative enough to established religious dogma, Mandeville's larger point was directed at the elite secular philosophers of the era who were attempting to construct elegant rational models of the value of virtue in contemporary society. His challenge to them was that any new system of moral philosophy that was founded on traditional concepts of individual virtue was an edifice built on a flawed foundation. Virtue did not properly exist, and one might as well confess the point and surrender any pretensions that rational reflection on virtue would yield meaningful laws on how one should conduct oneself among others. The operative concept was clearly human selfishness.

Mandeville was slippery enough that to this day there is no real consensus about what his own outlook really was. He was either a shocked moralist condemning the licentiousness of mankind and its allegiance to material wealth, or a hardened cynic who could not resist kicking the foundations away from underneath mankind's pretensions to virtue. Perhaps he was a bit of both; perhaps he was neither. He may well have been a keen observer of

12

humanity and a disciplined thinker whose conclusions outran his own moral comprehension. But regardless of his personal outlook, his reasoning was seductive and his conclusions were discomfiting to anyone who sought a rational confirmation of their claim to either virtue or worldly success, not to speak of those who aspired to both.

Anyone who could administer a healthy intellectual drubbing to Bernard de Mandeville was bound to be a hero to polite society, and Mandeville-bashing became great sport and almost a rite of passage to generations of intellectuals in England and on the continent. Among those philosophers who sallied forth to engage in a noble intellectual joust with the vulgar pretender were David Hume, William Law, John Dennis, George Berkeley, Francis Hutcheson, Edward Gibbon, Denis Diderot, Jean Jacques Rousseau, T. R. Malthus, James Mill, John Wesley, Immanuel Kant and Montesquieu. But the attention the philosophical community directed towards Mandeville had just the opposite of its intended effect. Like pouring water on flaming oil, their unremitting critiques only served to disseminate Mandeville's influence further, frustrating attempts to deal with his assertions decisively.

Some critics, despite their protestations, set out to refute Mandeville only to be strongly influenced by him. Rather than resisting the notion that self-love was at the core of all human action, they were persuaded to redefine vice and virtue in terms of what the effect of the action would ultimately be on a larger segment of society. In this rephrasing of Mandeville's tale, virtue is redefined as action that has the effect of making a great number of people happy, so that virtue should be gauged by its utility in society as a whole despite the animal motives that may have been its direct inspiration. From this strain of thought emerged the ethical notion of utilitarianism that was central to the concepts of classical political economy. Among those who originally set out to denounce Mandeville only to be profoundly influenced by him was an obscure, amiable and infamously eccentric Scottish academic named Adam Smith, who went after Mandeville with vigour in his first major work only to be accused of plagiarizing Mandeville in his later masterpiece.

Adam Smith's assault on Mandeville came in his first book, entitled *The Theory of Moral Sentiments*, published in 1759 when Smith was 36. At the time of its publication, Smith was a popular lecturer in the field of moral philosophy at the University of Glasgow and the book was a recapitulation of some of his lectures. Abstractly philosophical and academic in tone and firmly rooted in what might now be termed a bourgeois perspective, the book was hardly a work of fearless conviction. When it was critical of the privileged in society, its jabs were frequently couched in vague rhetoric; when it drew metaphysical conclusions, there was clearly an appeal to liberal Deist and fundamentalist Christian alike. Like his later masterpiece, the outlook of the book was unapologetically optimistic about the future of human society, but the basis for its optimism was fundamentally different.

There was explicit reference to the 'invisible hand' of the Author of Nature that guides the individual actions of men, and the pronouncement that individuals' actions in society serve to advance the plan of providence, themes for which Smith would later be renowned. But in contrast to his later development of these ideas, in this early work it was primarily the moral behaviour of the individual that advanced the providential plan, not his self-interest, and it was the individual's virtue that was primarily the fountain of man's worldly success, not his prudence and industry.

The point of departure for the book was doubtless a fine point of contention between Smith and his mentor Francis Hutcheson, who was a devotee of rational natural law and a passionate advocate for individual liberties, as well as a staunch critic of the bothersome Mandeville. Smith developed in a rather dry manner a theory of ethics that relied upon each person's inner self being sympathetic to the plight and concern of others, while understanding that total empathy with the experiences of others was impossible. This, according to Smith, left to each individual the quite natural responsibility to evaluate and pursue what are in his own best interests. Smith implied that one should show some concern for those in misery, but argued that a tempered concern for the plight of the miserable along with a heightened awareness of those who are successful is a natural, socially productive, and ultimately moral perspective to assume. It was in this vein that Smith took his turn at sniping at Mandeville. While confessing the popular appeal of Mandeville's arguments, Smith claimed that Mandeville's philosophy confused the pride that comes from legitimate success with vanity of a ridiculous or fraudulent sort. The search for fraudulent acclaim was a deceit upon the just sympathies of other people, and it was this that distinguished virtuous from vicious acts. According to Smith's philosophy, there was still a very important place in moral philosophy for both virtue and vice, and it was still immanently possible virtuously to pursue wealth without being overly distracted by those who are less fortunate.

Largely because Smith's book elegantly reaffirmed that worldly success was not antithetical to virtue, and in fact was often a manifestation of virtuous conduct, it was a hit among the upper class in England and served as his entrée into elite intellectual circles. Among those who were impressed by the book were Charles Townshend, a feisty nobleman and politician who was in and out of several high-ranking government posts in the period, none it seems without controversy. Townshend was a man of tremendous wit, ambition and vanity, a passionate and skilful orator described as 'one of those statesmen whose abilities are the misfortune of the nation they serve'.[1] It is ironic that this one man's vanity and poor judgement led to the two most significant events of the incendiary year of 1776. In the first instance, as chancellor of the exchequer, Townshend impetuously supported the reinstitution of the Stamp Act that was so hated in the American colonies, this as an attempt to balance the British budget on the backs of the colonies following a stinging rebuke of his domestic tax bill in Parliament. In the second instance, he had made the peculiar selection of the infamously idiosyncratic Dr Smith to serve as his stepson's tutor for his continental tour, a curious choice that was assumed by many to be an attempt to share the limelight with the newly fashionable philosopher. The former miscalculation created a storm in the northern American colonies that erupted into a riotous frenzy when Townshend foolishly compounded his error by attempting to subjugate colonial resistance to his new tax regime. The latter misjudgement forced the retiring Scottish academic to face the disordered real world, and to accommodate within his tidy and cloistered system of philosophy the messy details of the petty affairs of men as well as the discordant philosophies of the continent. Townshend's first misjudgement erupted in the summer of 1776 with the American Revolution, his second had led to the publication a few months earlier of what must be the most influential polemic ever penned – Adam Smith's *The Wealth of Nations*.

As a young man's continental tour, the two and a half-year excursion that was Smith's responsibility was uninspired, if not a total failure, but in terms of its effect on the tutor it was a historical event. The trip was undemanding enough to give Smith ample opportunity to reflect on his new book and boring enough to force the sometimes lazy philosopher to do so. He observed at first hand the indigenous economies of the Toulouse region in southern France and noted with interest the benefits of far-sighted government investment for canals and roads. He became incidentally embroiled in the fractious French politics of the region and the ongoing dispute over regulatory authority between the provinces and the crown. He stayed in Geneva, where he visited frequently with Voltaire, and rounded out his trip by spending ten months in Paris, where he dined in the fashionable French salons. He was saturated with French thought on government and society, and it is clear that these discussions had a profound effect on him. He dined frequently with Helvétius, who advocated creative legislation to steer individual behaviour towards social justice, and with Turgot, a brilliant champion of rational and practical government policy. He made acquaintance with the French Physiocrats, a group of reform-minded economists who advocated minimal taxation and a move away from mercantilist economics. He discussed political economy at length with François Quesnay, who popularized the phrase *laissez-faire*, and is reported to have considered dedicating *The Wealth of Nations* to him had the French economist not died before its publication.

Smith returned to England in 1766, when the tour was rudely terminated by the death of the brother of the pupil in his charge, and dedicated himself for the next ten years to writing the book that would be his masterpiece. He poured himself into the effort and, always a bit of a hypochondriac, suspected that the sustained intellectual effort would be the death of him. When it was finally published, it sold well and caused a stir but not a tremendous one. It went through several editions in Smith's lifetime, but the powerful interests in England were not yet anxious to embrace the book, for its lesson of liberal reform was unmistakable and perhaps more disconcerting than its promise of expanded wealth was attractive. The French Revolution was a frightening spectacle for English observers to behold and since the book had the air of French influence the upheavals in France had the effect of dampening enthusiasm for the book until after Smith's death in 1790. But as commercial interests grew more powerful with the widespread use of power machinery and manufactories assumed the more recognizable form of the modern factory, Smith's polemic became increasingly popular with capitalist interests, and liberal-sounding *laissez-faire* became the norm among conservative moneyed interests.

The philosophy contained in *The Wealth of Nations* is the result of formal academic analysis blended with real-world understanding, and of keen original insight made to meld with the cutting edge of the era's social philosophy. It is this dual nature of the book that so impressed critics of later eras, because the book represented such a startling comprehension between orderly theory and the inherent messiness of human relations. This ability to describe sundry human affairs in terms of a formal theory of human relations was the most compelling aspect of the book, and its claim to being the progenitor of the modern science of economics.

The Wealth of Nations skilfully incorporated the thoughts of many of the finest thinkers of the time into a comprehensive and compelling description of a social system that could bring material comfort to all elements of society, if only the rational principles that underlay human relations were correctly understood. The notions of *laissez-faire* and the rational utility of individual liberty were borrowed from French economists with whom he had spent so much time, from Voltaire whom he revered, and from his mentor Francis Hutcheson and his life-long friend David Hume. Smith was able to adopt the most salient liberal philosophies and moral instincts of his time into a consistent system of social relations that gave them the ring of practical utility and sound national policy.

As with his previous book, a well-reasoned rationale for the morality of self-interested behaviour was bound to be popular, and running through *The Wealth of Nations* is a masterful and memorable line of reasoning for the morality of self-love, a sophisticated and worldly-wise philosophy of how self-love in individuals plays the key role in sustaining a flourishing social order. According to Smith's oft-repeated aphorism, it was 'not from the benevolence of the butcher, the brewer, or the baker, that we expect our dinner, but from their regard to their own interest'. Self-interest is the fabric that binds individuals in society, and so it should be allowed free expression in most day-to-day manifestations. This is a philosophy that, rather than chaffing at Mandeville as his earlier writing did, actually surrenders to Mandeville's theme in many important ways without, of course, ever mentioning the troublemaker's name.

Any philosophy that hinges on allowing free expression of self-interest in individuals begs the question of how abusive acts of self-interest should be regulated, and Smith, borrowing again from continental philosophers, had a ready answer. Self-interest in one individual is naturally regulated in commercial relations by the self-interest of other individuals, so that if one individual wishes to extract an abusive price of others, that person is inviting competition from others for whom an opportunity is being conveniently created. In rational creatures like people, who are able to imagine how their best interests will be served in exchange, a system of markets quite naturally develops. When markets serve their true social function, self-interest and competition become like the yin and yang of modern society, each defining the bounds for the activity of the other, and in a most elegant way regulating the myriad details of contemporary social life. Rational self-love is the vital element in the social mechanism of the market, and it was pervasive market behaviour that formed the vast machinery of society. To a closet Deist like Smith, this was ample evidence of providential design in the workings of human society. Men's relations were guided as if by an 'invisible hand', an oblique metaphor for the design of the Author of Nature, towards what was just and towards what would inevitably make mankind wealthier and happier.

This was touching and optimistic reasoning, couched in the keenest observation and sophisticated logic. It led inexorably to the central policy recommendation of the book: that government is most effective when it leaves largely to markets the job of regulating social relations. This was delivered at a time when there was really no consistent vision of what the proper domain of governments was. It was common at the time for private commercial monopolies to importune among European governments for policies that served narrow business interests, and the rationale for the government intervening on behalf of these private interests was that the intervention would benefit the government's finances directly or that it would best serve the interests of the nation generally. Once one accepted that the government should intervene in major areas, there was no reasonable limit as to what details of commercial life might also fall under the purview of the government. Additionally, in international relations the failed paradigm of mercantilism still had a powerful appeal among many in influential places. Smith was not a controversialist, and he put forward his argument in his characteristically tactful manner, but the unmistakable message of his book was that in all but some well-defined areas of public policy the best interest of the nation and of its government was to leave to markets the adjudication of socially responsible behaviour.

Had Smith simply been repeating parroting what he had read and heard, his achievement in spinning together such a compelling and systematic policy recommendation from the disparate philosophical insights of his era would have been less than an epic achievement. His practical resolution of the moral quandary of selfishness in society, though elegantly and evocatively presented, was not a tremendous improvement over the social commentary of the time. By itself, a concept of rational, self-interested mankind moving within a subtly self-regulating society fitted well within the dominant outlook of the Enlightenment, where man was thought to move rationally and rhythmically within an ordered and essentially unchanged social sphere. But *The Wealth of Nations* was much more than a pretty Enlightenment treatise. It pointed to a different kind of world, a world that was progressing in a linear and wholly unalterable pattern, a world in which social relations would forever expand and become more complex, a world that in any event was pressing itself into his readers' collective consciousness. This was a book that suggested that society was evolving into unprecedented forms and was doing so according to a process that should not – and in any event could not – be restrained. For at the very core of Smith's economic paradigm was a mechanism that would continually push society forward, a fundamental dynamic that would never let social relations rest, a force that was at the very foundation of money, trade and wealth. This force was the division of labour.

As Smith described it, the division of labour was a process of almost mystical significance. Smith demonstrated that the division of labour increased the total output of any set of people, and posited that it was the only real way to increase the wealth of nations. This was the pivotal process in enriching society, because increased productivity increased society's stock of goods and it was this stock of goods that determined the real wealth of a nation. It was in this point that Smith was drawing a distinct line between himself and competing theories. In particular, it nailed down the coffin on mercantilists, who compulsively insisted that national wealth arose from accumulating stocks of bullion. It was also a major break from the French Physiocrats, who acknowledged that wealth lay in stocks of goods, but, immersed in the exigencies of an agrarian economy, insisted that capital was only a relatively trivial rearrangement of what could only be obtained from nature, so that the only real increase in total wealth came from agriculture or resource extraction. Smith, hailing from a country that was already beginning a process of industrialization and was palpably more materially wealthy than the France of the Physiocrats, understood that productive labour of any kind is the source of value. Labour was the true fountain of wealth, and the division of labour was the one magical way to increase its flow.

The division of labour was applied with varying degrees in all areas of activity that were related to markets, and in fact the division of labour and market exchange were parallel and complimentary processes that arose out of the primal motive of self-love. As the stimulator of markets and the division of labour, self-love assumed a role far more significant than merely keeping human excesses in check: it became the vital ingredient in a process that would systematically enhance the nation's wealth. Simply put, markets were instruments of exchange, and the act of exchanging was a process that only rational beings are capable of doing, because it is only through reason that each of us can accurately assess how a trade can enhance our individual selfish crusade. Markets encourage the division of labour by providing a method of exchange as well as an opportunity for increasing one's wealth by exchanging for the increased products that resulted from the division of labour. Market society, then, encouraged division of labour by appealing to individuals' self-interest, which in turn enriched society as a whole by boosting its stock of goods.

Smith's concept of the division of labour was an extremely broad one that existed on the level of nations as well as among individuals within a nation. Just as individuals analyse work into discrete elements in order to boost productivity, nations that divide work between themselves and exchange their products freely are only boosting their mutual wealth, while nations that arbitrarily restrict trade, or try to boost only exports in exchange for money as the mercantilists proposed, were hampering their own economic growth. So in addition to spawning exchange, boosting national wealth and providing the social machinery through which selfish actions benefit society, Smith proposed that the division of labour was also the reason for free trade among nations.

The division of labour was such an important component in Smith's view of the social order that he opened *The Wealth of Nations* with a detailed analysis of why the process is employed and how it works to boost productiveness. In presenting this detailed analysis, Smith used his famous example of how the division of labour is employed in the production of pins, and extended the argument to all productive processes. (The choice of pin manufacture is an interesting one to some observers, who note Smith's childhood fascination with the operations of the local nailery in his home town in Scotland. It is interesting to contemplate how a production function like the manufacture of nails in a tiny Scottish village might have made a tremendous impression on the future founder of modern political economy, especially considering the custom at the time of paying the nail-makers' wages in nails.) Smith observed that a modern manufactory which employs ten skilled men in the making of pins can produce upwards of 48,000 pins per day while an unskilled worker crafting pins individually and in sequence could never expect to produce more than 20 in a day. Smith pointed out that in this not atypical instance each member of the organized team could claim to produce the equivalent of 4,800 pins every day, some 240 times the productivity of unskilled individuals working alone. This allowed pins to be sold at a trivial price per pin, whereas if they were produced by individuals they would doubtless be very expensive commodities. The division of labour was certainly a process of tremendous productive potential.

The reasons behind this remarkable boost in productiveness were hardly mysterious: there were exactly three reasons, according to Smith, that the division of labour enhances productiveness. The first was due to specialization. The division of labour divides productive functions into discrete sub-functions so that labourers develop a certain dexterity for the specialized function they assume. Their minds and bodies focus their efforts on specialized, repetitive tasks, and they become capable of performing these tasks faster and more competently than if their skills encompassed a broad range of functions. This is the aspect of the division of labour that quite naturally leads to a multiplicity of trades and professions in advanced countries, and conversely in areas of production where specialization is appropriate the advanced nation will normally produce commodities for a much lower cost than less advanced countries can produce. The second reason the division of labour increases productivity was that it reduced the time lost in transporting intermediate products between stations in a productive process. A labourer would not carry a product through the process, but would simply repeat a special function over and over, concentrating on the repetitive task at hand without being distracted by the need to move the goods to other stations or by the psychic disruption that comes from changing tasks. Intermediate productive processes would not be so frequently interrupted in order to pass products on to other intermediate processes.

The third and final of Smith's reasons that the division of labour boosted productivity was that it laid the groundwork for the introduction of machinery in the productive processes. He noted that the division of labour had the effect of breaking tasks down into simpler, more routine tasks, and that at some point these tasks are inherently well-suited to being performed by a machine. Though machinery's role in reducing labour and boosting productivity was a common object of speculation in Smith's time, the model Smith was proposing was subtly different from what had been said before. Mechanization and the division of labour were not two among many distinct processes that contributed to social progress: there was really only one such process, and that was the division of labour. Machinery was to Smith just a special case of this mystical process by which mankind inexorably moves to greater wealth and happiness, and being inspired like all other aspects of the division of labour by selfish concerns, was itself a cog in the great social machine that was created and is constantly enhanced through the abiding instinct of self-love.

The division of labour was a pervasive and unremitting social dynamic that, like the selfish instincts that propelled it, was bound to persist with little regard for the moral reservations of philosophers. This was the element of Smith's vision of society that could not be contained within the neat balance of virtuous reason that marked the waning Enlightenment. Those who understood *The Wealth of Nations* now had a philosophical paradigm that confirmed their suspicion that society was dramatically changing into something it had never been before, that the introduction of new productive processes and new machines with new capabilities would become a permanent element of life in the new era. As it happened, Smith was writing before the widespread introduction of power machinery in factory settings, and so he sat on the very brink of large-scale heavy industry and the mechanical world that was to come. In this new era of industrialization, the general outline of Smith's paradigm proved to be remarkably prescient: people continued to be fundamentally rational and self-interested in their behaviour and the division of labour proceeded and accelerated in all aspects of productive life, dragging social science behind it kicking and screaming.

In more recent times, the pervasive application of increasingly capable power machinery has freed most labourers in advanced societies from manual work and created a new work force engaged in what might loosely be termed knowledge work: work whose raw material is information and in which the most-valued skills involve making decisions that are based on information. As the process of making these decisions came to be better understood and as machinery came to be more capable, these intellectual tasks came to resemble in their own way the kind of tasks that could more economically be performed by machines, specifically by electronic digital computers. Now, as then, each rational innovation contributes to a society that is tremendously more productive than would have been anticipated even in the recent past; and now, as then, the motive behind the process is to be found in individuals predictably and rationally acting out of self-love.

In his early work, *The Theory of Moral Sentiments*, Smith paused to reflect on the aesthetic allure of machinery and other useful artifacts. It is obvious from his discussion that he had a particular reverence for machines, a common fascination for people of his social station and era. Smith opined that a source of machinery's beauty was that it suggested to the beholder its utility in operation, how by dint of its design the user is relieved of onerous effort and fatigue. The more elegantly the design of the machine expresses its utility, the more beautiful it seems. But there was more to the appeal of machinery than an expression of utility, in fact, Smith said, if one observes closely enough he would agree that the allure of fine machines frequently exceeds any rational assessment of how useful they really are. It was obvious that the appeal of machinery was much more than a simple attraction to manifest convenience, but was a symptom of an overriding human instinct towards systematic order. This instinct was a key ingredient in the progress of mankind, since it guided individuals to seek systematic solutions to important endeavours, and to remove from existing systems all encumbrances upon their orderly operation.

Smith was describing an attraction to system that was inherently aesthetic rather than rational, a sentiment that ultimately guided people's appraisal of a system more than strict rational deduction of its appropriateness. People, it seems, have an aesthetic instinct towards elegant order, and this instinct guides them towards adopting systems of order to worldly situations and improves their lot in the process. It is a remarkable insight from an unexpected source and says much about the modern world, from the underlying ambition of modern architecture to the seemingly compulsive behaviour of computer hackers.

In Smith's mind, this same attraction to systematic order could be observed in people's appraisal of social institutions. He explicitly compared systems of governance to machines, saying that in each case their creation sprang from the same human attraction to systematic orderliness. In each a judgement of its appropriateness springs as much from an aesthetic judgement of its orderliness and consistency as from a more detailed assessment of how well individuals are being served by the mechanical or administrative apparatus. This is an interesting insight coming from Adam Smith, whose lasting intellectual appeal is primarily the aesthetic attraction of his system of political economy. As it happened, the allure of Smith's system is said to have spawned the modern discipline of economics, and the opening era of the new science was marked by acrimonious debate among dogmatic proponents of competing economic systems.

In this light, an oblique warning Smith inserts into his discussion of the appeal of systems is particularly poignant. Though the aesthetic appeal of systems is generally a benign influence in the affairs of humanity, there is a danger that one can be charmed by the innate orderliness of a system and maintain allegiance to a system of thought even when in certain instances it forsakes its fundamental purpose in serving humanity. This is a warning that went unheeded by generations of both adherents and critics of the Smithian paradigm of capitalism to the current day. In particular, modern-day adherents of what is supposed to be Smith's legacy of *laissez-faire* seem to be more enthused with what is supposed to be the simple mechanism of Smith's social philosophy at the expense of the full subtlety of his argument. Smith was obviously spirited in his presentation of a self-regulating and expanding social order that was based on the judicious expression of selfish interests and he believed strongly that the paradigm would serve well to make more rational the actions of governments, but he eschewed the dogmatic zealotry that characterizes many of his fans today. The basis of Smith's polemic is patently pragmatic, a straightforward appeal to the powerful on how best to regulate the affairs of a nation. Smith was not a proponent of a universal retreat of government from human affairs, and he was painfully aware that government must actively intervene in areas of public interest that were not the natural domain of markets, particularly those that pertained to fundamental tenets of justice.

But even Smith seemed to get carried away at times by the allure of his ordered view of social relations. He would neglect, selectively, to examine with rigour the ramifications of his system, as evidenced in several instances where he displayed in tactful prose an unmistakable callousness for the plight of the downtrodden. In his early work, he rationalized that a disproportionate concern for the wealthy over the poor in society was a quite reasonable and healthy human impulse, leading as it did to an attraction to those things that inexorably guided mankind to greater wealth and happiness. A prejudice for examining the forces behind the creation of wealth and power over delving into the mechanisms of misery was part of the beneficent machinery of social progress. Whether consciously or not, Smith betrayed this prejudice in all his writing, including his mature masterpiece.

In this vein, *The Wealth of Nations* broached the issue of slavery on a few occasions, a topic of general debate at the time, but Smith just could not seem to bring himself to condemn the practice as being fundamentally unjust. The worst Smith could muster for the institution of slavery was that it was economically inefficient, and so it was a condition that the forces of the marketplace would eventually move to correct. There is no real concern shown for the misery of slaves, and no reflection on how long one should be willing to wait for economic forces to free them. This was among the more glaring examples of how Smith embraced a philosophy of individual self-love as the core of benign social relations, but was unwilling to probe the process more deeply when faced with the disturbing prospect that in the real world the self-interest of some individuals might systematically conspire against the self-interest of others.

The example of slavery was only one of several curious passages in *The Wealth of Nations* where the brilliant thinker seemed to have encountered an unseemly aspect to his system and responded with the philosophical equivalent of sweeping it under a rug. These difficulties all pertain to the limitations of his genteel outlook on human self-interest and its role in the division of labour. In one passage, Smith reflected on the psychological effects that the continuing division of labour would produce in workers. He conjectured that a person's intellectual character is fundamentally shaped by his employment, and that the division of labour would inevitably restrict the working person's functions to a very few simple operations. The lack of intellectual stimulation would lead to an atrophied intellectual capacity, so that labourers would become 'as stupid and ignorant as it is possible for a human creature to become'.[2] This would have the doleful effect of rendering the labourer a poor conversationalist and retard his ability to understand even the most petty aspects of his daily life, but these apparently self-evident effects were not of particular concern to Smith, who was more concerned that the worker would become a poor judge of the affairs of national politics and so effeminate and disdainful of adventure that he would lose his value to the state as a soldier. It was in this practical regard for its self-interest that the state should intervene to provide public education to offset the effects of the division of labour, not out of any non-rational concern for the worker's diminished capacity as a human being. The self-interest of the state was elegantly elucidated, as was the self-interest of those the state's army would serve to defend, but one wonders if Smith had carefully considered the self-interest of the worker in this situation.

In another example, Smith delved into the process of innovation in industry, with similar garbled conclusions. He felt that it was primarily workmen who introduced innovations into the productive process and that it was in their rational self-interest to do so. Theoretically, the innovation would free the workman who proposed it of the necessity to perform the task, and he would be re-employed elsewhere. The net result would be that the workman's real wages would increase, because he could work at something else while the economic engine of society had been enhanced in some small way, so that the goods he bought with the wages from his new job were less expensive to him.

It was certainly plausible to suggest that working people were the primary initiators of innovation, for at the time it was largely so. This was before the era of the professional engineer or factory manager, or even the factory itself properly speaking. The owners of capital were not as totally in control of the production process as they are today, or even as they would be thirty years after Smith's death. Craft and guild workers had long been in a position of knowledge and control over individual aspects of production, and they were the ones who understood the processes best and were in the best position to improve upon them. But there was a very fundamental difference between a self-employed craftsman introducing an innovation into his work and a labourer doing the same thing. Quite simply, the self-employed worker would keep the product of his boosted labour, while the wage worker did not, and Smith did not seem to have fully considered the ramifications of such innovation within a prevailing social ethic of self-interest. Smith used the apocryphal story of a young boy employed in monitoring a rudimentary steam-engine. The boy's task was to open and close a valve on the machine in tandem with the stroke of a piston but, since he naturally preferred to play with his friends, he tied the valve to the piston, so that the valve would open and close itself automatically. Smith closed the story at that point, with the implication that technology had been advanced, that society had been enriched by some minuscule but positive extent, and that the boy was free to his leisure. More cynical readers might wonder what really happened to the boy when it was discovered that he was no longer required to monitor the engine and that instead of working he was playing with his friends.

These were elements of his social system that Smith chose not to pursue, for whatever reasons. Perhaps Smith's comfortable life and bourgeois perspective blinded him. Perhaps it is asking too much of a great innovator to develop rigorously all the tributaries to his insights, or perhaps in some points the ever-political professor chose to conceal his true feelings in order to avoid alienating the powerful people he was trying to persuade. But one suspects that having glimpsed a new vision of the path mankind was destined to follow, Smith retreated to the comforting Enlightenment conviction that the system he saw was in fact evidence of a divine rational being's benevolent intentions for humanity. One wonders if, despite his warnings to others, Smith fell prey to the allure of a new systematic social order fashioned by the machinery of self-love, and if the beauty of his system was ultimately too warm and comforting to subject to scrutiny.

2

Machinery and Labour

Bitter cold gripped London on the evening of 12 January 1820. It wafted through Buckingham Palace where George III, the blind and feeble symbol of a passing England, was dying. It bit at an indigent army in the streets and menaced the more fortunate who huddled in cramped boarding houses around meagre coal-fired stoves. The Thames had frozen over, disrupting the unloading of desperately needed grain from overseas. Darkness fell early, as the incessantly sooty air and foul weather conspired with the season to obscure the sun by late afternoon, when only the flicker of gas street lamps and carriage lanterns remained to protest the gloom.

Coming on the heels of several years of war and fitful commerce, the unusually harsh winter was misery to the common citizens of the grey and grimy Flower of Cities, but to society's elite, the winter – cold as it was – signalled the beginning of the social season.[1] Shunning their cool and airy summer estates for the warmth of their town houses, they convened in the capital, mixing in a blizzard of dinners, balls and purportedly casual 'at-homes'. With the early darkness came the clacking of carriages on the cobbled streets of the fashionable West End, the beginning of one night's clamorous transit to jovial intrigue, in which there were very serious ambitions behind the social choreography. Social intercourse was a sophisticated skill, and one that could bear heavily on the worldly success of its practitioner. The clever reveller, anxious to achieve the maximum social advantage from the evening's festivities, knew the wisdom of maintaining a flexible itinerary, and it was possible to modify one's plans on the spur of the moment due to the fact that in many circumstances it was considered unseemly for a hostess scrupulously to abide by her guest list. Arriving at the proper location or receiving the proper attendance for one's purposes was the result of the gambits and feints, bids and calls of each evening's social market.

While scurrying for advantage, the upper crust knew to avoid the rowdy Mayfair district that inconveniently skirted the regal homes of St James and the West End, and would not think to broach the vast breeding grounds of discontent in the east and south of London, particularly after dark. The sturdy quaint contraptions that wheeled the gentry above the heads of the unfortunate were curiously provocative to society's dregs and were scant defence against an unruly mob. The King's Horse Guards and the city militia, though admirably loyal, required precious time to know of a riot and respond. These were dangerous times – everyone knew it – times when a traditionally autocratic and feudal society was being twisted and rent by unprecedented forces one could not understand.

An eccentric parson, Thomas Malthus, had set the dismal tone for the era in 1798 with the anonymous penning of his foreboding economic treatise, *An Essay on the Principle of Population as It Affects the Future Improvement of Society*, which disavowed Adam Smith's promising prognosis for society and substituted for it a disturbing model. England's population was increasing geometrically due to the populace's unfortunate predilection for the flesh, the reverend gentleman said, while the less fertile land that was being forced into agriculture could only produce with a declining efficiency. As long as the land produced at a level greater than the minimum required for subsistence, there would remain some motivation for the people to reproduce, and the declining productivity of land would continue to lose its race with human fecundity. Only when the species was locked in the meanest level of subsistence would the biological engine sputter and stop, and all humanity would be destitute.

Events seemed to corroborate Malthus's theory. Though many at the time found it politically inconvenient to concede the point, the fact is that during the period between the writing of *The Wealth of Nations* and the death of George III the population of England ballooned, an increase that confounds analysts even today.[2] The press of excess population, along with their forced removal from the agricultural regions in the wake of the Enclosure Acts, spawned an awareness in the public of an unprecedented mass of hungry, unemployed and apparently dangerous paupers.

Enclosure was to agriculture what industrialization was to become to manufacture. Before enclosure, the primary agent of agricultural production had been the tenant farmer, who tilled a tiny strip of land while paying rent in the form of surplus produce to the landowner. For the tenant farmer, the produce of his rented plot represented a major component of his family's sustenance, along with husbandry from common lands and intermittent wage labour. Though the arrangement had held since feudal times, with the coming of the eighteenth century political and technological trends conspired against the tenant and small landowner. Agriculture was becoming a profit-oriented industry, and more rational agrarian techniques favoured the enclosure and tillage of larger plots of land. In thousands of separate actions effected by Parliament at private request along with numerous local actions, tens of thousands of tenant farm families and small landowners were evicted from their traditional plots and denied access to common lands by a new industry bent on efficiency. Denied the opportunity to farm or raise livestock, they were forced to rely on the last remaining mode of sustenance available to them: wage labour. But the informal part-time labour they had known before was obviously not available to all of them on a full-time basis in the rural areas. Torn from their sustaining agrarian existence, they were transformed *en masse* into wandering paupers whose only hope was to secure scarce wage labour in the new capitalist enterprises, or somehow to flee to American colonies where land was in abundant supply.

England's war with Napoleon had finally ended with triumph at Waterloo, but it had seriously disrupted trade. Grain prices rose precipitously, starving the peasants – many of whom were unaccustomed to relying on money to provide for their food – while handsomely increasing agricultural rents to landowners. Not willing to accept the lower profits that renewed trade with the continent would bring, the landed gentry petitioned Parliament to maintain the high cost of grain through a set of import restrictions known and reviled as the Corn Laws. The hungry mass of humanity in London's slums grew restive, and bread riots throughout England haunted the public's conscience. Notable among the down-and-out were recently decommissioned soldiers, so that on urban streets the English were forced to confront the embarrassing spectacle of the once proud vanquishers of Napoleon clamouring with the rest of the hopeless for food, while still wearing their ragtag uniforms.

As an agrarian population staggered towards capitalism, it encountered a fierce physical and psychological adversary – machinery. With the rapid substitution of steam power for manual power, the manufactories that Adam Smith had described so glowingly were transformed into turbulent, shrieking factories. Their voracious steam engines demanded huge quantities of coal and coke. To feed them, the output of the coal mines tripled in this period, and with it the number of those who depended on that dangerous work for their livelihood. The era witnessed singular cleverness in the design of machines, machines that rationalized the production of commodities, that could combine in one operation the work that had previously been performed by many. With the widespread use of machinery came a concomitant diminution of the demand for adult male labourers, as craft skills and brawn, with the higher wages they commanded, were suddenly superfluous to the evolving modes of production. What the new industries increasingly needed were nimble, docile workers who could squeeze into the smallest crevices, would work the longest hours, and commanded the most meagre wages. Women, and then children, were drawn into a barbaric new system of production while many of their husbands and fathers languished without wages.

Mechanization was the darling phenomenon of the elite, but to workers it was a pervasive ogre. The contraptions wealthy pundits praised as proof of social progress represented unemployment, discomfort and physical danger to the common worker. Not surprisingly, tensions came to a head and exploded in the Midland textile region. Weavers and spinners, who in generations past had made a tolerable living on the value of their skills and labour, witnessed a stream of 'labour-saving' innovations – the spinning mule, the flying shuttle, power machinery – each of which made their labour more routine, more dangerous and less valuable. The product of a score of weavers only a generation before could now be produced by a single power loom, several of which could be monitored by a solitary child, and as a result textile workers and their families were undergoing inhuman hardships. Wages were meagre and the demand for labour swung madly with the cycles of business and fashion. Many locales came to subsidizing textile workers' wages with private charities in order that the workers could feed themselves and their families.

To many among the workers the obvious cause of their misery was the machines that displaced them from the wage labour they needed for their bread. Uprisings became commonplace in the Midlands, as bands of displaced workers broke into textile manufactories and hacked the dreaded machines to bits in response to the obvious threat to their livelihoods. Initially the bandits only attacked the textile mills at night, but as time progressed they became increasingly bold. Pamphlets surfaced claiming responsibility for the raids and encouraging the populace to enlist with the armies of Ned Ludd, who was sometimes referred to as the general of the movement and sometimes its king. There was no Ned Ludd – his name was that of a mentally disturbed youth who had attacked his weaving machine in a rage a generation before – but to the Luddites his name was a balm to their burning frustration, a unifying symbol with which they could strike back at the machines that had ensnared them. To those whose interests were threatened by the Luddites, Ned Ludd represented a terrifying solidarity among the workers that was vastly out of proportion to reality. English ruling society had witnessed the violence of the French Revolution with horror, and the spectre of English peasants rising in revolt in the industrial heartland haunted their thoughts. The army was called in, and the scattered uprisings were put down with just a tinge of desperation.

In addition to their physical wants, the Luddites and their sympathizers had a profound need for a theoretical model of their predicament. Adam Smith's intellectual regimen, intended to arrest government intervention on behalf of powerful private interests, had been arrogated by those very interests and Smith's theories became their rationale for forswearing any government intervention on behalf of the paupers capitalism was savaging. Those Englishmen drawn to the economic discipline Smith had pioneered came exclusively from the ranks of the educated and comfortable social strata. Strikingly insensitive to the rest of society's anguish, the new economists belittled the workers' contention that machinery was impoverishing them.

Of those who clicked and whirred over the cobblestones of the West End in the chill of that January evening in 1820, a handful headed for a spacious but relatively unpretentious Georgian house in Upper Brook Street just off Hyde Park. Upon arriving, custom required the guests to linger in their carriages until their footmen's deft rapping of the knocker elicited the proper response from their host's house-servants, and only then to make the two or three quick steps from their conveyance to the warmth of their destination. When they finally assembled for dinner they represented the new elite of the ruling class – members of parliament, wealthy businessmen and distinguished political economists. Their motives for attending lay in the stimulating discourse these regular meetings unfailingly spawned about literature, society, art and politics, but principally about political economy, an area in which their opinions held considerable sway. The guests relished this banter and had made a habit of congregating here for some time, testing their economic theories like kindred vintners savouring one another's wine. None suspected that the evening's conversation would contain the seeds of extraordinarily radical notions.

Their host, David Ricardo, was enjoying his first anniversary in the House of Commons as the member for Portarlington, a tiny Irish borough that he would never see, for like many things of value in this emerging bastion of *laissez-faire* the seat had been sold to the highest bidder.[3] Though this process of purchasing seats was distasteful to Ricardo, it was far from uncommon, and he pursued this unseemly avenue into national office as a means towards participating in the economic affairs of the nation without having to resort to the messy responsibilities that a legitimate political constituency entails, and after a rough start his colleagues in the Commons came to appreciate his presence. David Ricardo was the era's pre-eminent political economist, and his incisive and decidedly non-partisan commentary was carefully considered by his fellow politicians and economists. He was a nervous orator in Parliament, with a shrill voice and an unfortunate stammer, but when surrounded by thoughtful friends in more familiar surroundings he was transformed into a most agreeable and engaging host. He presided over these intimate gatherings with notable grace, seldom failing to impress his guests with his famous talent for elegant and abstract reason.

Unlike his dinner guests, it had been Ricardo's wit, rather than his birthright, that had propelled him to the top of English society, and his independent path to wealth may have freed him later in life to reach conclusions that his peers insisted upon ignoring. His emigrant father, a devout Dutch Jew, was a successful member of the London Stock Exchange. His equally devout English mother had borne him 22 children, of whom 15 survived and six, including David, became stockbrokers. Young David dutifully joined the family business at 14, after an abbreviated mercantile education, but his propensity for abstraction and independence soon led to conflicts with his parents. He had difficulty concentrating on the detailed aspects of the stock business, and his free-thinking spirit became increasingly entangled in his parents' devotion to Jewish tradition. Their tense relationship erupted when, having just turned 21, Ricardo married his Quaker sweetheart and renounced Judaism. His parents, who had laboured all their lives to attain prominence in the London Jewish community, mourned his conversion as if it were a death. David was banned from the family business, by one account with a legacy of just £100 as a 'token of forgiveness'.[4] But amazingly, within four years David Ricardo had used this initial investment to build a fortune far in excess of his family's, having speculated with wild success in stocks, real estate and war-related loans. He became widely respected in commercial circles for his business acumen and scrupulous ethics.

Characteristically, Ricardo lost interest in the affairs that had brought him such extraordinary wealth. He turned to intellectual avocations, alternately devoting himself to the study of mathematics, chemistry and mineralogy. Idle and bored while on holiday at Bath, he chanced upon a copy of *The Wealth of Nations*. He was immediately intrigued with the rising discipline of political economy and within a few years its study was to dominate his thoughts.

England was confused and alarmed by the wild lurching of its inchoate capitalist engine, and Ricardo began to distinguish himself in the public eye with his cogent appraisal of the nation's interest in the employment of money, gold bullion, taxes and trade. His views, modestly presented in pamphlets, were widely read and influential among legislators and economists, and he befriended the most prominent economic thinkers of the era, principally Malthus, his life-long theoretical rival, and James Mill, his intimate mentor and posthumous exponent.

By 1815, Ricardo's new-found friend's entreaties that he produce a comprehensive summary of his economic theory finally met with reluctant acquiescence. He began *Principles of Political Economy and Taxation*, a book that directly addressed the baffling and worrisome issues of the day: fluctuations in the value of money, the effect of taxation on profits, the impact of trade protectionism on grain prices, rents and wages. Inspired by the contribution he recognized in *The Wealth of Nations*, Ricardo set out to explore issues that he felt Smith had left only approximately resolved.

Principles of Political Economy distinguished itself with its emphasis on how society distributes its product to its members. The key to understanding this distribution, according to Ricardo, was that rather than viewing society as a mass of individuals pursuing their own self-interest, it was

31

more instructive to consider society as being comprised of distinct 'classes' of individuals who shared selfish concerns and whose corporate interests were in constant competition with the corporate interests of other classes. This was a seemingly innocuous innovation that was to have considerable impact on the political debates of the future. For the next century and a half, political economy would be preoccupied with defining and redefining class interests and constituents, but it was sufficient to Ricardo to place all of humanity into one of just three classes: the landowners, the capitalists and the labourers. Though this three-part division may seem quaint to the modern reader, to Ricardo's contemporaries it rang true.

The events attending the Corn Laws controversy in 1815 demonstrated the model's practical relevance. The landowners were universally interested in high food prices, which increased their rents, and so petitioned Parliament for import restrictions. The labourers, already squeezed by enclosure, mechanization and industrial capitalism, ransacked London to protest against the bill while insisting upon a minimum wage law. The capitalists joined with the labourers in protesting against the bill, since the price of food was a major component in labour costs, but invoked the deceased Dr Smith's *laissez-faire* against the labourer's call for a minimum wage. The contemporary observer had no difficulty discerning the outline of Ricardo's class competition in the newspaper headlines.

The most profound issue in the book, and the subject on which Ricardo most conspicuously contradicted Smith, was the source of value in commodities. Ricardo opened his book with 'On Value', a chapter whose details were to endure endless equivocation in subsequent editions. Its point of departure was Smith's prevailing notion that the price of any commodity is simply the sum of the *price* of the labour embodied in it. According to Smith, common sense stated that if the price of the labour necessary to produce a commodity increased, the price of the commodity (and of any commodity of which the initial commodity was a component) would rise with it.

It is significant that Ricardo's initial difficulty with Smith's doctrine of value, and the difficulty that would eventually lead to his own momentous reformulation, involved the special case of human labour in its relation to machinery. He noted that when machinery is involved in the production of commodities an increase in wages does not cause all commodity prices to increase; in fact the prices of some commodities have been seen to fall after an increase in wages to the workers producing them. He posited that when there were mechanical alternatives to human labour available at an equivalent price, a rise in wages would make the mechanical option more attractive to the capitalist, who would not hesitate to replace the workers with machines. But having employed the machines, if the capitalist maintained the same absolute profit as before, his profit margin would begin to look attractive to rival capitalists whose profits had just been squeezed by the general increase in wages. It would be impossible for the original capitalist to maintain his rate of profit, for if he maintained his prices at the old level while his costs had been cut through the use of machinery, he would find his market flooded with rivals who had forsaken less profitable enterprises, and prices would fall with the intensified competition until profit levels fell in line with the rest of the economy. Ultimately he could attribute no profit to his machines.

Ricardo had discovered a profound paradox involving the profitability of machinery. The profits to be made by replacing labour with machinery had the elusive nature of the Cheshire cat: labour is consumed by machinery in pursuit of profits (to reduce the costs of production and thus increase profits), but as labour is extracted from productive processes, competing interests are drawn from less profitable labour-intensive enterprise, driving down profits until they are roughly equivalent across the economy. Eventually, the profits derived from machinery would have no more substance than the cat's tantalizing smile.

Armed with this startling premise, Ricardo attacked Smith's stated belief that the price of a commodity was the numerical sum of the price of the various labour employed in its production. According to Ricardo, Smith's formula applied only to primitive societies or areas of production where machinery could not displace human labour. But whenever capitalists have the option to replace human labour with machinery, the relative quantities of machinery and labour employed in producing a commodity must figure in the calculation of the commodity's value. Ricardo completed the line of reasoning by simply stating that since machinery could not contribute to value because its profitability was inherently fleeting, the relative values of any two commodities are determined solely by the amount of labour that each contains: if commodity A requires twice the labour of commodity B – regardless of the amount of machinery employed in either case – it must be twice as valuable.[5] He had formulated the Labour Theory of Value.

It should not be surprising that a reactionary social order resigned to protecting the interests of the traditional landowners and their upstart capitalist rivals would hesitate to embrace a philosophy that emphasized the role of human labour in the production of value, and the initial chapter of Ricardo's book met with criticism from many colleagues. On the whole the book sold well, however, and soon there was an opportunity for Ricardo to revise the troublesome chapter on value while preparing for the book's second edition. The second edition also sold well, expanding Ricardo's authority among the elite thinkers of political economy, and by the evening of the dinner party, plans were under way to prepare a third edition. No one, foremost among them Ricardo himself, expected the third edition to diverge significantly from the first two.

*   *   *

Dinner, we are told, proceeded amiably enough. The conversation meandered through literary criticism, copyrights and parliamentary reform. When the topic inevitably turned to economics, an issue arose that most economists considered settled but which incited much discussion nevertheless: does the introduction of machinery into the manufacturing processes benefit or harm the working class? From an account left in the diary of one of the participants, we can infer a rough sketch of the arguments presented.[6]

One would expect Ricardo to figure prominently in the conversation, not only because of his labour theory of value, but also because of his recent association with Robert Owen. Owen, who like Ricardo had emerged from humble beginnings to amass his own fortune, was a brash English industrialist with an unusually genuine social conscience. He had stirred both England and the continent with his model factory at New Lanark, where labourers worked reasonable hours in a clean, comfortable environment and young children, who were prohibited from working, were educated in free communal schools. Bolstered by success and public acclaim, Owen challenged the government to endow a daring pilot project: a model community of unemployed paupers who would be fed, clothed and employed in a new manufacturing town. Employing the logic of the Luddites, the new town would employ no machinery, in order that the maximum number of poor people could remain employed.

Though Owen's prescience may in some points seem chilling to the modern reader, to influential observers of the day it seemed dangerous mischief intentionally to collect the most poor and frustrated elements of society into one locale. It was with some embarrassment that the hapless Ricardo was cornered into serving on a committee charged with examining Owen's proposal. Though he unequivocally opposed Owen's notion that machinery was labour's adversary and bristled at even his indirect association with the scheme, the scientist in Ricardo could not resist the argument for conducting the proposed experiment, and even argued weakly in Parliament for funding that would never be forthcoming.[7] But he was resolute in his objection to Owen's opinion that machinery was an enemy to the working class: scarcely a month before the dinner party Ricardo had declared from the floor of the Commons that he was 'completely at war with the system of Robert Owen, which was built on a theory inconsistent with the principles of political economy'.[8]

Ricardo professed to his dinner guests his abiding concern for the plight of the poor, but would not retreat from his well-known contention that machinery had nothing to do with their misery, and that in fact mechanization was universally beneficial to all classes of society, including the labouring class. He had always acknowledged that mechanized processes decrease the amount of labour necessary to produce a given amount of any particular commodity, but insisted along with most of his privileged colleagues in the language of Adam Smith that the perceived displacement of labour was merely a temporary phenomenon. In his view, capitalists were commanded by their self-interest to re-employ any idle worker in new endeavours. The re-employed labourers would again receive wages, with which they could purchase cheaper, machine-produced commodities along with the rest of society. The argument was a familiar shield for deflecting the protests of the labourers, whose refusal to accept its subtle reasoning was generally taken as another example of their thick-headedness.

At that point a Mr J. L. Mallet, a government bureaucrat and dilettante economist, briefly joined in the debate and thus became an obscure footnote in the history of economic thought. Though he had long respected and been a bit intimidated by Ricardo's economic brilliance, privately he confessed some irritation with Ricardo's sweeping opinions, and on this occasion he took issue with Ricardo's cosy argument, arguing that what the uneducated louts were saying was indeed true, that they were losing their jobs to machinery. Mallet's precise line of argument is unknown, and Ricardo was unconvinced when the guests departed one by one into the foul night. But, as he was later to confess to Mallet, the discussion had triggered a momentous shift in his thoughts on labour and machinery.

Within a year, Ricardo had finished the third edition of *Principles of Political Economy and Taxation*. The initial tortured chapter, 'On Value', was mercilessly modified again, along with numerous minor changes throughout the text. But the most startling and controversial change was the addition of an entirely new chapter, one wholly unintegrated with the rest of the book, entitled 'On Machinery', which began with a gentle confession:

> In the present chapter I will enter into some enquiry respecting the influence of machinery on the interests of the different classes of society, a subject of great importance, and one which appears never to have been investigated in a manner to lead to any certain or satisfactory results. It is more incumbent on me to declare my opinions on this question, because they have, on further reflection, undergone considerable change; and although I am not aware that I have ever published any thing respecting machinery which is necessary for me to retract, yet I have in other ways given my support to doctrines which I now think erroneous; it, therefore, becomes a duty in me to submit my present views for examination, with my reasons for entertaining them.[9]

Ricardo acknowledged his mistake in assuming that the employer of capital and labour would produce to maximum capacity with any given assortment of productive factors, a misjudgement he shared with Adam Smith. He now recognized that it is in the capitalist's self-interest to produce no more than that quantity from which he realizes the greatest net income; in other words, he would seek an *optimum* production level rather than his *maximum* capacity. This subtle modification in his characterization of the capitalist's goals combined with Ricardo's pioneering emphasis on class competition to yield a sinister model: machinery was a tool for redistributing the social product between competing classes with an increasing portion of the labourer's share going to the capitalist. With machinery, the capitalist is no longer bound to expend his resources exclusively on labour in order to produce the greatest gross product: he also has the option to invest in techniques and equipment that give him no immediate return, but allow him to produce cheaper – i.e., less labour-intensive – products in the future. Since the capitalist does not necessarily produce at a maximum capacity, there is no selfish impulse on his part to employ all available labour, and therefore with the continuing introduction of machinery an increasing percentage of the population may become, in Ricardo's word, 'redundant'.

The only scenario that could be of universal benefit would be when the economy expands at a certain minimum rate so that the capitalists' profits will always be greater as production increases. In such an economy, workers would become wealthier because it would always be profitable to the capital- ist to re-employ any displaced worker, and everyone would become materially wealthier due to the abundance and cheapness of machine-produced goods.

But it would not suffice for the economy simply to expand, it would have to expand at some specifically high rate. Ricardo did not attempt to characterize the conditions necessary to attain such a high level of production, but he did imply that it was an unrealistic level to maintain. If the economy did not expand, or if it expanded too slowly, only some of the labourers made idle by machinery could be re-employed, and then only as servants to the vastly enriched capitalists and landowners. But for the labouring class as a whole the damning conclusion was unaltered:

> [T]he opinion entertained by the labouring class, that the employment of machinery is frequently detrimental to their interests, is not founded on prejudice and error, but is conformable to the correct principles of political economy.[10]

Ricardo immediately tried to muzzle the wild theoretical beast he had unleashed. Machines are only introduced gradually, he said – ignoring the obvious evidence to the contrary – and so tend to absorb only surplus capital as opposed to directly displacing labour. But perhaps more to the point, if there is an attraction to capital investment in machinery that English society crushes, competing societies on the continent might not be so accommodating. If England tried to manage the introduction of machinery on its shores, it risked the loss of heavy industry to foreign competitors who were not as troubled by the prospect of exploiting their own working classes. Better to suffer partial unemployment among domestic labourers due to the introduction of machinery than more general unemployment and financial hardship due to the loss of industry to foreign competition.

Within three years of the dinner party, a painful ear infection suddenly seized Ricardo's life. Though not as dismal as Malthus's prognosis for humanity, his theoretical legacy had a disturbing twist to it. In a society already strained by nascent capitalism, he inserted a theoretical basis for legitimate class conflict. To frustrated workers who had previously been slighted by economic science, he provided the first theoretical acknowledgement of their plight.

His colleagues at the pinnacle of English society would pick up where he left off on the issues of free trade, taxation and money within the bounds of what is now referred to as classical economic theory. A later generation of economists would come to recognize the costs of production – upon which Ricardo's generation had almost exclusively focused – as being balanced with the social demand for commodities. They would begin to dissect the capitalist's decisions with mathematical instruments. Combining Ricardo's dictum that the capitalist will produce at the highest net revenue with Malthus's insight that all productive processes necessarily reach a point of diminishing returns, this later generation, the 'neoclassical' economists, made the capitalist's decisions more explicit: if the capitalist perceives that he makes less and less money off each commodity by which he increases the level of production, he will increase production only to the point below which every commodity produces net income, and above which some commodities cost more to produce than the revenue they command. The crux of the capitalist's decision, according to neoclassical economics, is the 'marginal' revenue at each level of production, giving rise to the method of marginal analysis that dominates Western political economy today.

But the unique aspect of Western economics is its foundation on a moral axiom it inherited from Adam Smith and David Ricardo's culture: the right of the capitalist to command labour and machinery in order to extract profits from the production of commodities. Smith's Enlightenment rationale that society is best served by just and unabetted profit-making was as much an article of faith to the gentlemen of Regency England as it is to capitalists today. Mathematical marginalism, considered in the perspective that competitive market forces guide capitalists to perform an indirect social service in pursuing profits, is today the core of the rationale for Western industrial capitalism.

Ricardo broached two topics that would become of enormous relevance but did not pursue them. The first was that the answer to the question of whether machinery benefits the working class is dependent on the rate of expansion that accompanies the introduction of labour-saving devices.

Mechanization in economies that were rapidly and consistently expanding was consistent with the working class's interests; mechanization in sluggish economies would probably be at the working class's expense. The second topic is that the introduction of machinery systematically shifts the composition of the labour force away from physical production towards the direct service of the rich. No one would suggest that the Western labour force of the past has been transformed into the house servants of the present, but the notion did anticipate some of the more worrisome characteristics of the economies of Europe and North America today: the rise of subsistence service sector employment coupled with the flight of high-paying blue collar jobs, and the loss of the relative numbers of the middle class as the ranks of both the rich and the poor swell.

Ironically, less than a mile from the house where the genteel discussion had strayed to machinery and labour, a lonely and impoverished figure, a bitter and failed revolutionary, would pour over the volumes of political economy in the library of the British Museum and discover Ricardo's work. The descriptions he would find – of class conflicts in society, of machinery's impact on the labouring class, of the Labour Theory of Value, and of a systematic decline in capitalist profits – would fuel his revolutionary fire. David Ricardo, independent thinker though he was, was prevented by his social standing from concluding that the capitalist class systematically exploited the working class in the employment of machinery. Karl Marx suffered no such handicap. With all the venom Marx reserved for the mainstream economists of his day, Ricardo was largely spared. Just as Ricardo's free-market thought spawned the modern rationale for industrial capitalism, his dark prognosis for labour in association with machinery spawned the rationale for revolutionary Marxism. Ricardo's thinking, wedded to two opposing social perspectives, has fathered two very quarrelsome children.

On the same frigid evening that Ricardo dined over machinery and labour, another group of learned men was dining at Freemason's Tavern in Lincoln's Inn Fields about a mile to the east. The thirteen voted to form the Royal Astronomical Society that evening, and one of the fledgling society's first actions was to undertake the computation of extensive mathematical tables useful for the practice of that science. It fell to the two youngest members, Charles Babbage and John Herschel, fresh and invigorated by their recent exploration of continental scientific methods, to act as 'computers' for the tables. After months of drudgery and frustrating errors, Charles Babbage turned to his comrade and asked if he thought it feasible to apply machinery to their intellectual labour. Herschel thought it an interesting idea.

3

The Division of
Mental Labour

There seems to be no more frustrating earthly experience than that reserved for the prophet who sees too far ahead or counsels reform in times of apparent prosperity. The proof of the assertion can be found in the life and work of Charles Babbage, a nineteenth-century Englishman whose thinking on many subjects was so far ahead of his time that there is an almost comic aspect to his life, as though he were a thoroughly contemporary soul stranded in a primitive and obtuse culture.

Today Babbage is remembered primarily as the man who discovered the operational principles behind modern computers, and who did so fully a century before they were realized by technologies that were not available in his time. He is seen as an inventor of unusual persistence and originality who struggled vainly throughout his entire life to bring his machines to life. This rendering of Babbage is true as far as it goes, but it neglects to mention Babbage's considerable skill as a political economist in addition to his well-known facility with mathematics and engineering. It was Babbage's facility with economic principles that informed his evolving concepts of the operation of his machines and led him to understand the role machinery of all kinds would play in the national economies of the coming industrial order. Babbage proposed much more during his long life than the construction of computing machinery: he made remarkably far-sighted recommendations for a new approach towards integrating science and technology into the economic agenda of England, and ultimately his inability to bring about the social reforms he proposed may have been a far more tragic failure to his country than his inability to build his machines.

Babbage's prescience as both an inventor and a proponent of a new social and industrial policy for England was a direct result of his command of several different disciplines. He was a capable craftsman and an inspired political economist, a canny socialite and skilled mathematician, a creative inventor with a fiery sense for liberal reform. He owed his productiveness to the fact that, although he was never an extremely wealthy man, his life was one of relative financial freedom, and he moved smoothly through the upper echelons of London society. But, unlike most of those whose company he frequented, Babbage had the highest respect for the skilled mechanic and the technology of the modern factory. He was most comfortable in the company of engineers and mechanics; he spoke their language, and he saw the development of industry as central to the continuing economic might of England. His peculiar genius lay in the manner in which he was able to draw inspiration from social theory for his inventions, and how his command of technological principles informed his social theory.

Babbage was born in 1791, the son of a wealthy, though somewhat curmudgeonly banker who grew up in London. His father's forebears had been goldsmiths, the evolution from goldsmith to merchant and banker being a common one at the time. His modern biographer, Anthony Hyman, cites such an upbringing as critical to Babbage's future work in at least two ways. First, Babbage was probably exposed to craft handiwork from a young age, which was unusual in England at the time, where it was far more common that the upper class would be raised in an environment totally divorced from any craft tradition. Secondly, as a banker's son Babbage from a young age would have developed an intuitive sense of the integral relationship between business development and capital expenditure.[1]

Babbage was a bright, cerebral and sociable child. The year 1810 saw him entering Cambridge, which was at that time only beginning to recover from the severe doldrums into which all English university education had declined in the previous generation. The years at Cambridge were undoubtedly pleasant ones for the gregarious young scholar, who soon established friendships that would last for the remainder of his long and eventful life. Babbage seemed to integrate friendships, scholarship and recreations with unusual aplomb and counted among his friends John Herschel, the son of the great astronomer William Herschel, and George Peacock, who was later to become an innovative mathematician. These three men were to figure prominently in the development of mathematics in England and to rescue it from the neglect into which it had recently fallen.

Babbage, Herschel, Peacock and a small cadre of other sympathetic students came together in the spring of 1812 to form a short-lived, informal association that was to have a great bearing on Babbage's later life. The Analytical Society was a club formed among these friends for the purpose of mingling continental mathematics, serious scholarship and a bit of boyish intellectual mischief. Due to circumstances at Cambridge at the time, the very forming of the society was a not-too-subtle political act, and its activities betrayed a distinctly liberal, reform-minded agenda on the part of the group's founders. Though the Analytical Society lasted less than three years, the spirit of the Analyticals would survive among the principals for many years after and would contribute to a touching cohesion in their later lives, while also assuring that they would always be a bit outside the stodgy mainstream of the English gentry.

The Analyticals' *cause célèbre* sprang indirectly from a nasty and petty tiff that had occurred more than a century before between two of the giants of mathematics, Isaac Newton and Gottfried Wilhelm von Leibniz. The dispute revolved around who should be given credit for the invention of the calculus, a mathematical innovation of monstrous significance. In fact the two geniuses had arrived at the discovery wholly independently of one another, Newton apparently hitting upon it first but failing to publish it until after Leibniz had published his version. At first the men were cautiously civil about the coincidence, but with time vitriolic innuendo and vague accusations of plagiarism swirled about them. An open and vicious squabble erupted between their adherents that was fuelled by nationalistic passions, and inevitably the two principals were drawn into the fray. What had begun as a closed academic squabble festered into an almost political controversy made more ridiculous by the fact that many of the men involved had only a vague understanding of the calculus that was said to be the cause of the dispute.

Disastrously for English mathematics, there was an easy way for an English mathematician to affirm his national allegiance to Newton's claim, a way that seemed innocuous enough but was actually destined virtually to cripple mathematical inquiry in England for more than a century. The two men had quite naturally arrived at two entirely different systems of notation for denoting the central concept of differentiation, and quite naturally the English adopted Newton's and the Germans favoured Leibniz's. The problem for the English was that Leibniz's notation was a far more elegant and evocative expression of the concept and lent itself much more easily to various innovations that rippled through mathematics in the wake of the discovery of the calculus. Primarily because of its utility, Leibniz's notation was in general use throughout Europe and precipitated significant innovation, particularly by the French, while in England mathematical progress was tortuously slow, in part because of the burden of Newton's notation and in part because English mathematicians had effectively isolated themselves from the common language of continental mathematics.

The Analytical Society flagrantly expounded Leibniz's notation specifically, and in general promoted a liberal reform spirit associated with French rationalism. They looked with sympathy and envy to the prominent role men of science played in European countries, and in particular in Napoleon's France, where scientists and engineers were frequently given generous government support and played prominent roles in the bureaucracy. In conservative England, these general sympathies were suspect, and at

Cambridge the specific sympathy for Leibniz's notation was particularly irksome. To propose adopting Leibniz's notation and to promote French mathematics at Cambridge, the very institution to which Newton had lent such prestige, was a provocative and overtly political statement.

Babbage's leadership in the Analytical Society was the first expression of themes that ran prominently through his life. It placed him firmly on the side of rational, liberal reform, and revealed a tendency to turn to private learned societies as an agent in this quest. It sharpened his focus on French mathematics, allowing him to contribute to the revitalization of the moribund mathematics of his country, and endeared him to continental methods of blending science and technology under the aegis of government. But perhaps most interestingly, it must have impressed him with the huge significance and utility of cogent notation, and with how quickly a great country can intellectually ossify when it becomes entrenched in mindless orthodoxy.

After leaving Cambridge, Babbage married and settled in London in 1814. His wife, Georgiana, was precious to him, and the two were blissfully happy with each other until her untimely death only thirteen years later. For the next few years Babbage lived the life of a scientific polymath, doing significant work in mathematics, lecturing in astronomy, and reading with interest the emerging literature in political economy. He ingratiated himself with London scientific society and was admitted to the Royal Society in 1816.

Babbage's liberal spirit had scarcely abated since his college days, and it was during this period that his political sensibilities first began to have an adverse impact on his career. English society was thoroughly reactionary, and a liberal reputation had the practical effect of barring a young intellectual like Babbage from the academic appointments to which he aspired. He cast about for any of several teaching positions and was undoubtedly qualified, but was rejected at every turn. The Babbages and their children were forced to make do on a modest budget based largely on an allowance from Babbage's father, augmented later by a legacy from Georgiana's parents.

It was through his association with scientific circles that Babbage first embarked upon the task of inventing accurate calculating machines, for among the scientific circles in which he moved there was a recognized need for more accurate mathematical tables of all types. At the time, this was an issue of tremendous import, since the manual calculation of these values was a lengthy and costly process, but more importantly the tables produced were notoriously fraught with errors. The social costs of not having accurate mathematical tables were significant, since the absence of these values impeded astronomers and other scientists and engineers in their work and even endangered navigation on the high seas, since precise mathematical tables were critical for navigation. Even the inaccurate tables that existed at the time were the result of very expensive computational labour, and the person who could perfect a machine for doing fairly recondite mathematical computations could do much to rationalize and eliminate error from entire scientific and technical disciplines. Here was the perfect task for a mathematician and scientist who subscribed to rational reform, and Babbage talked about the prospects of such machinery to his new associates in London.

Babbage had at times reflected on various strategies for mechanizing the computation of mathematical tables, but had not approached the problem seriously until he and Herschel took an extensive tour of France in 1819 for the purpose of acquainting themselves at first hand with the French methods they had long revered. While there, Babbage became acquainted with a monumental set of mathematical tables that had been prepared by Gaspard de Prony, an engineer in Napoleon's administration. The tables, which filled seventeen folio volumes, dwarfed anything Babbage had ever seen. They were said to be remarkably free of error and had been prepared in an incredibly brief period, and it was the organizational genius behind their computation that was to leave a lasting impression on the young men.

There is a poetic elegance in the fact that Babbage's inspiration for his first machine came indirectly from Adam Smith, as interpreted by a French technocrat under the regime of Napoleon Bonaparte. Gaspard de Prony was the most highly acclaimed civil engineer in France, the director of the *École des Ponts et Chausées* and highly desirous of the political fortunes that were being meted out by Napoleon. The Republic had trumpeted its resolve for rationality in all things, and in that spirit commissioned numerous projects for rationalizing science, engineering and social relations. Among the reforms instituted at this time was the metric system, which Prony helped to plan, and the new system of decimal measures mandated the task of a new comprehensive set of mathematical tables for decimal increments to replace the old tables. The computation of these tables fell to Prony, and the task was as grandiose as the rational revolution that inspired it. Prony's task was to produce, in one massive publication, the trigonometric values for 3,600 divisions of a circle and the logarithms of all the integers from 1 to 200,000, all to be calculated with an unprecedented precision. This was the most comprehensive set of mathematical tables that had ever been contemplated, and a spectacular undertaking that promised vastly to facilitate the work of geometrists, architects, engineers and scientists. M. de Prony was well aware of the time and expense required to produce such a document, as well as the immense practical difficulties in assuring its accuracy. Skilled mathematicians would have to find a suitable algebraic expression called a polynomial that approximated each requested value, and each of the values in the table was derived from tedious and error-prone arithmetic based on these polynomials. For the algorithms alone, this process would have to be applied to 200,000 values.

Prony was an ambitious man, and had taken on the technical assignment largely to advance his political fortunes in a nation where scientific men could hold prominent positions in government. As he surveyed the requirements of the project, it became obvious that this was an assignment that would require many highly skilled and expensive human calculators many years to perform, and Prony was hardly enamoured with officiating over a project that was bound to require a generation of drudgery to complete. He became so absorbed in his predicament that he took to wandering the streets of Paris, oblivious to his surroundings as he contemplated the enormous problem he faced. He wandered into a second-hand bookshop, where, in the midst of his reverie, an attractively bound book by an Englishman caught his eye. The book was *The Wealth of Nations*, which he had never read. He opened the book at random to inspect it, and it fell open at its first chapter, 'Of the Division of Labour'. In a creative flash Prony saw the solution to his problem.

Smith had employed his famous example of how the division of labour dramatically speeds the production of pins, but Prony saw that the same principle could be applied to mathematical calculations. He instituted a system in which an elite group of the most skilled mathematicians in France would develop mathematical expressions that sufficiently approximated each of the values needed for the tables. This team, consisting of only five or six men, would pass its formulae to a second team of seven or eight somewhat less skilled mathematicians, who would labour to convert the expressions they received into a form that could be easily solved using only very simple addition and subtraction of numbers. These simplified problems were then passed to a group of sixty to eighty unskilled arithmeticians, who would simply do the computations, and pass them back up the hierarchy for interpretation. According to Babbage's later account, nine-tenths of this lowest class of calculators knew nothing more of mathematics than the mechanical operations of addition and subtraction, and the work of these was more accurate than their peers whose understanding of mathematics was greater.[2] Prony's arrangement was a fabulous success – the completed tables were prepared in only a fraction of the time that it would have taken using previous methods – and Babbage was greatly impressed with both the technique and the economic lesson that it expressed.

There was obviously a profound economy in Prony's method. Prony's team was systematically tearing mathematical problems apart until each original equation had been exploded into a myriad of simple additions and subtractions. By the time the problem reached the bottom of the pyramid of calculators, it had been transformed from recondite concepts that only a sophisticated mathematical mind could apprehend to a mass of purely repetitive functions that were so mechanical in nature that a knowledge of mathematics actually seemed to interfere with performing them. It is no accident that Prony's system is in fact an excellent analogy for the way modern computers really work, by systematically breaking up higher-level operations into increasingly less sophisticated operations until the processes are so devoid of any meaning that they can be performed by circuitry. But that gets ahead of the story.

Though it would deny the man the full credit he deserves for his creativity, it is tempting to say that to someone with Babbage's unique perspective, Prony's system offered an obvious opportunity. Here were a mass of calculators who had, through the division of labour, been reduced to doing almost purely mechanical work, inspired by Adam Smith's characterization of how the division of labour can improve upon productivity. Babbage was certainly familiar with *The Wealth of Nations* and facile with its principles, and in it Smith had intimately connected the process of the division of labour to the introduction of machinery. As it happened, Babbage's first calculating machine was little more than a mechanical analogue to Prony's human pyramid.

Though it is not necessary, a little mathematics will go a long way towards the reader's understanding of the concept for Babbage's first machine. The central concepts are of polynomial expressions and a particular method of solving them. Polynomials are mathematical expressions similar in form to

$$1/3 * x^3 - 3/2 * x^2 + 3x - 11/6$$

where x is a variable that is holding the place of any particular number. The useful aspect of polynomials is that they can be used to approximate the value of many useful functions, such as the logarithm function. As an example, the polynomial above gives a rough approximation of the natural logarithm of x within a limited range: if a number within this range is substituted in the polynomial and if the resulting expression is computed, the value that results is close to the logarithm of the number. It was the function of the skilled mathematicians in Prony's arrangement to define polynomials that suitably approximated the value being sought. Once the polynomials were defined, it fell to the unskilled arithmeticians to calculate the consecutive values given by each polynomial for succeeding values of x.

The problem of calculating a table of values for a polynomial can be thought of as just slightly more complicated than listing the squares of every integer between 1 and 500 – which is the same as solving the polynomial 'x^2' for five hundred consecutive values. One would be tempted simply to set out to perform five hundred multiplications, starting at $1 * 1 = 1$, $2 * 2 = 4$, etc., through $345 * 345 = 119,025$, until finally arriving at $500 * 500 = 250,000$. Most readers have probably forgotten how onerous a task this can be without some kind of electronic aid, but there is an additional problem: when you had finally reached 500, you could not know if you had made any mistakes.

Prony used a different method, the so-called 'method of differences', in his tables that saved labour in the calculations and made them easier to check. In solving the example problem, one might notice that if a vertical list were made of the first few answers 1, 4, 9, 16, 25, etc., that a second column could be made of the *differences* between successive values in the first column. This second column would consist of 3, 5, 7, 9, etc. (4−1= 3, 9−4= 5, 16−9= 7, 25−16= 9). There is an apparent trend in this second column, and with a bit of thought one might deduce that a third column could be created that simply consisted of 2s: (5−3= 2, 7−5= 2, 9−7= 2). In these columns lies the crux of the utility of the method of differences, and how they can be employed to produce the example table: if one simply continued the second column by adding 2 to the previous number 498 consecutive times (until the final number in the second column equalled 999), then the column of squares could be produced directly by simply adding the last number in the first column to the next number in the second column. Instead of doing five hundred multiplications, we have reduced the problem into 1,000 additions, and if we check occasionally to see that the value we arrived at through the method of differences is indeed the square of the intended number, we can be virtually certain that all the values above it in the table are also accurate.

The method of differences was an ideal mathematical technique for computing tables based on successive values for polynomial formulae, because it allowed each value to be calculated directly, by calculating the next 'difference' between table values and adding it to the previous value. The more complicated the polynomial, the more nearly it could be made to approximate a particular mathematical function such as a logarithm or trigonometric function, and the more complicated the calculation for each table value. But no matter how complicated the polynomial became, a process could be specified that allowed successive values to be produced using only addition and subtraction. In Prony's system, it was the most knowledgeable mathematicians who derived the proper polynomial, the lesser mathematicians who specified how to solve the polynomial through successive additions by defining the 'differences' in the list, and the lowly arithmeticians who did the computing.

Babbage's concept of what he would call the 'difference engine' was an elegant mechanical calculator that could display the results of subsequent values for polynomial expressions using the method of differences: it replaced the lowest group of arithmeticians in Prony's pyramid with brass gears and wheels. The machine was to be a system of vertical axes with numbered wheels attached to them, rather like an array of automobile odometers turned on their side. Each axis represented a number, and was geared to another axis so that the second axis would advance by the value shown on the first axis. To solve a polynomial, the wheels on the axes would be set to an initial value by hand so that they corresponded to the values for a particular polynomial. Once set the machine would display successive values for that polynomial, as successive differences rippled through the machine from axis to axis.

The problem with Babbage's concept was one of implementation, for the machine Babbage envisaged was a severe challenge to the machining technology of the time. There was no single action of the machine that was particularly difficult to embody in gears and wheels: the challenge lay in the complex action of the completed system's hundreds of interconnected moving parts, and of the requirement of precise movements to ripple flawlessly from one component to the next. One of the primary reasons for mechanizing this activity was to eliminate error in human calculations, and if the machine were itself susceptible to error it would hardly be useful. Every component would have to be machined to extremely fine tolerances for the time, on the order of ten thousandths of an inch when the industry standards were more on the order of thirty-seconds of an inch.

Babbage found himself in a difficult position that is familiar today but was rare in his time. He had an idea for a device that could potentially be of tremendous benefit to society, but it could not be built without advancing the state of industrial technology by a significant degree. To build his device would require a significant investment in funds, but the nature of the device was not such that he or any investor could be expected to risk the money for research and development. In Smith's terms, he had a wonderful plan for the productive division of labour, but his idea was not inspired by markets but out of an abstract conviction on his part that such a device would be useful. But the utility of the device was too abstract for many people to grasp, and even if influential laymen could be brought to understand the utility of the machine, solving polynomials was hardly as attractive an area of innovation as the more monumental examples of engineering that were presently capturing the public's attention, such as tunnels, bridges, steam engines or electrical devices. Babbage's only recourse seemed to be to petition the government for funding.

Babbage first formally proposed his machine in a letter to the Royal Society of London in July 1822. The Royal Society was the premier scientific institution in Great Britain, and though it was clear to those in Babbage's liberal, reform-minded clique that it was in severe need of overhaul, the society's opinion on the worthiness of such an enterprise was clearly necessary before the government would act upon it. With the fairly enthusiastic support of a committee of experts from the society, Babbage was able to secure an agreement from the chancellor of the exchequer calling for at least partial government funding of the construction of the difference engine.

The work on the difference engine was to proceed for almost a decade, when it would be suspended in a fog of resentment and ill will between Babbage, his sub-contractor who actually machined the parts and the government. By 1833 only a portion of the instrument had been completed, and though it was slow in dying, the difference engine project was dead except in Babbage's mind and on paper, and Babbage's later schemes for more ambitious calculating machines never had any real chance of being built. The model that was constructed worked excellently. It was testimony to the great strides in engineering that had been fostered by Babbage's project and a tantalizing glimpse of the potential of his later machines. In retrospect, it is clear that Babbage's inability to secure and maintain government funding for his inventions was more than the personal tragedy he felt keenly. It was a tragedy for the future economic health of England because even the work that was done was of seminal importance in advancing the state of the art of technical drawing and precision engineering, and if the project had proceeded it is reasonable to suppose that the economic spin-offs would have been even more significant.

Within a short time of work commencing on the difference engine, it was apparent that there would be problems. Foremost among them was a misunderstanding about the extent to which the government was underwriting the work. Babbage left his initial meeting with the chancellor thinking that he had been offered only an initial advance of £1,000 to commence work, but the chancellor seemed to think that the entire machine could be built for that amount. Incredibly, there were no notes taken at the meeting, and the principals' memories diverged. The work was more expensive and time-consuming than Babbage anticipated, and it became increasingly frustrating to explain his additional requests for funds as different governments were voted in and out of power.

Through it all, Babbage was forced to deal with high-level conservative politicians who were not ideologically predisposed to the government funding the project in the first place. Babbage did not have the advantage – as he would have had in much of Europe – of being able to deal with a bureaucracy that was peopled with scientists who could understand what he was doing, or with a government that embraced the need to stimulate national technology.

Babbage was not blameless in any of this, however. He was not skilful in the political art of give and take, and was more than a bit brittle in his belief that the government was treating him unfairly. But his fatal error was his lack of close management of his immediate sub-contractor, Joseph Clement, who was villainously opportunistic in exploiting the uncertain terms of his employment. Babbage's understanding with Clement was as vague as the government's understanding with Babbage, and Clement used the project to finance the construction of many valuable machining tools which he then, citing custom, claimed to own. Babbage, a firm believer in delegation and one who respected the skilled worker's craft, gave Clement a significant amount of free rein in his work, a trust that was tragically misplaced. Babbage was away for much of the time that important work was being done on the engine, and by the time Babbage finally confronted Clement with issues of cost and ownership, the arrangement was already out of control and their disputes vastly complicated his requests to the government for more funding.

In 1832, in the midst of Babbage's ongoing wrangling with Clement and the government, Babbage instructed Clement to assemble a portion of the machine for which components had been completed, apparently in an effort to have a working model to demonstrate the potential of the final engine. This model was to represent the furthest that this machine was to progress, as the dispute with Clement together with the government's impatience conspired slowly to strangle the project. Babbage kept the model in his home for a time, where it became the centrepiece of his social gatherings, but he was reticent to accept ownership of the contraption because he was becoming extremely sensitive to the perception that it had been he who had benefited financially from the arrangement when in fact the machine had represented a significant financial difficulty for him. This is the machine that is on exhibit in the Science Museum in London, and Hyman reports that it is still in very impressive working order.[3]

Despite individual failings in the matter, a primary problem that Babbage faced was that there was no institutional precedent for what he had set out to do. English government and society were structurally and ideologically unprepared to take advantage of the opportunity being presented to them. The reactionary spirit had firm control of England, and if an inventor had the temerity to request a government subsidy for his research, it was far easier to cite a policy of *laissez-faire* than it was to analyse systematically the inventor's proposal and judge its prospects for enhancing the public good. Additionally, polite society was curiously ambivalent about industrial technology anyway, full of pride for England's industrial prominence while disdainful of any direct involvement in manufacturing: it was still the goal of most who became rich as entrepreneurs to escape the unseemly squabbling of business for the refinements of a life of leisure. This was not a social system that was likely to embrace wholeheartedly an expensive innovation such as Babbage was proposing.

Babbage's experience with the government in trying to build his machine galvanized his long-held opinion that England's lethargy towards technological innovation was destined to bring it into economic decline, particularly in contrast to what he had experienced in his travels in Europe. The frustrations started to show in small ways and Babbage began to get rather irritable in his demeanour. But the man was dealt the cruellest of blows in 1827 when

Georgiana, to whom he was touchingly devoted, fell ill and died. Immediately after her death, and in the midst of his most trying experiences with the difference engine, Babbage plunged into a decade of intense reform-minded effort. Though his fervour was impressive, it seemed to his friends an empty effort, lacking the happiness and vitality of his earlier married life. During this period, Babbage railed against what he saw as the decline of science in England and, in print, blisteringly contrasted the Royal Society with the more sophisticated scientific societies in Europe. He was a forceful advocate for better scientific education, and bewailed the preference for theoretical over applied science, since he considered creative applied science to be central to England's future. He even ran for parliament on a sort of technocratic platform, trying to put industrial policy on the front burner of British politics.

Babbage was fighting the good fight, but his politics, like his inventions, could not find an audience outside of his coterie of friends. England was not receptive to the alarm he was sounding, and he was to be as frustrated in his efforts at reform as he was in his efforts to build his difference engine. He did, however, produce a book during this period that was interesting because it was a definitive presentation of his keen insight into the new economics of industrial societies, a book which had some provocative recommendations for England that in some ways were as far ahead of his time as the machines he had undertaken to build. The book was *On the Economy of Machinery and Manufactures*, published in 1832.

Babbage's book was a presentation of a sophisticated economic thinker, but though it gained him respect and was in general use as a reference among the economists of his day, today his contributions to political economy have been eclipsed by a fascination with his engines. The book betrayed Babbage's familiarity with industrial practices of the time and demonstrated his thoughts with appropriate examples in industrial practice, a unique approach for an economics text because it eschewed dry theory for practical examples and relied upon an empirical basis for its assertions. The book was notable in the history of economic thought because it emphasized for the first time the central role of industrial manufacturing in modern economies; and in its empirical observations and its characterizations of the development of machinery it was destined to have a significant impact on Karl Marx and John Mill.

Like Ricardo, one of Babbage's most significant observations had to do with reconsidering Smith's attitude toward labour and machinery. Babbage significantly added to the reasons Adam Smith had cited as the basis for the profitability of the division of labour, a subject to which he had devoted many hours of practical experimentation in the years he had worked on his machine, and of which he had gained such detailed knowledge in his many tours through factories in England and abroad. Babbage said that Smith had omitted one very important advantage to the division of labour;

that in addition to the three advantages Smith had cited (efficiency through specialization, saving time in transfer and the invention of machinery), the division of labour allowed a critical fourth advantage. With the clever division of labour, the manufacturer need only pay for the amount of skill that was required for the task, and no more. In other words, by dividing the work into many discrete tasks, the work could be parcelled out more efficiently to different people with different intellectual capacities. Those who were intellectually capable of handling more complex assignments could perform only the tasks that required their skills and that commanded higher salaries, and the less demanding tasks could be allocated to less skilled and cheaper workers, or even to machinery. This observation, the so-called 'Babbage Principle', was obviously what had led to Prony's success, and was noted with interest by Marx, among others.

Babbage was a fervent capitalist and a great believer in the wisdom of each man rationally pursuing his own self-interest, but he was more than a century ahead of his time in his sophisticated understanding of the true nature of his countrymen's rational self-interest. In this, as in his inventions, Babbage seems much more attuned to modern times than to the times in which he lived, and in many respects the book reads more like today's popular business-management tract than a nineteenth-century economics text. The book even recommends some policies that were entirely ignored by Western industry until they were rediscovered in recent times in the hugely successful industrial practices of Japan.

Babbage believed very strongly in a natural harmony of interests between workers and capitalists, and between private enterprise and government, and he believed that theories that promoted class conflict were tragically flawed and would inevitably lead to losses by workers and business owners alike. The problem with an adversarial worker–capitalist relationship, he felt, was that it embodied a hopelessly myopic view of each principal's self-interest, and if either side were niggardly in its demands the self-interest of both was bound to suffer. Rather than resisting workers tooth and nail on matters of compensation, capitalists should institute profit-sharing programmes with their employees to assure their motivation and hard work. Institutional innovation is the key to continued prosperity, Babbage held, advancing dramatically Smith's rather naive description of the innovative dynamic, and the wise capitalist would take care to assure that workers are handsomely rewarded for their inventions, and that funds are set aside in prosperous times for dedicated research and development in slack times. The workers also bore a responsibility for being reasonable in their demands. It was in the workers' self-interest to be loyal and flexible to the firm's requests, and he cited as an example that the net result of the Luddites' insurrections had been that textile manufacturers had moved their operations to more stable labour markets, making unemployment in the region even worse than it had been before.

51

Babbage even made the mildly shocking recommendation that the export of machinery to foreign countries should be encouraged without restriction. He saw machinery clearly as a commodity just like other commodities that were manufactured and sold abroad, and sensed that the economic health of the nations of the future would be linked to their ability to design and produce the finest machinery for export. He saw through the fears of many that the exporting of machines gave foreign competitors the means to compete with England, and sensed that it was in the factory that the economic health of future nations lay. The book is among the earliest of testaments to the need for a scientific approach to industrial production.

By 1834, the government had spent close to £17,000 on a machine that was still far from completion, and though it would take ten years to admit as much, its funding for the device had died. Babbage continued to press for a response to his claims for additional funding, but the government, through several administrations, waffled interminably. Part of the problem had to do with a lack of understanding of the machines, much of it had to do with uncertainty about the continued costs the government would face in continuing development. But the negotiations became even more complicated after 1834. In that year Babbage hit upon a whole new class of calculating machinery, and in his enthusiasm for the seemingly unlimited applications this new class offered, he persisted in including consideration of his new machine in the ongoing negotiations for funding on the unfinished difference engine. This was not a totally selfish inclusion on Babbage's part, for the machines offered quantum leaps in functionality over his original concept that was now over ten years old, and in the intervening years Babbage had developed new engineering methods that made starting from scratch a very viable alternative to completing the work using the older methods. Once again, his zeal for this new class of machines – which he referred to as the 'analytical engine' – was supremely well-placed but hopelessly ahead of its time, for in the conceptual development of the analytical engine Babbage was flirting with the fundamentals of modern computers.

It is significant that Babbage himself credits his formulation of the analytical engine's design to his reliance on the constantly improving system of notation he had developed for the machines. Babbage had originally developed a special notation as an adjunct to the reams of technical drawings that had to be prepared in building the first difference engine. The technical drawings themselves were significant advances over the drafting technique of the time, but even the excellent drawings produced by his shop were inadequate in fully expressing the full complexity of a system of components like Babbage's engines. The mechanical notation was developed to express much more about the operation of a machine than could be derived from a typical static engineering drawing of the components. Engineering drawings typically showed the proposed assembly in one certain state, the way an architectural drawing shows a proposed structure in one static view. But it was important to Babbage that a method be found to depict accurately the changing *state* of any component at any point in time, and with improvements the notation evolved into a formal system of representing the sequence of operations within the machine. Babbage's notation assumed an increasingly abstract and mathematical form, and became a sort of specialized calculus for perfectly mimicking on paper every operation of the machine.

The practical importance of an elegant system of notation had been impressed upon Babbage since his days at Cambridge and his co-founding of the Analytical Society, when he had realized that Newton's awkward and inflexible denotation of fundamental mathematical concepts was retarding British mathematics, while Leibniz's superior notational system had lead to significant advances in mathematics on the continent. With the Clement débâcle behind him and his prospects dim for ever building any of his inventions, the role of his notational system loomed much larger in his work. Since he could simulate states of his machines with symbols, it was sufficient in developing new concepts in machines to proceed somewhat in the mode of mathematical inquiry. In retrospect, it may even be said that Babbage was fortunate in being forced to develop his analytical engines almost entirely in the abstract, because the technological means for implementing the logical relationships he pioneered were more than a century away.

Though the analytical engines never existed in a comprehensive form other than on paper, Babbage's unshakeable grounding in engineering technique would never allow him to pursue a purely abstract engine whose components could not at least have been physically possible to build. But since he was confident that the mechanical notation accurately expressed the inherent operating characteristics of the various mechanical components, he was able to pull back a bit from a mechanic's perspective and work more productively in the abstract, still fully confident that his abstract design could be built with wheels, gears and axles. He worked feverishly on his new design for two years, focusing principally on the overall logical design of the machine, but also pausing occasionally to work in metal to assure that his concepts had not escaped practicality.

Freed by his notation, Babbage took a fresh look at the fundamental organization of his machine and began to conceive of machines with far greater computational power. In his old difference engine, results from one odometer-like wheel were mechanically geared to a second wheel, and results from this wheel fed in turn to a third wheel, so that turning the crank of the machine started a cascade of revolutions through the device, and the end result (the value that could be read off the final wheel) was a solution to the problem posed. The machine, complicated as it was, could serve no other purpose than solving polynomial expressions using the method of differences, just as Big Ben is designed to do nothing other than keep time and chime the quarter hours. But why, thought Babbage, should the process stop with the final wheel? What if the results from the final wheel were sent back to the first wheel, so that even more complicated expressions could be solved? What if the results from any wheel could be sent to any other wheel, or just recorded mechanically and re-read later when a problem required it? This was a new species of machine entirely, one which could, in Babbage's words uttered decades before Lewis Carroll, 'eat its own tail'.

The orderly rectangular array of identical wheels that characterized the design of the difference engine gave way to a design that looked from above like a mob of wheels pressing against a central cylinder and, like the pin makers in Smith's factory, the wheels now began to assume specialized functions. Some of the wheels were dedicated to performing specific arithmetic operations, which Babbage called the 'mill', because it blindly processed whatever values were fed into it just as a mill blindly grinds grain. Some wheels were simply locations for parking the result of the operations for later use, which Babbage called a 'store'. A few of the wheels were even dedicated to controlling mechanically the sequence of events that would take place in the machine. They looked something like large versions of the pinned metal cylinder in musical boxes, and as the pins rotated across other geared instruments, the machine's configuration was altered so that results would be copied from one location to another, or specific arithmetic operations would occur. Babbage called these pinned cylinders and their attendant machinery the 'control barrels'. A printing mechanism, largely developed even in the difference engine days, was integrated into the system to print results.

This was truly a machine that could be set up to perform a vast array of mathematical calculations. The control barrel could fetch any two values from any location in the store, feed them into the mill, and copy the results of the mill's arithmetic operation at some specified location in the store. It could cycle through any sequence of similar operations indefinitely, perhaps until a specified number of cycles had been performed, or until a certain value was calculated as the result of a specified action. But, though the sequence of operations the machine could potentially perform were vastly more complicated than in the difference engine, the analytical engine was originally designed to do nothing more than step through its mechanical fate like any other machine. Implicit in the initial state of the machine was the exact state of the machine when it had completed the operations represented by the pins in the control barrel. Initially, the only way to modify what the machine would do once it was set in motion was physically to modify the machine itself, such as by changing the location of pins on the control barrel. What was missing was a flexible way to guide the machine through any one of a limitless number of sequences of operations, and to do so in a way that would allow different sequences of operations to be retained for later use or modification. What the analytical engine still lacked that denied it the seemingly unlimited flexibility of modern computers was some sort of mechanism analogous to human memory, a mechanism that would allow it to store large amounts of information for later use. If the machine possessed some sort of extensive mechanical memory, it could retain a record of a series of mechanical instructions that it could run through in sequence, perhaps even modifying the instructions or their sequence as conditions warranted. This critical introduction of auxiliary memory into the design for the analytical engine came in 1836, when Babbage first began to integrate into his designs a card-reading device based upon a mechanism that was then in widespread use in weaving fine brocaded silks. The device was the Jacquard mechanism, also called, in an ironical anthropomorphism derived from its appearance as it sat atop the looms for which it was designed, the Jacquard 'head'.

The Jacquard mechanism had been perfected in the silk weaving capital of Lyons only three decades before, and at the time Babbage adopted it into his design there were already tens of thousands in use world-wide, including many in the Spitalfields area of London. The device was used to simplify the weaving of fine patterned silks in which amazingly ornate figures and patterns are formed by delicate arrangements of the warp and weft of the woven fabric. These patterned fabrics, or *façonnes*, had been produced for centuries in China and later in Italy and France on special looms called draw looms, and before the introduction of the Jacquard mechanism the process by which these fine silks were produced was an exceedingly tedious and expensive one.

In simple looms, fabric typically has two sets of threads woven at right angles to each other: warp threads that run longitudinally, parallel to the length of the fabric as it is rolled on to a bolt, and weft threads that run perpendicular to the warp and generally extend a metre or so across the width of the fabric. To create a simple weave, the warp threads are tightly stretched horizontally, parallel to each other in the approximate position they will assume in the finished fabric. Some of the threads – say, every other thread – are plucked upward out of alignment with the other warp threads, forming a triangular opening (called a 'shed') that extends across the width of the warp threads. The weaver can then slide a shuttle through the shed, above the flat surface formed by the plane of undisturbed threads and below the threads that were plucked out of their original position. The shuttle drags a weft thread behind it through the shed. The weft is then drawn tight and packed firmly against the previous weft with a device called a comb, and the warp threads that were plucked out of alignment are released. An alternate set of threads is then pulled out of alignment and the process repeats, so that woven fabric is produced one weft thread at a time.

A draw loom differs from a standard loom in its ability to pluck selectively and flexibly any one of many different combinations of warp threads for each weft rather than mechanically plucking the same combination of warps over and over for each weft. By carefully selecting the warp threads to pluck and modifying the colour and texture of the weft threads, draw looms create fine and colourful patterns in the finished fabric. In an effort to produce increasingly intricate and subtly shaded figures in the *façonnes*, inventors created increasingly sophisticated draw looms for identifying sets of strings to pull, and by the eighteenth century the draw loom had itself become a baroque contraption. To produce a brocade, a skilled weaver would set up a maze of cords, each connected to certain sets of strings, each of which was connected to warp threads stretched out horizontally in the draw loom. The operation of a draw loom would require, in addition to the weaver who set the wefts, one or more assistants, usually women or children, either sitting atop the loom or standing alongside, pulling any of a myriad arrangement of different cords for each weft. The beauty and intricacy of the brocades that were produced on draw looms in this manner is truly astonishing, but it was tedious work to produce these designs literally thread by thread and was in fact murderously difficult work for the assistants who pulled the strings, for the load of strings and counterweights that was required for each weft thread could be considerable.

What the Jacquard mechanism did was to read from a chain of punched cards the specification of the warp threads to be raised for each weft, and from this specification automatically to lift this set of threads from their horizontal position using the force applied from a foot pedal. The cards (which bore a striking resemblance to the punched cards used in postwar computers, of which they were the direct inspiration) had a regular array of positions upon them that could potentially contain a hole, and each of these positions corresponded to a warp thread on the loom below. Each card contained the specification for the position of all the warp threads for one throw of the shuttle. For each weft thread in the final fabric, the Jacquard device would repeat a specific sequence of operations. First, a punched card in the chain would be drawn into the mechanism and placed flat upon a wooden block in which holes had been drilled for every position on the card that might contain a hole. Next the entire assembly of wooden block and card would be impaled against a horizontal array of projecting spring-loaded pins, so that if there was a hole in the card that corresponded to a pin, the pin would pass through it undisturbed, but if there was not a hole the pin would be depressed. Each pin was attached to a vertical s-shaped wire hook in the heart of the mechanism. The lower portion of this double hook was attached by a string to a warp thread and the upper hook was held just above the bars of a horizontal grill above. This grill could be lifted by the action of a foot pedal, so that all the s-shaped hooks (and the warp threads tied to them) that remained in their original position could be lifted at once. But where the pins did not encounter a hole in the card, the corresponding s-shaped hook would be pushed aside, and the warp thread that was attached to it would not be lifted by the action of the foot pedal. In essence the presence of a hole corresponded to an instruction to the device to lift a warp thread for one throw of the shuttle, and conversely the absence of a hole meant to leave a warp thread undisturbed for that particular pass.

A card-reading mechanism along these lines was inherently useful in retaining a complex sequence of operations for a machine to replay, and had been a favoured technique particularly in France for recording the complex movements of mechanical automata. It is the direct precursor to modern numerically controlled manufacturing machines, which until recently were predominantly directed by continuous paper tapes with holes punched in them. The origins of the concept are a mystery, but the technique was developed principally in Lyons, where its practical applicability to the local silk-weaving industry made it the object of recurring interest. The Jacquard mechanism attached to a draw loom not only relieved the weaver of the cost of employing one or more string pullers, but it also made for a more consistent and error-free pattern, since a single slip by the string puller could ruin a fabric that had been many days in the making.

The experience of the man for whom the device is named, Joseph Marie Jacquard[4] of Lyons, bears an interesting contrast to Babbage's frustrations with his invention. The credit that Jacquard is given for inventing the device was the source of some local controversy at the time and still frankly rankles among knowledgeable authorities today who are more aware of the real story behind the machine. Jacquard did not appear to be an unusually skilled or creative mechanic and, unlike Babbage, seemed to have a very limited scope of interests. His very simple manner of speech was frequently commented upon and, stripping away the flattering portraits of him drawn by his friends – impressions that survive and continue to distort modern perceptions of the man – his life seems to have revolved around little more than desultory tinkering with machines and efforts to obtain public subsidy for his work, much of which was of dubious originality and frequently not of tremendous practical utility. But because the subject of his efforts was related directly to an industrial practice that the national and local governments were keenly interested in, and because the French in the time of Napoleon suffered no shyness about publicly sponsoring research and development projects, Jacquard worked under public subsidy for most of his life.

Jacquard's central innovation, which was made public to the city elders in Lyons in 1804, was in combining the inventions of two far more skilled inventors into one practical device. He drew from the work of Jean

Philippe Falcon, who made practical devices by which an operator could force punched cards against pins in order to obtain the correct pattern of threads for each weft, and from Jacques Vaucanson, who had discovered a clever way automatically to translate a series of holes into a shed, which eliminated the need for an assistant at the loom. Both these men had encountered political difficulties in Lyons as they tried to introduce their machines. Jacquard also had his political difficulties with the authorities in Lyons, but the stories that these arose from the petty machinations of workers who feared being displaced by his machines are largely mythical. There is no record to verify the accounts written shortly after his death that there were riots in Lyons against him or his machines; in fact the perfected machines were generally quite popular. There do appear to have been recriminations against Jacquard and the city elders did threaten to withhold the generous pension they had awarded him for the invention of his machine, but rather than being part of an illiberal working-class plot to obstruct the introduction of new technology, as it was frequently rendered during the nineteenth century, there seems to be another very different side to the story.

Jacquard's machines did not work well at first – they were rough on the silk, hard on the ears and lurched violently as they moved – and Jacquard did not seem anxious to improve upon them once he had received his lifetime pension. As to the council's threat to deny him his pension, the action was taken in 1813 not, as is frequently repeated, because of unjust intrigue against Jacquard, but because Jacquard was doing nothing to improve upon the device that was in the public domain and was in fact working with private investors on different devices while still on the public payroll. Ironically, the city fathers rescinded their threat because of a misunderstanding: when Jacquard travelled to Paris to argue for the reinstitution of his pension, the council apparently became seized with the suspicion that he might actually take his work to weavers in other countries, an early example of concerns for strategic technology transfer. Though this was never Jacquard's plan, the fear that he might do so apparently played a key role in the council's retreating from their threat, and Jacquard settled down to a comfortable retirement outside Lyons while the citizens continued to pay his pension in what cynics may consider as much a bribe as a wage.[5]

As it happened, another mechanic, Jean Breton, made a long series of significant improvements in the mechanism beginning in 1807 and continuing for a decade thereafter, and it was these improvements that made the machine truly practical. From that point on the use of the machines spread rapidly in Lyons and to other weaving centres in other countries and brought them to the attention of Babbage, who had made a sort of career of becoming familiar with the latest technology in use in industry.

*   *   *

Babbage was to continue work on the analytical engine for most of his remaining 35 years, but after the Jacquard device was assimilated into the design the fundamental arrangement of the components was essentially stable. It was the Jacquard device that seemed to make the machine's potential power unlimited. Cards would ratchet through the device much as they had on draw looms, but instead of triggering a sequence of operations that would ultimately move warp threads on a loom, the holes in the card would trigger a sequence of operations that could copy values from the store to the mill (or back from the mill to the store), or else trigger a set of operations in the mill that would yield the results of addition, subtraction, multiplication, or division of the two numbers that had been copied into it. As with draw looms, the results of each card might be trivial, but cards could be read through and operations performed with mechanical speed, and with supreme patience and accuracy.

The intermediary between the instructions represented by the holes in the cards and the actions of the mill and the store was the control barrels. The movement of pins on the barrels set into motion any one of a limited number of operations in the machine, and so the arrangement of pins and the operations they could set in motion represented the basic operations that the machine was capable of performing. Based on the value that was sensed in the card being read, the control barrel would move into a certain position, and start triggering one of the limited number of functions it was inherently capable of doing. Eventually in Babbage's design, in addition to moving values about the machine, the control barrels could move the cards backward or forward, keep the cards still for a certain number of operations, print values out so that the operator could read them, or pause for intervention from the operator as when an inherently flawed operation, such as division by zero, had been specified.

Though Babbage never even approached building his analytical engine, he was enthralled with the potential in his design. His enthusiasm for the system he envisioned has been more than vindicated, principally because the basic logical design he proposed can still be seen in modern computers. Babbage's card readers and printers correspond to modern input–output units. His mill corresponds to the arithmetic–logic unit in modern computers, his store to internal memory, his control barrels to control units, and the Jacquard mechanism to auxiliary storage units such as disc drives. The sequence of instructions on the cards would today be called the computer's program, and indeed punched cards and card readers persisted in computer designs down to the recent past. The pins on the control barrels correspond to the microcode in today's computers, and the set of operations the control barrels could perform correspond to today's notion of instruction sets. For those conversant with computer techniques, Babbage also invented the anticipatory carry, and anticipated the implementation of instruction pipelining and even the array processor.

As Babbage grew older, the constant frustrations of his life seemed to wear on him. The wit and warmth of the self-assured gadfly were gone, and increasingly in their place were the ranting and ill will of a bitter crank. Though Babbage's mind was lucid and he worked diligently on the design of the analytical engine well into his seventies, his death in 1871 was hardly noticed, and his funeral sparsely attended. His call for industrial and scientific reform had gone unheeded, his economics were freely borrowed but were themselves forgotten, and his ideas for calculating engines left scattered among a clutter of notes, drawings and partial models. Had his confidence in mechanical computation not been so startlingly vindicated in the next century, and had modern computers not promised so radically to change the modern world, history would surely have relegated Charles Babbage to the position of an obscure curiosity. As it happened, though, events dictated that modern historians unearth and reconstruct his technology in detail, and his views on political economy deserve a similar reassessment.

From the standpoint of Babbage's inventions, it is plain in retrospect that the technologies available to him – geared wheels and other mechanical devices – could never have been an economical medium for the logical devices he proposed. Even as late as 1879, the British Association commissioned a study to determine the feasibility of building an analytical engine along Babbage's design, but balked because its engineers could give no reasonable estimate of the costs involved. Every linkage in the analytical engine had to be machined and assembled individually, so that there were no significant economies in producing large quantities of them, and every moving component would have the physical mass of a sizeable metal component, so that it would require considerable power and time to set it into motion. Modern computers, though they operate on very similar logical principles, are composed primarily of an astonishingly large number of integrated electronic components which can be produced in huge quantities in a process somewhat akin to photolithography, so that there are enormous opportunities for taking advantage of economies of scale in their production. In a way, the components in modern computers are actually much simpler than those Babbage envisaged, but it is economical to manufacture so many of them at once that even the simplest computer today dwarfs the capacity of Babbage's design. In addition, the 'moving parts' in an electronic computer are electrons, and so the 'motions' in modern computers are much faster than anything that could have been achieved by the analytical engine.

Though electronic computers obviously proved economically viable where Babbage's design clearly was not, there is nothing to suggest that electronic computers represent anywhere near the ideal in economy. Given growing demands for computation, expensive research is under way to investigate the feasibility of using other media that can more efficiently perform these functions, such as electrical impulses moving through biologically produced cells, or photons moving through transparent crystals. Indeed, every function a modern computer performs can in principle be performed in almost any medium: in light impulses through crystals, electrons in circuitry, spinning mechanical wheels, or clamshells on strings. The only constraint – and the only possible opportunity, as Babbage sadly discovered – lies in each medium's cost-effectiveness.

The fact that every major sub-system in the analytical engine has a precise analogue in modern computers would have been more than sufficient testimony to Babbage's prescience if the concept for the modern computer had grown out of Babbage's work, but in fact his invention left only a very weak technological legacy. If research had been continued on the device, it is probable that electronic techniques could have incrementally supplanted components of the system over time, and the development of the computer technology would doubtlessly have been much more centralized in Britain, instead of in the United States as actually occurred. The spin-offs in machining and engineering design that Babbage engendered even in building his small difference engine would doubtlessly have been multiplied in myriad ways, and it is chilling to wonder if the long, downward economic slide that England commenced in the latter half of the nineteenth century would have occurred if Babbage's project had been funded and if his vision of state sponsorship of science and industry had taken hold.

As it happened, however, the design of the modern computer was to develop anew in tandem with the development of economical electromechanical and electronic techniques for processing information. The operation of electrical switching is fundamentally different from that of geared wheels, and so initially it was hardly apparent that the optimal logical design arising from this line of technological development would correspond with what Babbage envisaged. Babbage's prestige as an inventor is enhanced by the fact that his basic design was essentially forgotten and then later rediscovered, just as Aristarchus' notion of a heliocentric universe was forgotten and rediscovered by Copernicus, and Britain, like Alexandria before it, paid the price for the lapse.

One of Babbage's innovations, however, was not resurrected in the twentieth century. His mechanical notation, of which he was tremendously proud and which he tirelessly attempted to promote in engineering design, perished with him, barren. The mechanical notation was oriented to mechanical pieces and had little to say to electronic components. When researchers in this century found that they required a notation for predicting the states of the complex electronic circuitry they were designing, they would turn instead to the calculus of one of Babbage's contemporaries, who was not thinking at the time that it would be used to simulate the operations of machines, but had developed it instead as a way to simulate human reason.

4

The Laws of Thought

There is much that we will never know about what happened to George Boole out alone in a field on a winter day in 1833. We know that Boole had recently turned 17, that the considerable weight of an adult world was settling rather heavily on his young shoulders, that he was lonely and troubled and had taken a solitary walk to reflect upon the mysteries of life. We know that, in the midst of his reflections, Boole was struck by a flash of insight, a revelation so intense that he would refer to it throughout his life in almost prophetic tones. For the remainder of his life, George Boole thought that it was on that winter day that the essential secret to the mechanics of the human mind was first revealed to him.

Though the event was certainly momentous to Boole, it was not out of character that the young man would take to pondering such impenetrable mysteries, for Boole had since childhood displayed a cerebral, reflective and deeply spiritual nature. George was born in Lincoln, the first child to parents who were loving and dedicated to their son's upbringing. His father was a merchant of modest means, who was possessed of an unusually active intellectual spirit and who placed great emphasis on the value of continuous learning. He saw to it that young George's traditional education was augmented by continued reading and experimentation about the home. George's mother was a loving woman of deep religious convictions, and she passed on to her son her gentle and lively spirit. The twin impulses towards learning and towards concentrated reflection on the mysteries of God and man were to be prominent features in Boole's intellectual life.

George was a precocious and inventive child. His interests ranged from literature to optics, and a recent biographer reports his fashioning telescopes and possibly even a calculating machine under the watchful eye and active tutelage of his father.[1] While still a young boy, George began to display an amazing aptitude for the classics. With the aid of a friend of his father's, George rapidly learned Latin and began to translate Latin verse into English.

Immediately thereafter, he took it upon himself to learn Greek. His proficiency in these languages, and his talent for versification, in which classic poems must not only be translated into English, but the lyrical quality of the original must be reproduced, gave the young boy some local notoriety. By the time he was 16, he had also taught himself French, German and Italian. His talent for languages was to play a major role in his later life and work.

It was at this time, when Boole was 16, that his father's business collapsed, and George was suddenly faced with substantially supporting his parents, his sister and his two brothers. He sought employment as a teacher, taking a job as an assistant instructor at a Wesleyan school in Doncaster, some 40 miles from his home. His tenure at Doncaster was to be a brief one, as his religious instincts and his new-found interest in mathematics – those very things that must have stimulated his remarkable revelation out in the field – inevitably lead to friction with his stern Methodist taskmasters.

While at Doncaster, Boole rekindled an earlier interest in mathematics, which he had originally delved into largely because he felt he needed to understand mathematics better if he was to teach it. Being fluent in French, he borrowed a copy of Lacroix's *Differential and Integral Calculus*, and took to studying it in its original language in his spare time. The work was tedious, and Boole had no tutor to ease his conceptual passage, but he was absorbed with the task and persevered. Mathematics began to occupy more and more of his spare time, and Boole's intellectual attachment to it may have lead to some of the complaints directed against him at the school. His absorption with his own studies was seen as detrimental to his performance of his teaching duties by at least one instructor at the school who also felt that, though he did well with the few motivated students, he was unnecessarily impatient with the majority of students who required drill and discipline.

Since Boole was to excel for the remainder of his life as an instructor, it is easy to suspect that his religious views may have contributed to the unfavourable appraisals of his teaching while at Doncaster. Boole had since childhood displayed a keenly spiritual sense. He was widely read on religious themes – before the collapse of his father's business he had even seriously considered the priesthood in the Church of England – and from his knowledge of Latin and Greek was familiar with the classical concepts of ethics and metaphysics. By this time Boole had developed an intuitive distaste for the Christian concept of the Trinity. To Boole there was something vulgar about the concept that there were exactly three aspects to God. Boole felt that attaching any quantity to the concept of God debased God's universality and that the impulse to do so must have resulted from the limitations of the human intellect. Significantly for his later work, Boole developed a fascination for the Hebrew concept of God as 'Unity', and by the time he reported to Doncaster, he was a professed Unitarian.

When Boole struck out on his walk in 1833, it is clear that the pressure from some parents for his removal was already severe. His Unitarian leanings were scandalous enough, and reports circulated that he had taken to reading mathematics on Sunday and working on mathematical problems while in chapel. He was within a few weeks of being relieved of his post.

The flash of insight that struck Boole while out on his walk was that, just as there were consistent mathematical laws dealing with quantities that were useful in describing the external world, there were equally consistent mathematical laws that described the internal mechanics of human reason; that the mathematical laws of the mind were similar to those of the external world, except that they inherently ignored all concepts of quantity, and focused instead on logical relationships; and that by employing this new calculus of human reason, it was possible to reduce any logical problem to mathematical symbols, and to solve it in a mechanical fashion with mathematical tools.

Boole was not to express his idea for fourteen years, until such time as he had developed a significant mathematical mind, and he did not present a definitive mathematical treatment of his theory until the publication of his book, *The Laws of Thought*, seven years after that. He was given due credit as a significant and original mathematician and logician in his time and since. Bertrand Russell who, with Alfred Whitehead, was to take Boole's theories to the very foundations of mathematics fifty years later was even provocatively to declare that Boole had done no less than discover pure mathematics itself. But the metaphysical aspect of Boole's inquiries have always been given short shrift, and the excitement he felt at having discovered the fundamental laws of the human mind was an excitement that others never fully felt. Boole always felt that he had still not fully communicated the metaphysical profundity of his discovery: a grand treatise in which he hoped to make clear the relationship between his mathematics and the nature of the human mind was still a disorganized draft when he died.

But all these momentous events were ahead of the troubled young man from Lincoln in 1833, who had many pressing matters on his mind.

Boole remained an active educator for the rest of his life. After being relieved of his post at Doncaster and serving briefly in other teaching posts, he opened his own school close to his family in Lincoln in 1834. He was innovative and successful as a teacher, and he was able to assume successively more prestigious teaching positions. Throughout this period until the publication of his first seminal book in 1847, Boole maintained a keen interest in mathematics, and he was his own most passionate and accomplished student. He published his first mathematical paper late in 1841, and became acquainted with the prominent mathematicians of his day. Sadly, though, even as Boole came into his own as a mathematical mind and as his dedication to teaching flowered in the minds of his many students, his own longing to be taught never left him. He made several inquiries regarding admission to Cambridge to study mathematics, but was discouraged, as a university education in that day was still largely the province of younger and more affluent men.

Boole's wide-ranging interests and the unusual path of his intellectual development contributed profoundly to the freshness of the insights he was to bring to mathematics and logic. Elementary education was the centre of much of his adult life, an experience that contrasts sharply with that of most 'leading edge' academics who tend to engage exclusively in higher-level teaching or research, and Boole spent a considerable number of hours pondering and explicating the most fundamental aspects of mathematics to his students. Since his own understanding of mathematics was almost entirely self-taught, he was forced to read and re-read primary texts – often in other languages – until he understood them, a process that compelled him constantly to examine and re-examine the basic precepts of mathematics. His facility with foreign languages and his efforts at translation and versification as a child enabled him to read and reflect upon the thoughts of the great French and German mathematicians and the classical philosophers and logicians, and must also have stimulated his thinking about the very function of language and its relationship to reason.

The obvious trend in mathematics at the time was for greater abstraction and a more cavalier approach to manipulating the symbols of mathematics. Little by little, it was becoming clear that some of the symbols and operators of higher mathematics could be added, subtracted, multiplied and divided according to many of the same rules that governed numbers and variables representing numbers. This was a trend that was championed by the Analytical Society at Cambridge, and Babbage's colleague in the society, George Peacock, played a significant role in the development of the trend. The Analytical Society's attention to the matter is understandable, since their group was created as an outgrowth of the damage they had seen done to mathematics as a result of Newton's system of notation that did not lend itself to manipulation as well as Leibniz's more serviceable symbols. Boole, with his unique background in the varying syntaxes of different languages, naturally found the implications of this free-wheeling syntactical approach extremely evocative as he first experimented in mathematics. Even as early as 1835, it was apparent that Boole had formulated his basic idea that symbols could be manipulated in an almost mechanical fashion, as long as the manipulation was consistent with the original interpretation of the symbols.

Boole's mystical revelation in the field lay dormant in his subconscious throughout these years of young adulthood, but in 1847 an intellectual dispute erupted that crystallized his thoughts. It was an unimportant quarrel, as theoretical arguments go, whose only lasting significance was that it drew Boole into considering the operations of formal logic. The dispute was instigated by a firebrand Scottish philosopher, Sir William Hamilton, who accused Augustus de Morgan, a prominent British mathematician and close friend of Boole, of plagiarizing a not-too-original concept that Hamilton sought to claim as his own. Hamilton was a bit of a crank at times, especially when it came to mathematics and mathematicians. He clearly had only a vague understanding of the field and viewed mathematics as a bastard child of philosophy, one that created mischief in metaphysics and encouraged the development of vulgar, misshapen minds. De Morgan, by contrast, was a bright and original mathematical thinker who contributed generously and unselfishly to the careers of many of the finest British mathematicians of the era, including both Babbage and Boole.

Hamilton had focused upon the basic subject–predicate relationship from classical logic, whereby a subject A is related to a predicate B. According to the classical view, there are four basic logical relationships: all A are B, some A are B, no A are B, and some A are not B. Hamilton analysed these statements in the context of A's effect on B, saying that the relationship with A was in effect 'quantifying' the predicate B. De Morgan had been exploring classical logic from a mathematical perspective, and naturally encountered a similar formulation. Hamilton's charge of plagiarism caused quite a stir, and Boole, who was intimately familiar with both classical logic and mathematics, was quite naturally attracted to the dispute.

Just as it had fourteen years before, something snapped in Boole. A lifetime of inquiry and reflection precipitated into a single, elegant vision of how logic can be expressed algebraically by removing from it all notions of quantity, how the meaning communicated in language could be precisely translated into algebraic symbols, and how these symbols could be operated upon and transformed in a mechanical fashion that resembled the apparent workings of the human mind. But unlike his previous experience as a young man, this time Boole sat down at once to put his thoughts on paper. His idea gushed forth from his mind almost fully formed as he feverishly penned his first book, a slim volume entitled *The Mathematical Analysis of Logic*, which was published that same year.

The pace and breadth of the book reflected the rush with which it was written, and in its hurried development Boole did make some rash judgements, but on the whole the book is an excellent basic exposition of what would come to be known as Boolean algebra. The small errors in the book became glaring to someone with Boole's disciplined reason, and it was apparent to him that a more definitive explication was necessary.

But as he pondered his revisions, he became convinced that not only did his algebra resemble the workings of the human mind, but that it must necessarily reflect the mind's underlying mechanics, that the algebra of logic held the potential of revealing the most profound mysteries of man and his relation to nature. In 1854, he published a more definitive version of his paradigm, which he boldly entitled *An Investigation of the Laws of Thought*.

According to Boole's developed system, problems of logic could be expressed as algebraic equations, so that logical problems could be solved by manipulating algebraic symbols according to formal rules, just as symbols for quantity could be manipulated by the rules of traditional algebra. This was a truly pregnant concept, for it lent to all problems of logic a technique for rationalizing and formalizing the solution to any soluble problem, and used a system of symbolic manipulation that was inherently amenable to mechanization.

To understand the potential power of an algebra of logic, it may be useful to consider the power that was well established in Boole's time that could be derived from the ordinary algebra that related to problems of quantities. Ordinary algebra consists of a system of rules with which one may manipulate and transform symbolic expressions representing quantities into other symbolic expressions. The reason that this is done is simply because it is useful: it allows the mathematician creatively to seek out new relationships between quantities purely in the abstract, while still being confident that the new relationships he discovers are still valid in the real world of actual numbers. In this, the traditional algebra of quantities serves exactly the same purpose in relation to numbers that Babbage's mechanical notation served in relation to the gears, wheels and axles that made up his machines. In both, a set of assumptions were developed about the relationship between the symbols being used and the things being symbolized, whether quantities in algebra or mechanical components in Babbage's notation. In both cases, the symbols could be manipulated and transformed into different expressions according to certain laws that respected the assumptions underlying their creation. New, useful arrangements of symbols could be formed in this way – new algebraic expressions in algebra, new machine designs in Babbage's notation. As long as these new expressions were produced lawfully according to the underlying assumptions regarding their respective symbols, these new arrangements would be sure to be 'true': correct characterizations of quantity in traditional algebra, or the design of a useful analytical engine in Babbage's notation.

As an example of how these manipulations were known to have worked in traditional algebra, consider the complicated-looking algebraic statement:

$$x^2 - yx^2 + y^2 = y$$

What this statement represents, in essence, is the relationship between two quantities, which are represented in the statement by the symbols x and y. The fact that the quantities in the statement are represented by symbols and not by specific quantities implies that this relationship holds true for a whole range of values that might under certain circumstances be substituted for x and y. The statement may have been derived from scientific observation, where x and y have been observed always to maintain the relationship expressed in the formula. The power of an algebra of quantities is that it defines a series of rules that are permissible for re-expressing relationships whose truth has been established as other relationships whose truth is also known. Using the rules of algebra, a mathematician could deduce with confidence that, if the statement above expresses the true relationship between x and y, that the statement:

$$x^2 = y$$

expresses precisely the same relationship. Both equations express the same fundamental truth of the relationship, but the second equation states the relationship more profoundly than the first. If one wanted to know the value of y for any particular x, he could use the algebra of quantities to simplify the problem in the abstract before he actually did any arithmetic, confident all along that while he was manipulating the symbols of quantity, the new expressions he was developing were as true as the original.

Boolean algebra successfully translated into the realm of logical relationships the same utility of manipulating symbols that had previously been used only in the realm of quantitative relationships. With Boolean algebra, complex logical relationships could be expressed as algebraic equations and 'solved' in a manner analogous to that employed in ordinary algebra. Using a very similar set of basic algebraic laws, symbols could be used that represented logical relationships, and these symbolic expressions could be manipulated into other more useful expressions of the original truth. Just as it was possible to isolate a single variable of quantity in ordinary algebra most efficiently to define it in terms of the other quantities, it was possible to isolate an idea to define it precisely in terms of other ideas. As in numerical algebra, this allowed the symbolic manipulation to be performed in the abstract, with no attention being paid to the meaning of the variables until the final, most general expression of the relationship had been revealed.

Boolean algebra shared with ordinary algebra the basic types of symbols that were needed. There were variables such as x, y, z, etc.; symbols that denoted operations such as '+', '−', and '∗'; and a symbol of identity, '='. But when these familiar symbols represented elements of thought, rather than of quantity, their meanings and the meaning of the expressions written with them naturally changed. Interestingly, Boole did not give an authoritative specification of what these symbols represent in Boolean algebra. There is not, strictly speaking, any one correct definition of what symbols in an algebra of logic must mean. There are instead many possible ways to employ what is broadly considered Boolean algebra, many different systems of interpretation that can be developed for the symbols, and all are valid as long as they remain true to their original assumptions. So instead of rigidly defining what the symbols *must* mean, Boole developed the examples of two systems of definitions that both worked, and from these derived the laws of Boolean algebra. He insisted only that the interpretations assigned to symbols correspond to the operations of the mind and that, once established, the interpretations remain constant with that original definition.

In the first of the two systems Boole described, the variables represented categories and the symbols of operation represented the basic operations of the mind that classify things. In this system, 'xy' (an abbreviated convention for '$x * y$') would be interpreted as 'the class composed of those things that have both the quality of x and the quality of y'; '$x + y$' would mean 'the class composed of all things that have the quality of x, in addition to all things that have the quality of y';[2] and '$x - y$' could mean 'the class composed of all things that have the quality of x, except those that have the quality of y.' Using this particular system of interpretation, variables could be assigned classes as follows:

w = 'humans that wear hats'
x = 'blue things'
y = 'tall things'
z = 'women' (or, 'things that are human, adult and female')

The variables could be used to define new classes. The class 'tall women who are not blue, along with anyone wearing a hat' could be written as:

$$yz - x + w$$

and the proposition 'there are no tall women who are not blue' could be written as:

$$yz(1 - x) = 0$$

This system, which pertained to fundamental perceptions of class, Boole referred to as an algebra of *primary propositions.*

In the second system Boole described, the variables represent whole propositions – those that might be expressed as an equation in the first system – that are either true or false, and the symbols of operation represent a quality of time. Thus '$x + y$' would be interpreted as 'the time when both x and y are true'; '$x - y$' would mean 'the time when x is true, except when y is true'; and 'xy' would mean 'the time when x is true, followed by the time y is true'. Thus, the proposition 'x is true when y is true and z is not true' could be expressed as:

$$x = y - z$$

Since this second system was derived from statements of primary propositions, Boole called this system an algebra of *secondary propositions*.

Boole demonstrated that, regardless of whether the system of interpretation was primary or secondary, many rules of ordinary algebra could be employed in Boolean algebra as well. For example,

$$xy = yx$$

is true in both the traditional algebra of quantities and in Boolean algebra. In traditional algebra, the statement asserts that the product of any two numbers is the same regardless of the order in which they are multiplied: $2 * 3$ must always be equal to $3 * 2$. A similar law applies in Boolean algebra: 'tall things that are blue' is the same class as 'blue things that are tall'; and 'the time when x is true followed by the time y is true' is identical to 'the time when y is true followed by the time when x is true'. Many of the laws that governed traditional algebra have their direct analogy in Boolean algebra, and this had the effect of making manipulations in Boolean algebra appear in many ways to be identical to the manipulations allowed in ordinary algebra.

But there was an apparent fundamental rift between the laws that applied to the operations of the mind and the operations of numbers. There were some laws that had to be true in a Boolean algebra of logic that were not generally true in the traditional algebra of quantities. An obvious problem was in logical statements such as 'the class of things that are blue that are also things that are blue is the class of things that are blue'. Though the assertion seems silly, it is obviously true. Expressed in the terms of Boolean algebra, however, it took the form:

$$xx = x \ (\text{or}, \ x^2 = x)$$

and a similar truism was required in the algebra of secondary propositions. And there were other statements that had to be true in Boolean algebra that were seldom true in traditional algebra, such as 'there are no things that are both blue and not blue':

$$x(1 - x) = 0$$

and 'all things are either blue or not blue':

$$x + (1 - x) = 1$$

The problem with these particular statements was that, though they complied in all respects to Boole's system of interpretation in the realm of logic, they were not considered truisms in the traditional algebra that was developed to work on quantities. In traditional algebra, each of these three statements was false if the value of x were 2, ½, or almost any other quantity.

The only values for which these exceptional statements would be true in both traditional and Boolean algebra were 0 and 1, for these values were the only ones that satisfied in all respects the laws of both algebras. But Boolean algebra would only accept even these two values on its own terms, since it had an additional constraint:

$$x + x = x$$

or, 'the class of blue things in addition to the class of blue things is the same class as the class of blue things'. The reader can be forgiven if it seemed with this additional constraint that Boole was on to nothing more than a muddle. Now his new algebra was not only constrained to work on values of only 0 and 1, but it also insisted that whenever 1 is added to itself, the result would always be 1!

It was in this apparently sticky issue that the insight that had been maturing in Boole's mind since his solitary winter walk many years before enters into the discussion. To understand the laws of logical thought, according to Boole, one had to leave the world of quantity behind. The '1' in Boolean algebra does not in any way pertain to the notion of the quantity '1', in the sense of one-half of two or one-twelfth of a dozen. Instead, the '1' in the algebra of logical thought was that value that could not in any way be appended to, more akin to the concept of 'the universe' than of 'one (out of many)'. Depending upon the various interpretations that were allowable in Boolean algebra, the dichotomy between the two permissible values of '1' and '0' might be variously interpreted as the dichotomy between 'all of creation' and 'oblivion', 'eternity' and 'never', or 'truth' and 'falsehood', weighty concepts all.

Here was a mathematician, a linguist, a logician, an educator and a profoundly philosophical and reflective soul, who in attempting to reproduce the laws of reason in mathematical form had been lead by his own reason to the mystical notion that the laws of human reason assumed the same mathematical structure that applied to the most fundamental concepts of metaphysics. He had discovered a mathematical system that, through the simple device of refusing to admit to quantities, was capable of manipulating not only reason but also statements comparing the concepts of 'unity', 'all of creation', 'truth' and 'eternity' to the obverse concepts of 'nothing', 'oblivion', 'falsehood' and 'never'. Not only did it seem that a fundamental law of the mind had been discovered, but it also appeared that the laws of the mind were the same laws that could be applied to the most persistent issues of religion and metaphysics. The mechanism of the mind seemed tied to the fabric of the cosmos.

Boole galloped through what must have seemed an unbounded region of metaphysical speculation on the nature of creation and its relation to the human mind, as previously unrelated philosophical concepts seemed for the first time to suggest a single truth. With his authoritative grasp of ancient philosophy, he waxed reflectively on the Greek ideal that truth lies in unity. He recalled the Hebrew notion of God as 'All' or 'Unity', the idea that had had such an intuitive attraction for him since he was a boy. He sympathetically quoted Aristotle's approval of his fellow Hermotimus' statement that in intelligence was the cause of the world and its order, and quoted the medieval Saint Anselm, who modelled the universe on analogies between thought and being and eventually came to think of the universe as an expression of the self-reflecting thought of the Creator.

The mysteries to be derived from the new algebra of thought seemed inexhaustible. Boole pondered the significance of his own derived truth that

$$x + (1 - x) = 1$$

or, 'the universe consists of all things possessing the characteristic x, in addition to all things that do not possess the characteristic x' and found the mathematical expression of the enduring philosophical concept of dualism. The point of departure for all systems of dualism is that the elements of the universe can be constructively divided into two classes, based on whether the element possesses or does not possess a particular characteristic. He saw the truth behind the ten fundamental theses and antitheses of Pythagoras – finite and infinite, even and odd, unity and multitude, right and left, male and female, rest and motion, straight and curved, square and oblong, light and dark, good and evil – and even the dialectic of Hegel.

Whatever one thought of its metaphysical implications, Boolean algebra was an obviously powerful analytical tool in reproducing the results of human reason, and could in the process of replicating reason significantly reduce the effort required in ratiocination. Boole demonstrated the practical utility of his method by replicating in elegant mathematics a taxing logical exercise that had been performed by Aristotle in antiquity. In a lengthy series of arguments that had been of particular interest to the philosophers of the Enlightenment, Aristotle had undertaken better to elucidate the relationship between virtue and other human characteristics such as passion, faculty and habit. Boole began by taking Aristotle's premisses:

1   Virtue is either a passion, or a faculty, or a habit.
2   Passions are not things according to which we are praised or blamed, or in which we exercise deliberate judgement.
3   Faculties are not things according to which we are praised are blamed, and which are accompanied by deliberate preference.
4   Virtue is something according to which we are praised and blamed, and which is accompanied by deliberate preference.
5   Whatever art or science makes its works to be in a good state avoids extremes, and keeps the means in view relative to human nature.
6   Virtue is more exact and excellent than any art or science.

He associated a symbolic variable for each of the classes involved in the premisses:

v = virtue
p = passions
f = faculties
b = habits
d = things accompanied by deliberate preference
g = things causing their work to be in a good state
m = things keeping the mean in view relative to human nature

Using the symbols he thus defined, Boole restated Aristotle's premisses in algebraic terms:

$$v = q\{p(1-f)(1-b) + f(1-p)(1-b) + b(1-p)(1-f)\}$$
$$p = q(1-d)$$
$$f = (q-1)d$$
$$v = qd$$
$$g = qm$$
$$v = qg^3$$

Boole had now captured Aristotle's observations in the symbols of his algebra. Having done so, he could ignore what the symbols meant, and manipulate these expressions according to the various rules of Boolean algebra. Using his own rules, he was able quickly to reproduce Aristotle's conclusions. For example, he was able to demonstrate that, given the Boolean assumptions above, the statement:

$$v = h \, (1 - f)(1 - p)$$

was true, which, interpreted according to his original definitions, means 'Virtue is a habit, and not a faculty or a passion', or

$$v = hdm$$

which means 'Virtue is a habit accompanied by deliberate preference, and keeping in view the mean relative to human nature'. In this way was the wisdom of Aristotle made knowable through the operations teachable to anyone competent in fundamental mathematics.

Boolean algebra described a way for symbols to be manipulated in a manner that was wholly unmindful of the symbols' meaning. In theory, any logical problem could be described as Boolean statements, and a mathematician facile with the laws of Boolean algebra could proceed to derive more general or more detailed statements of truth from the original statements, new statements that could be useful to the person who had originally posed the problem. This recalls Prony's system of employing the division of mental labour in the computation of logarithms, down to the detail that the mathematician in this hypothetical case, like the simple arithmeticians in Prony's case, would not need to know, and in fact would be completely unaided by knowing, the meaning that was attached to the symbols. There were opportunities for real economies along just these lines, as could be seen in the practice of large insurance companies, who used to use Boolean algebra to test the logic of their complex legal contracts. With the dizzying array of situations covered by modern insurance agreements, the only practical way to predict when the insurance company was liable and when it was not was by reducing the terms of the contract to Boolean expressions, and having teams of mathematicians discover the underlying patterns of responsibility the way Prony's team discovered logarithms. Today, of course, this function would be done by electronic computers.

Boole's discoveries subjected logical problems to *algorithmic* solutions. An algorithm is a recipe by which a type of problem can be solved, a finite set of specific operations by which a set of symbols can be lawfully and reliably transformed into another set of symbols: long division and income tax forms reflect two commonly employed algorithms. Using our theoretical example of the mathematician and the logician, if certain types of problems were repeatedly encountered, it would be a perfectly natural development if the mathematician decided to employ the Babbage principle in his work, so that he simply listed a detailed sequence of operations for these types of problems that a less skilled employee could carry out, and spent his valuable time on other activities. Since the meaning of the symbols has been extracted from the process, it makes no difference if the operations are performed by a child, a monkey, or even a machine, as long as the mathematician's instructions are faithfully carried out and the rules of Boolean algebra are not violated. Boole's formalizing of logical operations, which were later found to encompass all mathematical functions, set the stage for the ultimate mechanization of these functions.

Boole also made a giant theoretical step toward mechanical computation with his unshakeable intuitive attraction to binary systems. Binary systems permit only two fundamental symbols, like a language that has an alphabet of only two characters. There is an inherent, absolute economy in binary notation, and the story of the early years of computing technology after Boole's time can be fairly characterized as the recognition and technological exploitation of binary notation's potential. Machines are inherently better suited to sensing and recording binary values, since the mechanical discrimination required to distinguish between two possible entries is invariably more accurate and faster than that required to distinguish between more than two values. The Jacquard mechanism, and all the punched card technology that was its progeny, is asked only to sense whether a hole is present at a given position in a card or not, a question that inherently admits of only one of two answers: yes or no. The mechanism would have to be much more complex, and practically speaking either slower in operation or more prone to error, if it had to distinguish between, say, no hole, a round hole, and a square hole. The profound economy of recording information in binary code is inescapable and the practice persists in computers today, from punched cards that have 'holes' or 'non-holes' at specific locations, to integrated circuits teeming with electronic gates that are 'on' or 'off', to such mundane things as the universal product codes that mark supermarket commodities with 'black' and 'white' stripes. Even the characters on a computer display are recorded in the computer's memory as a string of ones and noughts.

In his time, Boole was widely considered the greatest logician since Aristotle, and today he is commonly considered the father of both information theory and computer science, as well as a pioneer in discovering the true relationship between logic and mathematics. However, his name is almost never associated with what he considered a most fundamental subject of his investigations: the operation of the human mind. Boole's readers have always politely ignored his assertion that within his model must lie fundamental insights into the operation of the human brain, preferring instead to focus on the practical benefits of the remarkable system of symbolic logic he devised. Boole considered his discovery to have profound psychological ramifications. He compared his work with Kepler's discovery that the planets moved in precise, mathematical shapes, the discovery that laid the groundwork for

Newton's law of gravitation. If the paths of the planets followed a mathematical law, it was generally acknowledged that therein lay some profound insights into the physical laws that guided them. Why, then, when it was so positively demonstrated that reason itself could be described mathematically, was it so difficult to persuade sceptics that fundamental laws of the mechanics of the mind would follow? Sceptics readily agreed that Boole's formal system could *mimic* human reason, but would balk at going along with his assertion that the system must in some way shed light on the actual mechanism of human thought.

Boole never seriously contemplated a mechanical model for his system. Had he set out to do so, he would surely have encountered the same sort of practical difficulties that dogged Babbage all his life. It was intuitively apparent at the time that any useful mechanical model of Boolean algebra would have to be enormously complex and precise in order to reproduce even the most basic logical operations. It is tantalizing to consider what may have happened if Boole and Babbage had ever collaborated in any extensive way. Babbage was tremendously impressed with Boole's innovations and with the quality of his thinking, and both men shared many interests in common. Boole did meet once with Babbage in 1862 and apparently got the full treatment from the inventor who was by now well on his way to being known as a cranky eccentric. Babbage explained the workings of the difference engine and apparently the two men also discussed his ideas for the analytical engine, for Boole promised to learn more of the Jacquard mechanism.[4] Boole demurred from a second meeting, citing an unexpected development, and there is no evidence that he gave the man or his machines any further thought.

Boole's assertion that within his algebra lay some of the secrets of the human mind was almost totally forgotten. The value of his mathematics persisted in two ways, one broadly abstract, the other narrowly practical. On the abstract side, he showed the way for a broad theoretical comprehension of the unity between mathematics and logic. On the practical side, he left a powerful formal tool for understanding the operations of any system that deals exclusively with values akin to 'all' or 'nothing'. This is a prominent characteristic of electrical circuits, and as war clouds gathered over Europe and the Pacific in the 1930s, a graduate student in electrical engineering was to discover that complex electronic circuits followed the rules expressed in *The Laws of Thought*. Ironically, Boole's formal systems are today at the heart of the very machines that claim to possess artificial intelligence, even as a philosophical debate rages over whether these machines can actually think, or merely mimic thought.

5

Origins of a System

In his master work, *Economy and Society*, which he prepared as the world's economic powers moved inexorably towards the outbreak of the First World War, the seminal German social historian Max Weber stated that the historical seed for all social discipline was military discipline, and that in all societies the social discipline developed for warfare would always have some significant influence on the structure of the state and the economy. Weber considered it self-evident that the second great agency of social discipline, and the one most likely to borrow lessons from the warriors, was the large-scale economic organization: the Pharaohs' workshops, the slave-owners' plantations, the capitalists' factories and, presumably in our time, the corporate office.

The need for war discipline arises from the utility in warfare of directing individuals so that masses of individual actions can be channelled into what from their leaders' standpoint is rational group behaviour. In Weber's time, it was apparent that the desire for discipline was the motivating force behind the formal nature of military life and the impersonal bureaucracies the military engendered. The adoption of these same mannerisms in production and economic competition was supremely rational on the part of capitalist enterprise, and part of the pervasive social dynamic of rationalization and formalization of work that was apparent throughout human history.

To many contemporary Westerners, Weber's description of warriors being in the vanguard of socio-economic organization may seem quaint: interesting, perhaps, in illuminating their distant cultural history or perhaps in understanding barbarous cultures like the Russians, but hardly relevant to the dynamics of their own sophisticated commercial culture. It may surprise them to learn that the computers they encounter every day are essentially military spin-offs, and that most of the computer giants that design and manufacture them had to be persuaded by the military – frequently against their own pecuniary judgement – to invent the components that comprise today's computers. Related technologies were being developed before any military potential was perceived, of course, but at a cautious mercantile pace that contrasts sharply with the velocity this development assumed once it became an integral component of modern total war.

The fact is that perceived military demands in Great Britain and the United States were the agent for the technological breakthroughs that led to the modern computer, and military demands continue today to play a major role in defining the computer technology of tomorrow. Between Babbage's time and the outbreak of the Second World War research continued in a number of venues on techniques for mechanical computation, but after the outbreak of hostilities the perceived needs for computational devices became an issue of vital social importance in America and Europe, with the result that government funding for innovation in computer technology accelerated dramatically. In the United States, government subsidy for computer research during the Second World War continued apace into the initial muted conflicts of the cold war, and then expanded radically into a broad, continuous and well-endowed programme to push the leading edge of computer technology systematically to new limits. The result is that today there is hardly a single component of modern computers that was not initially funded in whole or in part by the military. Magnetic disc drives, solid state circuits and integrated circuits, the concept of the stored program, higher-level programming languages, graphic displays, even the popular icon-type interfaces and hand-held mouse pointing devices owe their discovery either directly or indirectly to military research and development, primarily in the United States.

The continued political consensus in the USA for a sustained military role in developing computer technology did not arise solely from a general concern for an apparent military challenge, for it was obvious early in the 1960s that the economic benefits from this research that had accrued to US industry were profound. In the presence of robust domestic capital markets and a burgeoning commercial market for computer technology, this continued American military investment spawned a domestic computer industry that quickly outpaced those of its military allies and, by the economic threat it offered to these countries, shocked them into responding in kind. Though the huge corporate conglomerates that dominate the landscape of the computer industry today were forced into adopting their own pitched research and development efforts just to stay abreast of their competition, it became clear that national governments were almost as frightened at the prospect of being dominated by a foreign computer industry as they were of being occupied by a foreign army. Research and development in computer technologies became a prominent part of a new type of nationalistic rivalry – founded upon nationally directed economic competition – that has come to overlay and is displacing the primal military rivalry of the postwar era.

And so Max Weber's observation rings true again in our time in the birth and diffusion of computer technology: the military discipline of broad and sustained research and development finds its way into private industry, and eventually becomes adopted by peacetime government bureaucracies that see themselves as directing economic organizations on a national scale. The wartime imperative of inducing continuous innovation in technology has been adopted by private companies and governments in peacetime, and as a result the pace of innovation in computer-related technology has been the swiftest and most sustained that the industrialized world has ever seen. The result is a systematic, headlong rush towards the industrialization of intelligence.

A recurring process of government subsidy followed by commercial spin-off fuelled the rapid development of computer technologies during and after the Second World War, but important precedents for this symbiotic relationship between government and industry had occurred much earlier. The seminal event in initiating this relationship between public investment and private enterprise in an industry that would be a harbinger to the modern computer industry centred around the US government's need to perform timely and accurate censuses.

Under the United States Constitution, the federal government is required to perform a census of the population every ten years, and census results were the subject of much interest in the latter part of the nineteenth century. There was a general public curiosity and pride in documenting the particulars of the United States' historic expansion, coupled with a popular progressive social movement that was intent upon cataloguing various characteristics of the population such as the extent of literacy and the incidence of sanitary plumbing in residences. But the American census was more than a dry foray into demographics, however informative: it was the computation upon which representation in the House of Representatives was apportioned, and so was pivotal in the shifting balance of power in the Congress as the population went through the heady process of massive immigration combined with simultaneous urbanization and western expansion. The census count every ten years was therefore both an immense computational task and a highly significant political event.

By 1880, both the importance of the census and the size of the undertaking had grown to the point where there were obvious difficulties in tabulating the results by hand. The population of the country had reached 50,000,000 and it required more than seven years to complete a census that had to be performed every ten years. The manual method of tabulation was so inefficient that as the population increased, the Bureau of the Census was faced with the prospect that it might have to commence future censuses before the result of the previous count became known. The chief bottlenecks were in collating the massive amounts of data on individuals and tabulating the results. In a precedent-setting move, the bureau sponsored a sort of 'shoot out' between three mechanical tabulating devices, the winner of which would be employed in the 1890 census. Obviously superior among the three was the machine created by a mechanical engineer and former Census Bureau consultant named Herman Hollerith, who had just the year before won a major contract with the US Army Surgeon's office for his punched-card tabulating device.

In Hollerith's machine, field census counts on groups of individuals were recorded on stiff paper cards the size of the US dollar bill, the information being represented by holes punched into the cards at appropriate places representing characteristics that were to be tabulated. The cards were stacked into a machine and mechanically scanned one by one. Where a hole appeared in the card, a pin was allowed to drop through it into a small cup of mercury below, completing a circuit and triggering a counter to advance by an appropriate number of positions. The machine offered the potential to tabulate very rapidly the results of numerous field surveys, by mechanically 'reading' the information contained in stacks of punched cards that were loaded into the machine, each card recording the answers to various queries from field surveys.

The Jacquard device was the immediate and obvious inspiration for Hollerith's machine. The weaving machine, which had come into universal use in the production of decorative fabrics, was a familiar and still fascinating contraption to those with even a passing knowledge of textiles. Hollerith was particularly familiar with the details of the Jacquard device, having previously investigated the device as part of an abortive weaving business venture. During his days at the Census Bureau he and colleagues had discussed in idle conversations the possibility of employing a Jacquard-like machine in mechanizing the mammoth tabulating tasks in the bureau that accompanied each census and occupied an army of clerks and tabulators.

By Hollerith's own account, an experience while commuting on a train made a deep impression on him and helped resolve in his mind the manner in which a card-reading device could be used to record census data. Hollerith was struck by the elegant and speedy manner in which the conductor was able to record each passenger's characteristics on his individual ticket so that it could not be reused by another passenger. A number of boxes were printed on each ticket that corresponded to the patron's physical features, boxes for light or dark hair, eye colour, etc., and the conductor would punch a hole in the box to mark conformance to the trait. In Boolean terms, the conductor was uniquely identifying each patron by classifying him or her according to various characteristics. Hollerith, an avid photographer, had a different comparison to make: he described the tickets as a 'punch photograph' of the patron.

This clearly was a revelation to a mechanical engineer reflecting on how to make machine-readable records for characteristics of millions of individuals, and one wonders if Hollerith, who had had to overcome a reading disability as a boy, may have been particularly impressed with this compact and speedy manner of recording and reading vital statistics. His early designs for punched cards closely reflected those he observed on the train. Ever the pragmatist, the cards he eventually designed were the exact size of the US dollar bill then in circulation, so that readily available filing cabinets designed to hold money could be used to store the cards. Computer punched cards to this day have retained Hollerith's format, and even the arrangement of holes in his early cards is still largely retained in computer punch cards of the current era.

From a technological perspective, Hollerith had done little more than reapply Jacquard's principle in an electro-mechanical counting apparatus, but in a larger sense he was reprising a long-lived system for mechanical memory. Hollerith-type card readers were a recurring basic technology in calculating systems down to the fairly recent past, when many business computing systems routinely employed punched cards. The basic role of the card-reading device was that it lent memory to the machine, in the Hollerith machine's case memory used exclusively for recording data. Even though the machinery Hollerith designed to employ the cards was very crude by today's standards, being only a simple counting machine, the use of his mechanical memory device encouraged a transformation in the census from a purely counting function to a more comprehensive data-gathering and storage exercise, and anticipated many of our current concepts of database design and management.

Hollerith achieved considerable renown in his day, and his work lead to several lucrative contracts with the US Army and other government agencies in the United States and Europe. There was clearly money to be made in tabulating machinery, and Hollerith created even more of an opportunity for competition by being averse to lowering the prices for his machines. After the 1900 census, the Census Bureau, concerned that Hollerith's profits were excessive, elected to subsidize another inventor and bureau employee, James Powers, to develop a competing tabulator. Both companies prospered in an environment of potentially lucrative government contracts, as well as burgeoning opportunities in the commercial sector.

There was at the time a very healthy commercial demand for fast and reliable tabulating machinery in what might be fairly described as the era of the clerk. Since the latter part of the nineteenth century, the economies and populations in the Western industrial countries expanded in such a way as to create a whole new demand for raw tabulation. The populations were growing and moving about frenetically, particularly in the United States. The expansion of the railroads and a general increase in mass production enhanced the importance of accounting and record-keeping in corporate businesses, and American companies responded as Gaspard de Prony had responded, by creating a hierarchically structured army of bookkeepers and clerks to handle the work. The creation of a clerical work force presented business and government with a new set of costs and limitations. Clerks required training and had to be maintained in large numbers in centralized locations, to be produced in the quantity required by large-scale operations. Clerical work was also tedious, and clerks were subject to error and fatigue, and could be painfully slow in the presence of large amounts of information to be recorded and tabulated. Unlike Babbage, Hollerith and Powers found a ready corporate market for the machines that would replace these clerks – whose development the Census Bureau had essentially subsidized – and the companies of these two men became the precursors of two of the computer giants of today.[1]

But for all the promise the punched-card machines showed, and all their obvious profitability in computation for government and business, the machines were nothing more than tabulators. They could count holes and non-holes, and perform mechanically built-in counting functions, and do this with impressive speed, but they were not designed to perform any complex computation and could not solve even the simple polynomial expressions that Babbage's difference engine could. In the period between the world wars, the need to solve higher orders of mathematical expressions became increasingly acute, and the demand for machines that realized Babbage's dream became more pressing. Science and engineering were becoming dramatically more refined and required more detailed and complex mathematical calculations.

For any liberal democratic society, the systematic and equitable subsidizing of technological innovation in the absence of a pressing national threat is an exceedingly difficult task. The opportunities for mechanical computation that surfaced between the world wars were precisely the types of applications that Charles Babbage had imagined for his machines, the funding for which he was unable to obtain from the British government. For those involved in the engineering and scientific problems of the early twentieth century, the situation was in many ways similar to what Babbage had faced: their needs were legitimate, but somewhat abstract in the minds of government bureaucrats and not in the forefront of public policy. The situation changed as the Second World War approached, however, when the military's demand for computing devices unleashed a steady source of funding for new techniques in computing.

An example of the vexing military problems that demanded complex mathematical analysis was the calculating of projectile ballistics for warfare. The specific problem of calculating the correct trajectory for a fired shell is exceedingly complex and virtually impossible to do manually. The calculation in predicting the path such a projectile would assume in a vacuum is relatively straightforward, but is complicated tremendously by the drag of the air as it passes over the moving shell, which varies with the shape of the shell, its velocity and the density of the air. In computational terms the problem proved so intractable that military scientists were forced to employ sweeping assumptions and rules of thumb in order to render it calculable. The net effect of simplifying the description of the problem in order to ease its computation became apparent during the First World War, when weapons were rushed into production and it was discovered in battle that their firing characteristics were significantly different from what their designers had predicted. One computer pioneer involved in trying to solve these problems cites the example of the German navy's discovery, upon their first firing of a new gun, that its range was over twice that for which it had been designed.[2] Other areas of science and engineering, including the design of structural components, accurately predicting the position of the planets and moon, and the design of complex electrical power networks offered their own serious computational challenges.

By the 1930s, the necessity for solving these types of problems, which among other things had profound military implications, and the particular state of technological development, led to what was for the time intense research and development into a computational strategy that within a few years proved to be a dead end for general purpose computing and is used today only in relatively few specialized computers. This strategy was embodied in so-called *analogue computers*, which for purposes of advanced mathematical computation had displaced the digital computation that had been proposed by Babbage a century before. The fundamental concept behind all analogue computers is that, since all physical processes operate according to mathematical rules, it is in theory possible to build a physical model that simulates any particular mathematical function. By measuring the positions of the elements of an analogue computer, one can derive results that correspond to the problem being considered. At the zenith of mechanical analogue computation, room-sized machines were developed that were capable of solving complex problems of integration and differentiation by 'analogy'. But though it enjoyed a brief stint as the state of the art in machine computation, the strategy was inherently limited and with the advent of new electronic technologies surrendered back to the digital strategy the best hope for fast, complex mathematical computation. The shift back to a digital strategy also had the effect of opening the door to new techniques that processed all types of symbolic information, not just the numerical computation to which analogue devices were limited.

The fundamental difference between the two strategies for computation is that analogue machines rely on continuous processes that require *measurement*, while digital machines rely on discrete steps more akin to *counting*. This contrast in technique can be likened to the difference between a slide rule, which is an analogue device, and an abacus, which is a digital device. In using a slide rule, one derives arithmetic results by sliding the continuously marked scales relative to each other and reading the results directly from the scales. To perform a similar function with an abacus, one needs to move the tokens in the abacus according to a rigid set of rules through a number of discrete steps, each step dependent on the current arrangement of tokens and the rules for operating upon them. The slide rule relies on measuring the relative positions of the sliding logarithmic scales against each other, while the abacus relies on the correct appraisal at each discrete step of the correct number of tokens in each position.

The immediate trade-off between the two approaches that is apparent in the example is that, while all measurements involve an unavoidable degree of error, counting is a process that can reliably occur with absolute precision. A machine can be built that can reliably relate precisely how many apples there are in a bin, but no machine can ever be built that can tell you exactly how much they weigh. While the process of arriving at a solution through a series of discrete steps in a digital artefact may seem byzantine, the fact is that there is a good chance that the result will be absolutely precise.

Of course, one must in some sense measure something in order to count it. The difference between counting and any measurement such as weighing is the meaning one attaches to the measurement that underlies both. In order to 'count' or sense the presence of a token, one measures for its presence, and if its measurement indicates a value within a certain range of permissible values, one counts that token as present. This process of testing within limits for the purpose of detecting a token points to why digital machines have so consistently converged on a binary format for storing data: it is inherently faster and more sure to test only for the presence of one token, such as a hole in a card, and assume that if it is not detected, then the alternate value should be counted.

Besides its advantages in precision, digital computation has an inherent potential for speed and flexibility. As long as each discrete step is carried out reliably, the potential of simply speeding up the step-by-step process while still obtaining precise results is huge, in contrast with analogue devices which as a practical matter give less accurate results as they are pushed to operate faster. This was a primary reason why digital computers almost completely displaced analogue computers during the course of the war, as electro-mechanical and then electronic means were devised that made discrete digital steps occur with blinding speed. As techniques for digital computation matured, opportunities arose for digital machines that had the intrinsic capability of solving many different types of problems. Analogue machines were intrinsically devised to solve certain types of problems, the way an architect designs a building to serve a certain purpose, and were of very limited use on problems dissimilar from those for which they had been designed to solve. A digital machine, in contrast, was designed to go through a long series of steps, and if the steps it went through could be easily modified, the types of problems it could solve seemed unlimited.

85

The move toward digital computation was given a substantial theoretical boost by the work of Alan Turing, a brilliant young English mathematical logician who in 1936 opened up a comprehensive and definitive vision of the nature and limits of digital computation. Turing was able to characterize the types of problems that were inherently solvable by machinery – so-called *computable* problems – and the types of problems that would by their nature always defy positive mechanical solution. For a machine to solve any non-trivial problem of mathematics or logic, it must be capable of carrying out a finite series of steps without any non-mechanical intervention, such as that of a human operator being called upon to interpret any intermediate results. This finite series of mechanical steps is an algorithm, and the question of what problems are mechanically soluble is one of what problems can be solved by algorithmic means.

As might be expected from a mathematical logician, Turing's proof was entirely abstract. Turing was able to characterize computable and non-computable problems by positing the functioning of an hypothetical apparatus that he was able to prove was capable of performing *any* calculation that *any* mechanical apparatus was capable of performing. If this purely imaginary device, which became known as the Turing Machine, could solve a problem without human intervention then that problem was computable; if the Turing Machine could not solve the problem then the problem was non-computable, and not soluble by algorithmic means, or indeed by any mechanical apparatus.

The specific device Turing described for the purposes of his proof was a digital machine that was capable of 'reading' and 'writing' symbols in a serial fashion to a paper tape that could potentially be unimaginably long but always of a finite length. By 'reading' a value Turing meant that the machine could mechanically sense whether the symbol that was being scanned was any one of a finite number of symbols (though a simple binary set of symbols such as '1' and '0' was perfectly sufficient) and by 'writing' a value Turing meant that the machine could modify the tape so that the value in the current position was one of these symbols. The machine was capable of assuming any one of a finite number of internal 'states' which were a consequence of its actions thus far, and was capable of advancing forward and backward along the tape, reading or writing values as it went.

Turing originally set out to prove that some problems of mathematics are intrinsically unsolvable by an automatic computing device, and he did so by proving that there were some problems the Turing Machine could not solve, and then demonstrated that his hypothetical machine had the inherent ability to solve any problem of mathematics that any machine could ever have. Though his original assertion was important in mathematical theory, the proof that his machine was as capable as any other machine was a practical revelation to the many teams of workers during and after the war who were trying to rationalize the operation of digital computing machines, because it demonstrated an essential equivalence between digital computers of all types.

It was well established by that time that problems of arithmetic were essentially problems of logic, and Turing had shown that there was a whole class of machines that only had to share certain minimal capabilities in order to solve any computable problem by digital means. Armed with this insight, researchers could view the continued development of computers as an engineering task: that of discovering the fastest and most economical means for having a machine assume different useful states, and for reading and writing its intermediate results to some sort of memory. By engineering increasingly economical arrangements of components, the computer was not assuming any ultimate capability that it could not have had with simpler or slower components, but it was allowing the computer to move through more complicated algorithms faster, and so was enhancing the practical utility of computers and opening up new applications that were economical to computerize.

An added twist to Turing's proof was that the imaginary digital machine was not limited to computing numbers: it was more precisely a consideration of mechanically processing one set of symbols in order to produce another set of symbols, and numerical computation was merely a subset of its functionality. This had obvious ramifications for the development of codes and ciphers for use in wartime and is still today one of the most advanced and secret applications of computers. Turing was later to contribute significantly to the allied war effort with his work in the British Code and Cipher School, where he developed pioneering digital computers for breaking German codes, and much of that research is still secret today. The other implication of the digital machine's ability to process symbols was that it invited the first serious speculations about creating electronic thinking machines, since in essence processing symbols is what human minds do.

At about the time Turing was developing his theorem of computability, another fundamental theoretical insight of tremendous practical importance was being propounded by a young American electrical engineering student at the Massachusetts Institute of Technology. Claude Shannon's discovery – amazingly made while a graduate student, and communicated in what is undoubtedly the most influential master's thesis ever written – significantly rationalized the design of complex electrical circuits, a problem not only to computer scientists but also to engineers in myriad other electrical and electronic applications. The very pressing practical problem Shannon addressed was how to predict the behaviour of very complex arrays of electrical switches and, conversely in the design of complex circuits, how to design very complex arrays of switches that would work as a system in the manner desired.

Shannon's startling discovery was that systems of electrical switches conform in their behaviour according to the laws of Boolean algebra. The basic reason why this is true is that simple electrical switches behave according to the assumptions that Boole laid down for his system of algebra: either the whole current is allowed through or the whole current is blocked, the electrical equivalent of 'all or nothing' in a switch corresponding to Boole's concepts of infinity and zero, or true and false, in a variable. Since switches (or 'gates') acted like Boolean variables, arrangements of switches could be modelled with Boolean algebra. Every switch design imaginable had a corresponding Boolean formula that precisely described how it would behave in any circumstance, and conversely every logical relationship, since it could be translated into Boolean algebra, could potentially be expressed in arrays of switches. Using Boolean algebra, a designer could render in circuitry any logical relationship that was required, so that the design of electrical circuits that compared values, that recorded them, or that even did simple arithmetic was possible and practical. In the same way that Babbage used his notation to design complex mechanical devices, a modern designer could use Boolean algebra to design incredibly complex arrays of circuits that were capable of performing any logical activity, and could do so with complete confidence that the behaviour of his creation was precisely described by the corresponding Boolean expression.

As an example of the analogy Shannon discovered between Boolean algebra and circuitry, consider the comparison between the Boolean operation '+' and how two switches wired in series work: if either of two switches or both switches in a series circuit were closed – in Boolean terms, had a value of 1, so that all the current was allowed to pass through the switch – then the circuit as a whole behaved as a closed circuit, allowing the full current to pass through. This is analogous to the Boolean expression $x + y$, which is equal to 1 if either or both of the variables x and y are equal to 1, and will be equal to 0 only if both x and y are equal to 0. Conversely, the Boolean '*' operator corresponds to a parallel circuit: it will not allow a current to pass through it unless both its constituent switches are closed, just as the result of a Boolean '*' operation is not true unless both operands are true.

The arrangement of switches in a series circuit is referred to as an OR circuit, since it produces current exactly analogous to that produced in logic when two propositions are joined by 'or': the total circuit will produce current if one or both of the switches allows current to pass, analogous to the logical statement 'c is true only if a OR b is true'. Similarly, a simple binary parallel circuit is referred to as an AND circuit, which mimics the statement 'c is true only if a AND b are true'. Other circuits that mimic basic logical relationships are imaginable such as the NOT gate, which transmits current if another switch is open and blocks current if the other switch is closed. The NOT gate corresponds to the logical statement 'b is true only if *a* is not true', or '1 − *x*' in Boolean terms, where *x* is the value of the switch.

Shannon discovered that since electrical circuits intrinsically reflect Boolean logic, complex combinations of electrical circuits perfectly model complicated problems of Boolean logic and so could solve them by analogy. An immediate corollary to this discovery is that since arithmetic operations were essentially operations of logic, arithmetic can be modelled by circuitry. Complex circuits could be composed of NOT, AND, and OR gates that behave just as if the circuits were adding, subtracting, or multiplying two numbers together. The term 'adding' does not imply that this still relatively simple circuit exhibits any intentional action in computing the sum of two numbers, but only that, if the arrangement of one particular set of switches is set to correspond to the binary values of the digits of one operand value, and the arrangement of another set of switches corresponds to the digits of the other operand, then by polling certain portions of the circuit one can reliably interpret its behaviour as the numerical sum of the operands.[3]

To computer researchers, Shannon's discovery significantly rationalized how logic could be modelled with electronic components and simplified the process by which complicated logical designs could be rendered in wires and switches. With the increasing use of electronics in computers that came from technologies pioneered in wartime and immediately thereafter, this enabled computer designers to manage more capably the technical details of what they were doing, to consider the design of computers as a more formal problem of logic, and to tackle electronic designs of previously unimaginable complexity. Complex specialized circuits could be designed that could perform arithmetic functions, comparison functions, or fetch and send data, and the circuitry could be designed so that it performed these specialized logical operations in many quick, discrete bursts that allowed step-by-step operation of the many logical operations that would be required to perform a calculation. Banks of circuits could even be quickly designed that stored data or instructions just as punched cards did, but this information could be retrieved and stored in a fraction of the time required by mechanical means.

During the Second World War, several teams of researchers worked simultaneously in England, the United States and Germany on various designs for automated digital computing machines, using various blends of mechanical, electro-mechanical, and electronic components. There was an underlying military purpose to each of the projects and each team had its own particular consortium of academic aegis, industry sponsor and government agency patron. Significant among the teams and projects were the Harvard Mark programme which was originally a joint project of IBM and Harvard University and was picked up by the US Navy during the war and sustained by the Navy and Air Force thereafter; the British Code and Cipher School located outside London at Bletchley Park, where Alan Turing worked in applying computing machines to pivotal allied work in breaking German codes; Bell Telephone Laboratories in New York, where a series of computers were produced under the direction of the US National Defense Research Committee for the Air Force and Navy; and the Whirlwind project at MIT, begun by the Navy and adopted by the Air Force.

Though each of the various teams at work on their own vision of computing machines can claim to have contributed technical improvements that would become significant in today's designs, from today's perspective each of these machines seems somewhat idiosyncratic, as each was designed to fit its particular patrons' mission, the team's assessment of unstable emerging technologies and the machine designers' personal proclivities. For this reason – coupled with the fact that some of the work is still classified – the birth of the modern computer tends to incite controversy and ruffle personal and corporate egos. What is clear is that at the conclusion of the war, the work of one particular team – the Moore School of Engineering in Philadelphia – established a new paradigm for computing machines that was rapidly disseminated to the other teams and to a spate of new research teams that sprang up after the war. This paradigm was a logical design for a digital electronic computer that served as a remarkably robust platform for the sustained riot of manufacturing innovation that was to follow, and serves today as the logical structure of most computers.

Though the Moore School researchers are given prominent mention in most histories of computers, the circumstances involving their breakthrough were the basis for bitter feelings among the principals. Led by J. Presper Eckert and John Mauchly, in association with Herman Goldstine, the Moore School team was working in 1944 on a high-speed ballistics calculator called the ENIAC (Electronic Numerical Integrator And Computer) for the US Army's Ballistics Research Laboratory. While working on the project, several improvements in streamlining the operation of the device and in making it a universal calculating machine became apparent; and while work on the ENIAC was still proceeding a proposal to the Army for a more advanced machine, the EDVAC (Electronic Discrete VAriable Computer), was under way. Certainly the seminal new concept of the stored program was already a pivotal part of the conception of this new machine.

While the proposal for the EDVAC was being prepared, a prominent mathematician and polymath, John von Neumann, came to join the team after a chance meeting with Goldstine. Hungarian born and of German descent, von Neumann had already established himself as one of the brightest and most influential minds in twentieth-century science, contributing profoundly to areas as diverse as mathematical logic, quantum physics and even economics. As the problems being addressed in the proposed EDVAC were being thought out, Eckert and Mauchly apparently tended to the technical aspects, while von Neumann and others focused on the more abstract problem of the optimum relationships between the logical components of the device. Von Neumann committed to paper a draft of the team's ideas that were being developed, many of which were the result of team discussions, and many of which bore the unmistakable stamp of his own genius. The draft report was widely circulated within the scientific community and was immediately hailed as a breakthrough, but unfortunately for later relationships, it bore von Neumann's name alone and the logical design it proposed came to be known as the von Neumann architecture.

The ideas developed at the Moore School that came to be credited almost exclusively to von Neumann spread rapidly due to several circumstances, including a series of important seminars given there in 1945 and 1946, the widely read report that bore von Neumann's name, and ultimately to the bitter dissolution of the Moore team itself. Eckert and Mauchly were unique for their time in seeing tremendous commercial potential in the machines they were developing, and their bitterness toward von Neumann's apparently unintentional seizing of credit was complicated by an ongoing dispute between them and Moore School officials over patent rights. Already heated, emotions boiled over when an Army agent opined that the basic design for the EDVAC was not patentable in any event, due to the fact that von Neumann's report had from a legal standpoint placed it in the public domain. When pressed to sign away their patent rights to their work, Eckert and Mauchly resigned and formed their own company, which after much travail produced the UNIVAC computer, later absorbed by Remington Rand.

The so-called von Neumann architecture the Moore School team developed was the foundation of the vast majority of general purpose computers to this day, including almost all scientific and commercial computers. The design owes its influence to the fact that it reflects an inherently elegant way to optimize the costly resources of computers, while making their operation as efficient and economical as possible. The basic dual strategy behind the von Neumann architecture is to minimize redundancy in costly logical components and to maximize the speed with which data and instructions can be read from and written to memory devices. In order to minimize redundancy in the logical components, a von Neumann machine opts to shuttle data between different logical components one step at a time, and so von Neumann architectures are associated with *serial*, or step-by-step, operations. In order to expedite the reading and writing of information to memory devices, von Neumann machines possess relatively large amounts of fast internal memory in which information is held. This fast internal memory can read and write data at speeds that dwarf those of mechanical devices such as card readers, which is one reason why von Neumann machines offered immediate boosts in the efficiency of computers.

But there was a more important aspect to von Neumann machines that opened up whole new vistas to the efficient and flexible manipulation of symbols. Data in internal memory could not only be stored and fetched at higher speeds than was possible with mechanical devices, it could also be accessed directly, or randomly, which is why fast memory of this sort is generally referred to as *random access memory* (RAM). When data is required of RAM, it is possible to inquire directly at the location within memory that the data is held, and conversely when data is to be recorded in RAM, it is possible to record it in exactly the position desired. This is in contrast to the *sequential access* that is associated with, among other memory devices, the Jacquard-like card readers: when information is required of a stack or chain of cards, the only practical way to fetch it is to read through the stack, bypassing unwanted information until the desired information is located.

This relative abundance of RAM in the von Neumann architecture allowed the crowning aspect of this seminal technological paradigm. Not only was there room in RAM for data, such as numbers or characters that were being processed, but there was also room in RAM to hold the instructions for the various computational tasks the computer was to do. Instead of the computer having to rely on a sequential access device like a card reader to find its next instruction, it could fetch the same information from RAM. To use an analogy from Babbage's analytical engine, it was as if all the information that was contained in the Jacquard card chain was instead held in a huge store, except that now the store operated at blinding electronic speeds. Each individual instruction could now be accessed at random, making it much easier to instruct the computer simply to skip over certain instructions, or repeat a set of instructions over and over, depending on the situation it encountered at the time. This breakthrough concept, where the instructions for individual computer functions were stored in RAM, was the *stored program*, and is the final vital aspect of the von Neumann architecture. The paradigm of a computing machine with a stored program, held within a generous RAM space, that directed an essentially serial operation was the *sine qua non* of the von Neumann architecture. This was the powerful concept that rippled outward from the Moore School and still dominates the design of computers today.

Von Neumann machines are special cases of Turing machines, and none can solve a problem that Turing's hypothetical machine could not solve, but the entire rationale behind the von Neumann architecture was that it was the most efficient, practicable Turing machine that could be built. In Turing's terms, the von Neumann machine with its internal program and large RAM space was simply a manifestation of the original Turing specification, with a preference for more 'internal states' (i.e., RAM for data and instructions) and less 'tape' (sequential access devices such as card reading machines or paper tape) than previous designs. This modification in the relative balance between random access and sequential access components was nothing more than a technical reaction to the relative productivity of RAM over sequential access devices, and only became practicable as much cheaper and reliable random access memory components became available. The von Neumann architecture was a major turning point in computer system design, not only because it was a major realignment of computer resources based on a shift in the relative economics of some computer system resources, but because it established a workable logical design for almost any computer system then imaginable. After its adoption, different hardware components of the computer system began to be explicitly considered as resources, as an industrial engineer might think of equipment on a factory floor, and issues involving the most economical balance of computational resources came to dominate the design of the computers.

From its first description in the 1946 EDVAC report, it was clear that the von Neumann architecture possessed a profound potential for performing complex and intricate logical functions in a physical apparatus. It offered the prospect of tremendous flexibility in solving any sort of problems at the expense of a mind-numbing complex apparatus that would have to perform an equally mind-numbing number of exceedingly simple tasks in a rigid sequence. Clearly, a programmable von Neumann-type computer would have to be the most complex instrument that had ever been conceived to that point, and its myriad of components would have to operate with a consistency that had never before been achieved. The approach was that which had been glimpsed by Babbage, but had been doomed to remain dramatically uneconomical as long as it was forced to rely on mechanical means. It was only with the advent of new, inexpensive electronic components that the feasibility of such an approach became apparent. With electronics, the von Neumann archetype became firmly established as a robust logical paradigm that served as a stout platform for a generation of frenzied technological innovations.

Since the war years, the efficiency of computer technology has undergone a remarkable, if by now familiar, transformation. With the adoption of the archetypical design a fundamental process of computation had been defined, and further advances of computer technology became in many ways a much more simple game: a game of making the established process more efficient. Any innovation that made components cheaper, faster, or more reliable, or more efficiently produced instructions for stored programs, was bound to alter dramatically the economics of computation and information processing. Fuelled in the early years almost exclusively by government contracts, which were in turn dominated by military demands, the von Neumann architecture benefited from a steady stream of incremental improvements that would radically enhance its practical utility, and ultimately made the new machines economical to adopt in commercial enterprises. There were three key areas of innovation that worked in parallel to enhance dramatically the productivity of computers in the postwar years: techniques for manufacturing electronic components and circuitry, technologies for auxiliary storage, and the techniques for producing instructions for stored programs.

Of the three, the most dramatic improvements have come in the manner in which wholesale improvements have been continuously made in producing complex, reliable and economical electronic circuitry. The innovations were the result of tremendous competitive opportunities seen for the manufacture of systems of circuits capable of memory and logic, so that today the capacity for these functions is mass produced on a tremendous scale. The pace of this technological advance is undoubtedly the most rapid and sustained of any economic activity in history. Each major innovation represented a quantum leap in basic computer computational speed and capacity over the existing technology, leading to such dramatic leaps in productivity that it is common to associate each major innovation with a 'generation' of computer hardware, though in these terms a generation may last as few as three or four years.

First generation hardware is associated principally with vacuum tubes for logic circuits and various techniques such as electrostatic tubes, delay lines, or magnetic cores for memory circuits, roughly spanning the period from the dissolution of the Moore School team to the end of the 1950s. Each of these technologies owed their existence to wartime military research and development programmes. The vacuum tubes played the role of Boolean gates in the manner that Shannon had described. Though the details are not important here, it is fair to compare each tube to a small and delicate light bulb. Each required a considerable amount of electricity to operate, each generated heat while operating, and each had a limited life before it burned out. Computers based on such devices were necessarily behemoths: ENIAC used 18,000 vacuum tubes; was 100 feet long, 10 feet high, and 3 feet deep,[4] and when operating used enough power to heat a block of apartments.[5] With so many tubes, each of which was essential to proper processing, hardware failures were an ongoing reality of computing, and extraordinary measures were undertaken to extend their operating life. Tubes were operated well below their rated capacity, and the operators of the machine were loath ever to turn the system off because of the stress to the tubes of cooling and re-heating. Despite all precautions, in its prime ENIAC could do no better than fail 2 or 3 times a week.

The heat these beasts produced was considerable, and the warm tubes in their bowels attracted flying insects. On occasion, a component would mysteriously cease to function while operating, and upon searching for the cause the technicians would discover that a bug had flown too close to an element and had met an untimely death, taking the sensitive component with it. With time, whenever the machine failed for any unknown reason, it was euphemistically declared that there was a bug in the machine, giving rise to the term that persists among computer users today.

The invention of the transistor signalled the second generation of computer hardware. Invented in 1948 by researchers at Bell Laboratories with partial funding from the military, the transistor was a rugged, compact and reliable substitute for vacuum tubes in logic circuits and used only a fraction of the electricity that their predecessors required. The military heavily subsidized the development of this technology after its initial discovery, both in direct funding and in assuring ready markets for the experimental devices, and the technology was made practical primarily because of the force of continuing US military contracts. Among the early programmes that pushed forward the development of the transistor were the Atlas intercontinental ballistic system, an airborne control computer for the US Air Force, and a Navy system for radar tracking.[6]

As transistorized electronic equipment came to be mass produced, the now familiar circuit board became common. A typical circuit board contained several transistorized components attached to plastic boards, with the electrical connections between components provided by silver or copper wiring that was applied to the surface of the board. In the early 1960s, the manufacture of the transistors themselves became more planar, so that cost-effective assemblies were being achieved by plugging planar transistorized components into planar boards.

But even as early as the late 1950s, the strategy of plugging discrete transistorized components on to circuit boards could not keep pace with the demands the military was making on electronic systems. With the increasing complexity of these systems, a dual manufacturing and performance constraint presented itself. The manufacturing bottleneck was in the cost required to interconnect reliably the increasing number of components on the boards, while the performance problem was that the speed with which the components could be operated was constrained by the amount of time it took for electrons to travel the longer distances between the components. The push was for a blurring of the distinction between component and connection in the presence of demand for higher quantities of more complex transistorized assemblies, and the ideal solution was a technique for mass producing complex, miniature integrated circuit assemblies in high quantities.

Using new manufacturing techniques that were based on established photo-etching technologies, it became possible to produce comprehensively the functional equivalent of entire circuit boards in a single, monolithic component. Precision drawings of the planar components and connections were photographically projected to very small images, which could be used as multiple acid masks on tiny silicon wafers. These were *integrated circuits*, which because of their small size and the close spacing between components offered yet another order of magnitude advance over the efficiency of the second generation transistors, and were the hallmarks of the third generation of computer hardware, generally considered to have begun around 1960 with the first implementation of integrated circuits in computer systems.

As before, military demands were central to the creation of integrated circuits. Though the integrated circuit was simultaneously invented by two private American groups, the motivation was for providing a technology that satisfied the announced specifications of the military, and the researchers intentionally eschewed government funding in order to protect its proprietary nature in the presence of virtually certain and lucrative military contracts.

With the manufacture of integrated circuits, technology had reached the curious point where a detailed drawing of components and wiring could be directly converted into complex electronic circuits capable of performing logical operations, so that, in a strange way, the distinction between the logic of the circuit and a detailed drawing of the shapes of its components became blurred. The strategy of photo-etching even more complicated integrated circuits was obviously a promising one, so that a chief economic obstacle to producing more advanced integrated circuits became the design and drafting of these drawings. Since the drawings were images of algorithmic processing, algorithmic processes came naturally to be applied in their creation. Special computer systems known generically as computer-aided design and drafting, or CADD, systems were employed to speed the design and drafting of the patterns for integrated circuits. Using CADD, repetitious logical circuit components could be quickly repeated in the drawing, design tolerances could be automatically calculated, and subregions of large integrated circuits could be designed separately and inserted when the finished design was being compiled. The final result could be drafted with a precision and speed unrivalled by human drafting. With these techniques, the entire essential components of a computer could be squeezed on to a single chip. This technology, so-called VLSI technology (very large-scale integration), is now generally referred to as the fourth generation of hardware, said to have begun around 1972.[7]

But by looking only at the very broad view of the natural evolution of manufacturing techniques that has occurred since the Second World War, one can easily lose an appreciation for the quantum leaps each step brought to the complexity and productivity of manufactured circuits. The first integrated circuit was invented in 1959, and contained only one logical device within its circuitry. For more than twelve years immediately following that, the number of devices that could be put on to a chip on average doubled every year, so that in 1972 integrated circuits were being produced that contained 20,000 transistors – about the complexity of the ENIAC – on a single chip. Since then, the annual rate of increasing miniaturization has slowed only a bit, to quadrupling every three years, so that now chips with hundreds of thousands of logical components are common commodities and chips with one million components per chip are not unknown, and according to some projections chips with one billion components should appear by the year 2000.[8] Additionally, new materials offer the prospect of providing quantum leaps in efficiencies entirely separate from those of large-scale integration.

The actual productivity being squeezed out of these advances in electronic logic is astounding. The Intel 80386 microprocessor (an integrated circuit that contains the logical components of a computer's central processing unit) being sold at this time of writing contains 275,000 transistors, more than fifteen times the complexity of the entire ENIAC system. The chip itself consumes less than 3 watts of power and works within a functional computer system that consumes less than 100 watts, compared to the 174 kilowatts of electricity required to run the ENIAC, and can perform a simple addition more than 25,000 times as quickly. The ENIAC required 1,800 square feet of floor space, weighed over 30 tons, failed every two to three days and took more than two years to build at a cost of about $800,000. The 80386 chip is a one-half inch square, cardboard-thick wafer that sells for a few hundred dollars and is engineered to last an average of 961 years between failures, and more than 2 million of them were produced and sold in 1988.[9] (Intel has under way the design for a new chip that is approximately 150 times as powerful as the 80386.)

The second major area of innovation since the Second World War was in the development of improved techniques for auxiliary storage. The circuitry in an electronic digital computer corresponded to the capacity of the machine to assume a vast variety of different 'states' as described in the Turing Machine model. Along with the improvements in manufacturing the circuitry of the machines came a steady stream of innovations oriented to improving the performance of secondary memory devices, which were analogous in the Turing model to the very long paper tape. In one sense, the written record was not absolutely essential: a machine could theoretically have so many internal states available to it that it could hold everything in circuitry, but as a practical matter this would always be very wasteful. Fast memory is always expensive relative to other forms of storage, which made ancillary storage techniques economical by virtue of Babbage's law: that specialization would allow the most precious resources to be used most efficiently. With secondary storage, data and instructions that were not of critical importance could be saved temporarily and removed from fast memory, so that precious resources could be most productively employed in other data processing. A sort of hierarchy of memory technologies became discernible in all computer systems, not unlike the hierarchy of human computers Prony had used to calculate tables of logarithms, with critical information being kept in the fastest and most expensive media and devices, and less critical and more numerous information being stored on mass storage media that was much more economical in cost, but required much more time to be read from or written to.

In addition to being inherently expensive relative to other forms of storage, fast memory is inherently volatile. In the electronic world, this meant that the information in fast memory would disappear with any interruption in the electrical current. This was another reason that ancillary memory was required: simply to keep stable records of any data that fast memory could not accommodate, such as information not currently being used.

Punched cards and paper tape adopted from the tabulating machine industry were the original auxiliary storage media, but being electro-mechanical were entirely too slow to be used as part of a memory hierarchy in direct association with electronic processing. Though punched cards persisted for holding information through the 1970s, the need existed for a non-volatile memory with a much faster *access time*, so that information could be quickly read and written. The requirement for speed was important because, though hardware and software had increased dramatically in complexity, both were still locked in the Turing/von Neumann model of sequential processing and were still performing algorithmic processes one step at a time. The ability to read and write to an auxiliary device gave the computer a theoretically unlimited ability to perform algorithmic processes, as Turing demonstrated, but there would be an unavoidable delay every time the computer read or wrote information to auxiliary storage. The faster the access time to the auxiliary device, the more efficiently fast memory could work in tandem with its slower cousins.

A significant advance in access speeds came with the first use of magnetic tape as auxiliary storage in the 1950s after being pioneered under government-sponsored research by Eckert and Mauchly's commercial spin-off from the Moore School. Magnetic tape records data very much as audio recording tape records sounds, except that individual binary digits are held as changes in polarity in the magnetic medium, rather than analogue values corresponding to sound levels. The 'herky-jerky' movement of magnetic tapes on the fronts of computers became a popular symbol of computer technology in the early years – satisfying as they did the public need to see these unintelligible contraptions move in a way that resembled more familiar mechanical devices – but ironically they also exposed the technique's principal drawback. The reason magnetic tapes were constantly in motion, spinning madly forward, then back, then back more, then forward, was that they were moving to the point on the tape where the data that was called for was stored, or conversely where there was free space to record new data. Though they operated much faster than punched tape or stacks of cards, magnetic tape shared with these older approaches the characteristic of being a sequential access device. If the position of the reading head on a magnetic tape drive were at the one thousandth item of data on the tape, and one wanted to read the first record, there was no escaping the fact that the drive had to move the tape backward past 998 records until it could read the record desired.

This was suitable in instances that involved information that was inherently sequential, such as archiving unused information, but it could be a serious detriment to the speedy process of a programme that had to continuously read and record individual bits of data at scattered locations on the tape.

Magnetic discs, based broadly upon principles developed under government contract for the US Navy and Air Force, met the perceived need for a more direct method of accessing massive amounts of data starting in the late 1950s. In magnetic discs, the recording surface is applied to the surfaces of a round plate, rather than to flexible plastic tape. Data is recorded in several concentric rings, or tracks, on the surface of the plate. The plate spins at a constant high rate of speed and a read/write head, which floats just above the delicate surface, moves inward or outward from the centre of rotation so that it hovers directly above a specified track. There it searches the data zipping past until it recognizes the label for the location it is trying to access, and at that point on the disc it either reads or writes data. This class of storage is referred to as *direct access storage*, since the device can move fairly directly to the area of the data it is accessing.

Magnetic discs designed for very low access times and large amounts of data came to be composed of several such plates stacked on top of each other and spinning in unison, with gaps between the plates large enough to allow finger-like arms to reach inside without touching the spinning surfaces. Both surfaces of each plate would have a magnetic recording surface, and each arm would have at its end a pair of read/write heads, one for each surface of the plate. These types of magnetic discs are commonly referred to as *rigid*, *fixed*, or simply *hard* discs. On the other extreme, *floppy discs* or *diskettes* were developed to hold much less data and with much slower access, but with the quality of being very inexpensive and eminently portable. These discs have a single 'plate', which is more precisely a round piece of flexible plastic held in a plastic sheath.

Magnetic discs and tape served admirably in their role of significantly reducing the cost and access time associated with storing information. The effects of this new technology went far beyond altering the dynamics between computer components to altering the dynamics between computers and society. With information so cheap to store and access, computer technology came to be seen as an economical way to store, shuttle and retrieve vast quantities of information, rather than merely do complex computation. The economic opportunity for computers to act as information processors became apparent, and it became feasible to develop and maintain electronic information data bases.

The third major area of ongoing innovation since the Second World War has been in the methods of producing the instructions for the stored programs by which computers operate. The instructions that the computer recognizes directly from its stored program are said to be expressed in *machine language.* These are the only instructions that a computer can act upon. All computers have a basic set of operations, an instruction set, that automatically occur in a knee-jerk fashion whenever a certain number is held in a certain electronic register. As a program is executed, a series of numbers is read from the stored program into this register, and the computer blindly responds with the logical operation that corresponds to each value. This correspondence is established with the design of the computer circuitry, so that different models of computers use different machine languages, and a machine language program developed for one is useless on another.

The symbols used as machine instructions are generally stored and transmitted as binary values, and are generally associated with other symbols that refer to memory locations or numerical values. A series of machine language instructions, if they were written on paper, might look like this:

$$10100111 \quad 10001011 \quad 11101010 \quad 11101010$$

$$10100100 \quad 10010100 \quad 10011010 \quad 10100101$$

$$10100101 \quad 10101000 \quad 10100101 \quad 10101010$$

This is the sort of stuff that IBM mainframes are at this moment doing 15,000,000,000,000 times a second. As instructions, they may be poetry to a computer, but exceedingly difficult to manage by the human programmer who is composing it. The ongoing need for computer software to operate computer hardware has been a persistent bottleneck in the delivery of functional computer systems, and has been the focus of intense research and development by the government and private industry in the postwar period.

With the first computers, the only way to create a stored program was to produce by hand long lists of instructions in this machine language format, and though it was a great improvement over actually manipulating the hardware by hand, it was tedious and fraught with errors. The programmers had to look up the binary expression of every instruction, and keep track of every location in memory in which a needed value had been stored. This was a tremendous amount of human intellectual effort to record an instruction that even then was going to be executed in less than a thousandth of a second.

Beginning in the early 1950s, a first giant step was taken to speed and economize the process of producing machine instructions. This step, like many of the significant ones that followed and continue today, was the result of applying software to the problem of creating software. Programs were written that would translate instructions from a list written in a higher-level language that was comprehensible to programmers into the basic machine language instructions that the computer could use.

As an example of how these early translators worked, a programmer would write out a series of instructions using English-like terms on a piece of paper that represented what she wanted the computer to do. (At the dawn of the discipline, computer researchers underestimated how considerable a cost component of computer systems would be absorbed by software development. Programming was originally such a tedious and menial task that women were generally expected to do it.[10]) There were strict rules for the vocabulary and syntax used in this first instruction list, known as the *source code*, but the terms for the operations were inherently easier to remember and the addresses easier to keep track of. Operations would have English-like names like MOV for 'move', CLR for 'clear', or CMP for 'compare'. These are called mnemonics, since their spelling jogs the memory as to their meaning. In addition, addresses at which data could be accessed could be referred to symbolically rather than by their literal numbers, meaning that an *ad hoc* mnemonic, or variable, could be assigned to any location and any further references to that variable would end up addressing the location that variable symbolized. This allowed the programmer to name an address 'A' or 'RALPH', making it much easier to remember. So instead of the machine language instructions listed above, the programmer might write a source program consisting of instructions like:

MOY AH,1
INT 21H
CMP al, 'B'

The source program would be transposed into punched cards on a typewriter-like device, and this stack of punched cards would be read as input by a computer being operated by the translator program, and output would be produced in the form of a second stack of punched cards. This second set of cards represented the same algorithm that had been abstractly expressed in the source code, except now it was recorded as machine language instructions that could be read directly into memory and executed. This initial venture into higher-level languages that allowed for mnemonic commands and symbolic addressing was called *assembly language programming*, since machine language instructions were being assembled from slightly more complex instructions. Assembly language is still routinely required today in many fundamental programming assignments.

Even higher level languages followed immediately. FORTRAN, contracted from 'FORmula TRANslator', was developed in 1954, and is still in common use today. This first class of symbolic languages, which included names such as BASIC, COBOL, Ada, and PL/1, and later languages such as Pascal, C, LISP, and PROLOG, offered programmers an even higher level of abstraction. The languages were developed with specific needs in mind: FORTRAN was and is still used by engineers and scientists, COBOL is designed for business and accounting uses, BASIC and Pascal were originally designed to teach programming to students, LISP and PROLOG are the languages of choice for artificial intelligence applications.[11] The goal of these languages, which is actually the underlying goal of all innovations in software production, was to make it possible to deal more exclusively with the abstract nature of the problem being addressed, and as much as possible to divorce the programmer from consideration of the mechanics by which the computer would solve the problem. A portion of a BASIC program might look like this:

```
100   LET X = 123.34

110   LET Y = 23.89

120   Z = (X * Y)/ASSETS

130   IF Z < PROFIT THEN GOSUB 300

140   PRINT ASSETS
```

(In BASIC, each line of the source code is normally assigned a number, after which follows the source code instruction. The instruction on line 130 says, in effect, that if the variable named 'Z' is at this point less than the variable named 'PROFIT', to skip to line number 300 and commence operations at that point.) This small segment of code, so easy to follow once one is familiar with the peculiar vocabulary and syntax of BASIC, might typically be translated into dozens of lines of unintelligible machine code. This generation of languages allowed algorithms to be developed much more quickly, with greater opportunities for catching errors in the logic of the program and revising the program for modified applications.

In the evolution of techniques for developing software, some persistent themes that have been present since the nineteenth century in the organization and management of intellectual activity re-emerge in vivid detail. As even a casual comparison between the examples shown above of BASIC and machine-language code graphically demonstrates, the unmistakable trend in programming languages is toward syntax and methods that are more abstract and more attuned to the thought process of the programmer, and less mechanical and less attuned to the physical needs of the machinery that will use the program. In this, the development of programming languages and the role they play in ultimately industrializing intellectual activity bears an interesting resemblance to the development of Babbage's notation and how it aided him in the development of his engines. As Babbage's notation became more abstract, the machines he was able to design with it became more complex and powerful; as programming techniques become more abstract, the system of algorithms they are able to produce becomes more sophisticated, and the functionality of the resulting system assumes increasingly subtle capabilities of reason. It is generally accepted in government and industry that by discovering new techniques in generating software, computer systems will in the future begin to assume much more of the intellectual load of humans.

The actual process that occurs as increasingly more capable methods of producing software are developed is a throwback once again to Prony's system, and an elegant exemplar of the Babbage principle being applied to the production of computer algorithms. Algorithms expressed in higher-level languages are eventually expressed to the computer as machine-level 1's and 0's through the operation of the software that translates one into the other. The team of programmer, translating software, and machine code/computer is a direct analogy to Prony's pyramid of high-level mathematician, intermediary mathematician, and rote arithmetician: the methods at the highest level are translated to the means of the most repetitive mechanical functionality, so that the most recondite processes the programmer can conceive are eventually translated into the mechanical operations of rote Boolean logic. The difference is that in the programming example the lowest two positions have already been surrendered to machinery.

The proliferation of faster and cheaper computer hardware has created a high demand for software of corresponding capability. Software production, which is a still a particularly labour-intensive activity, has not been able to keep up the pace. The military and private industry have responded in a number of familiar ways to cut costs, which means save labour, in the production of software, and as Adam Smith would have predicted, an integral element of the efforts to economize in software production has been the mechanization of higher and higher intellectual realms of algorithm design. Automated code generation, using computer-driven models actually to generate software, is a key area of research with the military, particularly as the software bottleneck is seen to be critical in the development of high-priority defence programmes such as the Strategic Defense Initiative, and it is widely predicted that computer programmers as such will largely be displaced by automated tools in the decades ahead. The division of mental labour that has already occurred in the software industry has, as it has in the past, cleared the way for the introduction of mechanical tools in the production process, and automating software production is a predictable turn of events in an ongoing process of reducing the judgement of humans to algorithmic processes, so that machinery can take over incrementally more sophisticated intellectual tasks.

Though a robust and fruitful paradigm, the serial operation of von Neumann machines presents obvious opportunities for improvement. With the introduction of new hardware technologies and software techniques, opportunities for improving the productivity of computer systems beyond that possible in a strict serial approach became apparent, and in fact efforts have been under way from the very beginning to chip away at the pure von

103

Neumann paradigm in order to enhance the computer system's throughput. The central inefficiency in a strictly serial operation was that, though the serial operation held tremendous potential for simply being speeded up, it would always necessarily leave the vast majority of the computational resources of the computer idle.

The limitations of a strictly serial operation can perhaps best be understood by way of analogy. In the pure von Neumann machine, data in the form of electrical values is shuttled from one computational resource to another in a rigidly serial fashion, and each computational resource modifies the data in some specific, mechanical fashion. The analogy would be to compare the computer to a factory, perhaps one that produces automobiles as a computer produces processed information. In this peculiar von Neumann-style factory, the components of the car being produced are shot around the factory floor between stationary workers, each worker performing a very simple assembly according to a set of rigid rules, just as data is shot between the resources of a computer under the control of software. An odd aspect of this car factory is that only one task can be performed at any given time: if any one worker is occupied with his task, all the other workers must freeze. This is the analogy for true serial data processing, where only one process can be performed at any time.

If anyone with any business sense at all surveyed this automobile factory from above the factory floor, the glaring inefficiency is that at any one time, all but one of the workers in the plant are idle. Speeding up the movement of the car components and making each worker work faster would proportionately increase the output of cars, just as new electronic techniques vastly increased the velocity with which data could move through the system, but could do absolutely nothing towards remedying the obvious problem that each worker was hardly ever producing anything.

The glaring inefficiencies could get much worse, because frequently computer systems of necessity need to send or receive data to and from mechanical devices that operate much slower than electronic components, as when data is written to or read from auxiliary storage devices or when a process must pause for some input from the user. In comparison to the speeds on the factory floor, the speed with which intermediate goods could be shipped outside the factory was extremely slow. In the analogy of the car factory, this would be as if subassemblies of the automobile had to be occasionally shipped to or received from distant factories on an ox-cart. Strict adherence to the serial archetype would mandate that whenever a delivery was required, everyone on the factory floor would stop working until the shipment had left and returned.

As the factory analogy shows how glaring inefficiencies can result by serial operations, it can also serve as an analogy for some of the solutions that were proposed and give a sense of the enormous potential for increased speed that these innovations held. The most obvious opportunity for speeding up the factory was to avoid it closing shop whenever a delivery was made. The common-sense solution in the factory example would be that whenever a delivery of a subassembly was to be made, a worker in the factory would note the status of that subassembly and declare the assembly process for that particular car suspended at least until the delivery was complete. A factory foreman could then select another car to work on, which could then proceed until it had to pause to await its own delivery (or perhaps until the delivery for the first car was received back). If the number of deliveries that were necessary for the complete assembly of each car were significant, it is possible that hundreds of cars could efficiently move through a factory organized in this manner, though only one step is still being performed at any given time. To anyone waiting at the plant door for a particular car, the time it took to complete their car might not be significantly different whether their car were the only car being assembled, or one of scores being worked on at the same time.

The computer technique that corresponds to this example is *multiprogramming*, which can allow for several programs (the several car assemblies in the example) to use a single computer, and each program makes serial use of the computer's resources as if, from its perspective, it is the only program being performed by the system. The practical benefit of multiprogramming is that it can allow for *timesharing*, where several users use a computer simultaneously, each user perhaps totally unaware that other users are using the system. As an individual program comes to a step that requires what to integrated circuits is an inordinate amount of time, such as input/output operations, that program is suspended until the sluggish operation is complete, and other programs are allowed centre stage for the intervening period.

Multiprogramming was not a universally tenable solution, but even if it were applicable to a particular computer system, the technique only skirted the issue of serial processing. Even with multiprogramming, strictly serial processing meant that only one operation was being performed at any one time, and all the other resources were being wasted. There seemed to be enormous opportunities for finding some productive task for idle computational resources to do while they were awaiting their next task, just as the factory manager might look for ways to organize the factory work so that workers could be doing something productive while they awaited their next primary task. One immediate opportunity is *pipelining*, which might be compared to putting certain specific sequences of steps on an assembly line. Each worker in a pipelined organization automatically looks ahead and performs a task on an upcoming ingredient, so that when the next worker down the line has completed his task, the input he needs for his next task already awaits him. Charles Babbage apparently incorporated the concept of pipelining into his early machines.

Another technique designed to keep idle resources more consistently busy was *multitasking*, in which a single process might be broken down into several sub-tasks that are able to move through the system simultaneously, either serially by a variant of multiprogramming, or concurrently by properly employing multiple processors. The analogy for the former approach would be a situation in which, if one subassembly such as the engine block were being assembled and ran into some exogenous delay, a single factory foreman would temporarily suspend that task pending the resolution of the delay, and turn his attention to directing workers in assembling another component, such as the suspension, that was not affected by the engine block. The multiple processor approach would correspond to a factory with several foremen, each of whom directed his team of workers and had access to some common resources shared by all the foremen: in this arrangement, the engine block and the suspension could literally be assembled simultaneously.

At a different scale, the drive to develop communication networks between computers responded to the same need as multiprogramming and multitasking: it is an attempt to distribute computational capacity economically while allowing communication of data between computers and sharing of some computational resources, but in a way that allows various degrees of autonomy for the different elements along the network. The co-ordination of the computational resources is left to a free-wheeling organization more akin to a market than to an industrial regimen, so that the analogy of a network might be more usefully compared to the transactions that take place between factories than any type of organization that is generally seen within factory walls.

Of course at some point someone will suggest that all the workers in a factory must be gainfully employed most of the time. The analogous strategy in a computer system is *parallel processing*, in which there is a high redundancy of key computational resources and problems are solved by dividing the tasks into many sub-tasks that can be pursued independently and in parallel. As might be imagined, even the slightest success with parallel processing offers tremendous boosts in the productivity of the system over serial processing, and this is an area of research that has largely been funded by the military from the very beginning. The principal drawbacks to more general applications of parallel processing are in making the procedures behind it universal: one can imagine a factory designed to produce a specific product that can work very efficiently in parallel, but designing a factory that can produce any of a wide range of products in parallel becomes a vexing organizational problem. Analogous problems exist in terms of parallel processing for general purpose computing.

Without going to absurd lengths with the automobile assembly analogy, suffice it to say that every incremental innovation in managing the manipulation of data in modern computer systems can be likened to intuitively

106

obvious concepts of how one would most productively organize a team of workers. The fact that direct analogies invariably exist between computational systems and productive labour systems is more than a happy circumstance that facilitates the understanding of the evolution of computer systems: it points to the fact that the two types of systems both serve the same fundamental economic purpose, and the process of rationalizing the two productive functions is motivated by the same desire to achieve an economical efficiency in the production of a valuable commodity, automobiles in one case and information in the other.

The fact is that computer systems *are* teams of workers, a point that becomes obvious if we surrender our insistence that 'workers' must have blood and not electricity coursing through their brains. The modern computer is an incredibly vast array of simple electronic components, each of which is capable of solving a specific kind of logical problem by analogy. The problems these workers can solve are exceedingly simple ones, merely simple issues of logic, but there are an unimaginably large number of these workers and they produce results with a speed that is difficult to grasp intuitively. The whole thrust of computer research since the promulgation of the von Neumann model has been how better to mass produce these logical armies, how to make them work faster and more efficiently, and how to produce their instructions for working together more efficiently.

The innovations in manufacturing, programming and process management that have transformed information processing in the past five decades are all supremely rational from the standpoint of what is required to process information with increasing speed, which accounts for the rapid incorporation of these techniques into commercial products and the astonishing increase in the power of modern computers. The principles of the division of labour as pronounced by Smith and appended by Babbage can be seen in virtually every innovation. Multiprogramming, multitasking and pipelining allow for a saving in time as intermediate 'goods' are being transported between processes, and are only feasible through detailed specialization of certain computer components. The von Neumann paradigm displays Smith's concept of specialization with rare elegance: its entire economy is derived from the fact that specialized logical components are developed for specific functions, and the work to be done is distributed between specialized components so as to maximize the efficiency of the system. At a different scale, the computer networks developed by the US military in the 1960s and widely used in business today are perfect examples of the Babbage principle, as they are blatant attempts to distribute the computational load of an integrated system of computers according to each computer's capabilities, expense and availability.

Purely economic motives can explain the technical rationale for each innovation, but cannot even begin to explain the unprecedented speed with which these innovations were aggressively sought out and continue to appear. The wartime desperation of a few countries to spur on computer technology at the fastest possible rate has now been augmented by the efforts of huge corporations of a new type, companies in which constant innovation is vital to continued market share and huge investments in research and development are an inescapable component of operating expenses. And as if to provide an ironical symmetry to the process, the vitality of these industrial companies has come to be seen as critical to the competitive interests of their host countries, spurring a new regimen of government-sponsored research for the purpose of bolstering computer technology within nations. This dizzy pace of increasing computational capacity was borne of the desperate efforts of industrial nations engulfed in a total war for their very survival and has never slowed down for similar competitive reasons.

Since computer companies today spend an inordinate amount of their incomes on research and development and so consistently produce products that leap-frog previous offerings' capabilities, the captains of this industry appear unusually bold and forward-thinking, and in many ways they are. This is an image difficult to reconcile with the industry only a few decades ago, when the industry leaders were singularly unwilling to assume any risky development in computer technology, and when the common wisdom was that computers represented lucrative but specialized government contracts with no real commercial potential. At that time it was unthinkable to industry strategists that there would ever be a demand for more than a few mainframes scattered around in government offices. It was only through the constant prodding of the military research establishment and the promise of continuous, secure government purchases that the very cautious proto-computer companies entered into and lingered in the new computer market.

In the 1960s the commercial potential of computers and computer software became apparent, and by then the American giants – IBM, Sperry, Control Data, Philco, together with the aggressive smaller new enterprises, Burroughs, NCR, Honeywell – seemed to have a stranglehold on the growing market. The companies were unique in being able to benefit from considerable wartime funding without suffering any wartime destruction. In contrast to Great Britain, where significant and seminal research and development occurred during the war, military and other government spending did not abate with the end of hostilities, and in fact accelerated with the significant cold-war military projects that relied heavily on American pre-eminence in computer technology.

Perhaps the most remarkable aspect of the rise of the American computer industry in the 1960s was the apparent ease with which government-subsidized innovation was translated into commercial applications. This was hardly an accident, for a primary goal of military planners in the cold-war era had been to aid in the development of a robust domestic industry in key industrial sectors. The diffusion effects of the technology pioneered on military contracts were considered much more than a pleasant ancillary side-effect to government-sponsored research and development: these effects were a separate goal to be pursued deliberately and vigorously. For much Department of Defense research, secrecy was a curiously ambivalent and short-lived directive. Though exotic new techniques in computing were being developed at considerable cost, relatively little concern was expressed for the rapidity with which these techniques were introduced into open commercial markets, for the adoption of these techniques by private industry and their ripple effects in US industry were seen as vital components in the smouldering rivalry with the communists.

From all indications, the results of the diffusion-effects strategy, which was not by any means limited to the computer industry, were spectacular. As certain key innovations appeared in commercial products, the demand for computers in private enterprise proved enormous. The American domestic market for computer products and services was singularly robust compared to Japanese and European markets. US domestic spending for computer products soared ten-fold between 1960 and 1968 to five billion dollars, and even that figure is deceptive because during the same period the cost effectiveness of computers soared.[12] American venture capital markets, critical to funding in new start-up ventures, were similarly strong and served to stoke the already heated fires of innovation.

Not only did the diffusion-effects strategy work well in stimulating America's technological capabilities in the computer industry, the approach could not have been better designed to accentuate the weaknesses of America's cold war adversary. Though supremely suited to state-sponsored research and development in weapons systems, the Soviet system was at a severe disadvantage in a competition that depended upon any sort of give-and-take between government and private industry. The Soviet domestic markets for computers and investment capital were of course non-existent, and the rapid and uncontrolled development of information processing technology was antithetical to the state control of information and presented a powerful threat to the Soviet bureaucracy. A nation that still closely monitors the use of photocopying machines could hardly be expected to embrace such an open-ended technology, and the development of broad-based and uncontrolled computer communication networks like that pioneered by the US Defense Department's Arpanet was unthinkable. The Soviets have been backed into a situation where they will for the foreseeable future be totally dependent on buying or stealing Western computer technology, and without significantly restructuring their economy the prospects for developing a sufficient pool of endemic human resources are bleak. It is stark commentary to consider that at the present time of writing, the desktop computer on which this manuscript was prepared cannot be legally exported to the Soviet Union, and the computers that do exist there of even this limited capacity are hardly in the hands of individuals for their own creative use.

The US computer industry's rise was so precipitous that it evoked a nervous reaction from Western industrial allies, who were soothed by American technological superiority *vis-à-vis* the Soviets, but were intimidated by the obvious possibility that their own economies would become hostage to US technology. By 1965, fully three-quarters of the electronic digital computers in use in the major Western industrial countries were in the United States, and over half the computers in use in England and France, more than 70 per cent of those in Germany, and more than a third in Japan were manufactured by American firms, while virtually all the computers in use in the United States were domestic products.[13] The European and Japanese responses to this economic threat were similar in that government stimulation of the domestic computer industries seemed to be the answer. The Europeans were particularly slow off the mark, due to a tendency present in England, France and Germany to encourage a single national firm to carry the technological banner for the nation. Without an element of competition for key contracts, which had been part of the American system since the days of Hollerith and Powers, the Europeans' initial efforts to create a viable industry stalled. The chosen companies were predictably slothful in performing key government contracts they were awarded and the American pattern of small, flexible start-ups responding to new business opportunities was slow to develop. By the mid-1970s, European firms were still as dependent on American computer technology as they had been a decade before.

The Japanese response was subtly different in many ways. The postwar Japanese government was forbidden the option to spur technology with military contracts, and so the Japanese government's efforts to stimulate domestic computer industries were much more naked acts of national economic self-interest and were never confused with military issues as they were in the USA and Europe. Though the concept of the start-up was probably more foreign to the Japanese than it was to the Europeans, the Japanese did not fall prey to a dearth of domestic competition as did Europe. Industrial Japan had long assumed a pattern whereby the domestic economy was dominated by a handful of integrated giant conglomerates who had the resources to enter aggressively into promising new businesses. The traditional role of the state and the bureaucracy blended well with the challenges of the new industry, and the success of the public–private partnership in Japan in response to this threat now borders on legendary.

Though it is dubious to draw a direct causal connection, the period from 1960 through to 1980, representing the precipitous rise of the computer industry in the Western industrialized countries, was also a period of rapid, if fitful, economic expansion and a pronounced shift in employment patterns. There was a strong shift in employment from manufacturing to service industry jobs, and rampant and anxious discussion of the high-technology industries' role in the relatively decreasing number of blue-collar jobs. Though muted in the overriding sense of technological prosperity, new fears began to surface about the prospects for unemployment due to automation, fears that had not been heard since the discussions of technological unemployment in the 1930s and that recalled the debates of Ricardo's era. The worst fears about computers displacing human workers proved to be unfounded, or at least consistently premature, but there was a subtle difference between this new technological onslaught and those of the past that threatened traditional patterns of work, for in this case the new technological developments were being systematically forced along by the national governments, and particularly the defence establishment in the United States. The days were long gone when the military directly guided the majority of computer-related research, but the military has retained a key role in pushing along technologies at the outer boundary of feasibility, most significantly artificial intelligence and parallel processing. Even today fully 70 per cent of all university research in computer science in the United States,[14] and nearly 80 per cent of direct government funding for information technology research and development is funded by the Department of Defense.[15] Private industry has its own uses for these technologies, but without continued government – and primarily military – funding the pace of innovation in these areas would be much slower. Military research and development still plays a key role in super-heating an already dynamic industry and in spawning a new era of nationalistic competition revolving around a continuous, feverish pace of innovation in computers.

To researchers in computer science in the United States, the defence establishment has proved to be a generous and patient patron, and defence-related projects were consistently the most far-reaching and creatively challenging research to be done. The anti-military academic backlash that accompanied the painful denouement of the Vietnam War caused some strained feelings between American academics and the US Defense Department, but on the whole so much of the research requested by the military was so open-ended that it was easy for many liberal-minded academics who would normally have shunned military contracts to remain loyal to their source of funding. Even today the most liberal computer science academics who are critical of defence-sponsored computer research shy away from calling for any general cut in military-sponsored research and development.

For two decades a shaky consensus developed in government and academia that allowed the military's generous funding of basic research in computer science and other key defence industries to continue. Conservatives who were pro-business and pro-defence as well as liberals who desired a national industrial policy and funding for basic scientific research were both assuaged, and the American public has been consistently responsive to calls for large defence expenditures to protect their freedom and to guard against communist encroachment. The political consensus for military research and development was much more sustained than that elicited by occasional calls for the civilian-oriented research and development which, in a manner that recalled Charles Babbage's difficulties with the British bureaucracy, was difficult to rationalize consistently through shifting administrations and ambivalent attitudes about the government mingling in private affairs.

Not surprisingly, two perspectives arose in the United States about the nature of the benefits of military research and development. One school emphasized the superior weaponry that was the direct result of applied research, while the other emphasized the economic benefits of the diffusion of the research into the larger economy. From both perspectives, the judicious employment of defence research and development was directly contributing to Western security: the 'smart weapons' school could claim that America's best hope for deterring Soviet aggression was by overcoming the Soviets' numerical superiority with qualitatively superior weaponry, while the 'economic diffusion' school claimed that a healthy, vibrant economy provided the industrial know-how needed to maintain a superior technology base that would indirectly be capable of producing superior weaponry, not to speak of providing the tax revenues for financing it.

The economic diffusion school largely held sway in these arguments throughout the 1960s and 1970s, when liberal and moderate politics ruled. Military spending on research and development remained strong but declined slowly in real terms throughout the period, while non-military R & D (excluding the civilian space programme) climbed consistently, from 17 per cent of the military amount in 1960 to over 82 per cent of the military amount in 1979. Funding for the civilian space programme, which was spawned in response to a quasi-military challenge from the Soviets but was largely rationalized because of its potential for economic diffusion benefits, experienced a tremendous real growth in funding between 1963 and 1967, after which it levelled off and has remained relatively constant since then.[16]

One embarrassing aspect of government-sponsored research into weapons systems that the 'economic diffusion' school did not have to contend with was the very mediocre record military research and development had in actually delivering working weapons systems that in any way fulfilled their original mission. The familiar pattern was to specify a system that was beyond the bounds of current technology, and during the course of the contract fundamental new techniques would be developed that made the original concept possible, but also frequently obsolete. This tendency now seems to be an institution among advanced weapons systems, and has been perpetuated to the point of caricature in the case of the Strategic Defense

Initiative. With each failure, however, it seems that computer technique is advanced another increment.

The SAGE air defence system was typical of the pattern. SAGE was an outgrowth of the Whirlwind project begun at MIT in 1943, a project that had itself spawned many basic innovations in computer technology but whose mission had drifted as technologies changed. Whirlwind's original purpose was to provide real-time flight simulation capabilities for training Navy pilots, but it ran into difficulties in its original mission, and became the focus of controversy in its time because of the huge share of US government research funds it attracted and the meagre results it returned. The Navy dropped Whirlwind, but the Air Force took an interest in the technology as it was considering the development of a comprehensive command and control system to co-ordinate defences against Soviet bomber attacks. Though SAGE was one of the most expensive defence projects of its era, its original mission was largely outmoded by the time it came into operation in the early 1960s, as by then the Soviets were deploying intercontinental ballistic missiles and the threat from Soviet bombers seemed insignificant.

But though it never enhanced America's military security, the project precipitated profound technological benefits throughout the US computing industry. Whirlwind pioneered important techniques in process control and transactions processing, and was one of the earliest computer systems to use magnetic core memory and graphic displays. Timesharing was pioneered by IBM, the prime contractor, in developing the SAGE system, and the knowledge gained in the project allowed IBM to undertake the SABRE airlines reservation system for American Airlines, which became operational in 1965. AT&T pushed the state of the art in high-speed digital communications on the project, and Burroughs found funding for what is said to be the first solid-state computer to be mass produced.[17]

The Reagan administration brought with it a radical reappraisal of defence research and development. Department of Defense funding for R & D soared after two decades of gentle decline, almost doubling in real terms between 1980 and 1986, while federal non-military research and development declined in real terms by over 20 per cent in the same period.[18] Along with the shift in funding came a less quantifiable but equally dramatic shift in attitudes, as the conservative ideologues in the 'smart weapons' school had their day. The new policy was for research that more directly came to bear on deployable weapons systems coupled with a new, sterner attitude toward secrecy. Research projects in more fundamental science were eschewed, as were liberal researchers who were not sufficiently loyal to the military purpose behind their research.

Ideologues within the Republican administration are quick to claim victory in the cold war with the unexpected attempts at liberalization that are being promulgated in the Soviet Union under the Gorbachev regime.

By their reasoning, the USA's vast array of marvellous weapons and its stalwart conviction to press others to deployment has doubtless brought the Russians to the arms control table, and intimidated the hapless brutes into seeking their goals via non-military means. Even granting the dubious assertion that the Soviets are helplessly reacting to what the United States does, the position is a curious one, given the Soviets' persistent public focus on economically restructuring their economy. Even a casual perusal of the debates going on in the Soviet Union reveals that this is a country that is not insecure in its military prowess, but is deeply concerned about its economy. The liberalization of the Soviet Union does not resemble a country straining under the load of maintaining a military balance of power as much as a government shocked by its society's inability to maintain the technology it will need to maintain any relevance in future global politics. If anyone doubts the appeal of economic diffusion, let them only consider the astonishing changes it is bringing about in this most unlikely setting.

Initially fuelled by nationalistic competition, both military and economic, and later joined by private enterprise as its profitability was assured, the push for power and economy in computers has continued unabated since the Second World War and will doubtless continue at a breathtaking speed for the foreseeable future. As the development of computer technology proceeded, the major functional bottlenecks in electronic digital computation were consistently addressed first in military projects, and the solutions that grew out of these situations filtered into the commercial economies of the Western industrialized economies with profound economic effects. This process is continuing, particularly in such key areas as parallel processing, robotics, automated programming and artificial intelligence.

The net effect of the combination of the improvements in manufacturing of computer components and the logical design of computer processes has been the celebrated continued increase in the power and cost-effectiveness of the computer. From the time of the first electronic digital computers in the late 1940s to the current state of the art, the most advanced computers have both increased in speed and decreased in price by a factor of 100 every ten years[19], or in other words have increased in cost-effectiveness by a factor of 10,000 four times over. It is generally acknowledged that the state of computer-related technologies is such that these rapid improvements should continue unabated for decades to come.

Breathtaking as these projections may seem, they are relatively conservative because they are basically extrapolations on current techniques and do not begin to take into account the additional boosts in cost-effectiveness that may result from wholly new means now under development. Just as it was impossible to predict the revolution in computation that would take place because of electronics in general or integrated circuits in particular, any breakthroughs in one of hundreds of areas may make even these estimates of future computing power seem hopelessly naive.

It is doubtful that we can really imagine the impact that the widespread diffusion of computing devices like this portends for society. At one level what is happening is perfectly clear – increasingly inexpensive machines that possess ever-expanding capacities to perform vastly more complex algorithmic processes – but one shrinks from attempting to consider how changes like this promise to ripple through the economic fabric of society. For as algorithms become increasingly complex they seem to take on an entirely different character, as their mechanical nature becomes obscured by the sheer magnitude and velocity of the blizzard of stupid logical inferences that comprise them. Tantalizing prospects appear, of robots that can learn complex procedures, of machine vision systems that can use video images and interpret them usefully or voice recognition systems that can listen to and respond in natural languages. Even from the dawn of electronic computers there were murmurings of machines that could reason like a human being, but with the speed and precision of a machine.

It is hard to imagine a more ideal military technology than intelligent machinery. Machinery that never panics, never tires, never forgets or makes careless mistakes, never hesitates in carrying out its mission; machinery that can handle immense amounts of data without confusion, that can make sound split-second decisions while dodging enemy fire and can flawlessly perform complex calculations while missiles are in the air; machinery that can shoot with incredible speed and precision, and will leave no widow when it, itself, is shot. To military planners, the promise of intelligent machinery is the prospect of reinforcing cold, rational, formal military discipline into the panic-stricken, ear-splitting, mud-splattered, dazed, disordered fog of war, and is the reason why military budgets have been generously funding research into artificial intelligence for over three decades.

The military imperative to displace human decision-making could be seen in the use of analogue fire-control servo-mechanisms during the Second World War to shoot down German aircraft. Human gun operators simply could not aim their guns fast or accurately enough to shoot down speeding planes, and the express effort was made to 'take the human out of the loop' as best as could be managed with the existing technology. The strategy of displacing humans from the critical and dangerous functions of war had an inescapable military logic. As computer costs dropped enough to allow plentiful resources for long-range research, machine intelligence was a vision that was pursued with singular vigour. With the military buildup during the Reagan years, military funding for mathematics and computer science doubled in absolute terms after remaining relatively stable during the 1970s, and three-quarters of federal funding for AI came from military sources.[20] During the 1980s, one military program alone, the Strategic Computing Program, will expend over one billion US dollars on artificial intelligence research, which does not include the 200 million dollars budgeted for the Strategic Defense Initiative's battle manager and dozens of other advanced computing projects within the individual military services.[21] Today, military AI research has resulted in sundry military test projects such as a battlefield manager, 'intelligent assistants' for jet fighter pilots in the heat of battle, unmanned tanks that can distinguish friendly implements from those of the enemy and rove and fire autonomously, and the aforementioned computational centrepiece for SDI: a vast intelligent computer network that could reason with blinding speed whether the United States was coming under ballistic missile attack, and wheel a complex array of purportedly defensive firing systems into action to engage them. The computer system that would control SDI would have to work so quickly that it has generated its own constitutional controversy as some speculate that it is the elected commander-in-chief who has been taken 'out of the loop'.

Progress in AI research was not nearly as rapid as it had been in other areas of computer science research, and only the ultimate appeal of the objective sustains the military's interest through some very disappointing early trials. The lesson of the early years of AI research was that human-like intelligence consistently proved to be more complicated than was originally thought, and one comforting off-shoot for those who were disturbed by the research was a new appreciation for the subtlety and power of human thought. For many years, there was no indication that any real breakthroughs were imminent, though the optimistic – critics would say disingenuous – proposals for further research continued to come.

There was little indication that government AI research would spawn the familiar pattern of commercial spin-offs and diffusion into commercial markets until the late 1970s, when the concept of expert systems emerged. Expert systems represented a sort of theoretical lowering of sights within the artificial intelligence research community, a backing away from promises that a computer system would reproduce many of the subtle aspects of human thinking in exchange for some more practical results in reproducing human reason within a very restricted sphere of expertise. The task of an expert system is to reproduce with a computer the reasoning of a human expert in some field with no pretension that the system is performing key aspects of thought. An expert system might not shed any light on how human minds work, but it could perform like a human expert within a limited field of endeavour.

It was clear from the beginning that there was an attractive pragmatic aspect to expert systems that other more theoretical research into artificial intelligence did not have. There was an explicit recognition that there was tremendous potential benefit, military and otherwise, from systems that could

116

mimic human reason, even if there was no prospect that any understanding of actual human thought was being gleaned. If algorithms could be found that reproduced what a reasonable expert would conclude given the same data, that was sufficient reward for practically minded men and women. The capacity for reason could be thought of as any other resource, such as the capacity to build ships, and there was no reason to suppose that all reasoning has to be performed within the constraints by which even the best human minds are limited. From a military standpoint one nation's ability to provide reams of rational decisions at blinding speeds during the stress of warfare could be critical to that nation's survival, and like any critical capacity that ability could only be obtained from a thriving, leading-edge industrial base.

The compromise toward expert systems precipitated the familiar process by which military and other government research and development could re-emerge in commercial markets. Anything that offered to take humans 'out of the loop' and replace them with faster, more disciplined machines had obvious commercial appeal, even if the prospect of wage-earners being taken out of the loop may have seemed a bit darker than that of foot soldiers being spared the dangers of battle. Researchers who had cut their teeth on government projects became entrepreneurs, and firms with names like TeKnowledge, IntelliCorp, and Thinking Machines Corporation began to spring up in the USA around the universities and think tanks that were heavily funded by the Defense Department and other government agencies.

The fervour for private investment in expert systems became even more pitched in the early 1980s, in response to what was viewed as an ominous Japanese commercial challenge in expert systems technology. The publication in 1983 of a book, *The Fifth Generation*, subtitled *Artificial Intelligence and Japan's Computer Challenge to the World*,[22] along with a spate of other related books and articles, captured the attention of the public and policy-makers in the USA and Europe, who began to think of themselves as being caught off guard while the Japanese prepared for their final assault on their economies. The ominous scenario was for a rapidly approaching future economy in which knowledge was an industrially produced commodity, and was produced with such speed and precision that systems of exclusively human knowledge could not compete. The call was for pragmatically minded government-sponsored research and development into expert systems, and the USA and Europe promptly responded with new government–industry programmes.

The period of the mid-1980s also saw venture capitalists embracing the expert systems start-up companies for the first time, causing a pitched speculative environment and a dramatic increase in demand for AI researchers in private companies. The speculative environment compounded the tendency within AI research to embellish immediate prospects for breakthroughs, and there has been a recent backlash from capital markets and critics, perhaps less tolerant of immediate results than the military, when progress was not made according to claims.

Though the progress consistently lags behind the stimulus, some impressive gains have been made in artificial intelligence in general, and in expert systems in particular. Ongoing and almost routine quantum leaps in hardware capacity and almost any improvement in software-generating techniques promise to go a long way towards making new breakthroughs in AI feasible, and the day may be closer than we generally imagine when artificial intelligence is commonplace. The idea of intelligence disembodied from human souls strikes deep and ancient chords of anxiety in the human psyche, and it is clear that the appearance of machines that do considerable intellectual work will require a broad re-examination of many of our most basic beliefs about humans and their place in worldly affairs.

The truly odd nature of awaiting the coming of mechanical intelligence is that its approach is the fruit of decades of persistent and stalwart government funding, enjoying the legitimate democratic support of the free peoples of Europe, the United States and Japan, yet in the abstract there has been no real discussion of whether or not mechanical intelligence is desirable, or even a disciplined examination of what its social impacts are likely to be. What has driven this technological dynamo along is a competitive atmosphere between national concerns about the security of their culture against foreign domination, either military or economic. The ultimate irony is that industrial society is racing headlong towards the creation of something that has haunted mankind's collective psyche seemingly for ever, and that nations are rushing toward this goal through a desire for, of all things, security.

6

Of Little Men and Monsters

It is said that a strange and powerful creature roamed the crooked streets of Prague's Jewish ghetto in the sixteenth century, a man-made, man-like automaton that had been created out of a desperate attempt to protect the Jews of that city from the unremitting stream of physical intimidation and libel visited upon them by the Christian population that ringed their crowded quarters. It patrolled the streets under cover of darkness, intercepting Christian interlopers as they planted false evidence against innocent Jews and carrying out secret missions for the Rabbi who had brought him to life. The creature was the golem, and his creator was the virtuous and scholarly leader of the Jewish community, Rabbi Loew, who had fashioned him of clay and brought him to life through a magical ritual in which the name of God was invoked to bring life to lifeless mud. The golem was a fearless and indefatigable warrior, since he was stronger than any man, knew no pain and feared nothing except his immediate deactivation, which the Rabbi could do at any time, and which inevitably became necessary.

Rabbi Loew was able to animate the creature through the mysteries of the kabbalah, an ancient oral tradition that was said to have been handed down from Moses. The kabbalah offered the promise of magical power over man and nature to those who knew its mysteries. At a time when the Jews of Europe were being systematically and cruelly persecuted in their urban ghettos, the urban Jews' fascination with kabbalah and its power was intense.

There are conflicting versions of the story of the golem, but all of them share certain powerful themes that resonate in the human psyche and were later borrowed in some of Western culture's most powerful stories of man and his creations. In all accounts, the golem was fashioned in a ceremony that evoked elements of the Genesis account of the creation of man. But the creator of the golem was not God, but a man, and though the Rabbi was the most virtuous man imaginable, the creature intrinsically lacked some qualities of a man that only God could convey to him. The golem would for ever lack a soul, and so, though it was possible to teach him rudimentary reason, it was impossible to teach him true wisdom or understanding. He was mute, because being devoid of a soul, he was devoid of free will and could only mechanically respond to the stimuli with which he was presented. He could follow instructions, but it was extremely important that the instructions be expressed simply and with the utmost care, because he had a disturbing tendency to carry out his instructions with insane precision. He always instinctively knew the precise time of day.

In all versions of the story, syntactical tricks played a prominent role in the activation and deactivation of the golem. The magical powers of certain combinations of letters and words were the practical foundation of all kabbalah magic, expressing as it did the belief that profound mystical forces could be marshalled through creative syntax. In one version of the golem story that would have chilled the imagination of Boole, the lump of clay was brought to life when the Rabbi scratched the letters AEMAETH (for 'truth' or 'God') on the forehead of the clay figure, and the golem was deactivated when the first two letters were removed, leaving the word MAETH ('he is dead'). The manner in which a knowledgeable rabbi could relate mystical meanings with the secret syntax of the kabbalah contrasted markedly with the limitation of the golem that was thus created, who had an inherent ability to interpret the syntax of the commands presented to him, but could never understand in any real way the meaning of the instructions he dutifully followed.

But by far the most powerful and consistent theme in the various versions of the golem myth, and the central motif in later adaptations of the story, was the inevitability that the golem would eventually come to present a threat to those who had created it in order to serve them, and that it must eventually be destroyed. The golem itself was decidedly neither good nor evil, but there was something intrinsic about human nature that made the relationship of humans with the golem dangerous. In some accounts, all golem intrinsically grew at a constant rate as soon as they were activated, so that the trick in using them was to get as much utility out of them before they became so large that they became a threat.[1]

A curiously evocative incident, suggestive of the dangers inherent in dealing with the golem, is said to have occurred when Rabbi Loew's wife set about naively to employ the beast in labour-saving housework. As the household was busy cleaning up in preparation for Passover, the rabbi's wife became incensed that the golem was not participating while the others were doing arduous work on their hands and knees. Ignoring her husband's advice that the strange mute was not to be used for chores and unaware of the golem's true origins or mission, she commanded the golem to carry water from the well to the barrel in the house, and admonished him to be quick about it. Soon, the household was startled to find water flooding the floors of the house, as the golem had faithfully executed his instructions and was continuing to ferry buckets of water to the household barrel long after the barrel had filled and overflowed. This haunting theme was later adopted by Goethe in his popular ballad, 'The Sorcerer's Apprentice', which in 1897 was set to music in Paul Dukas' orchestral work of the same name, and was ultimately brought to life for mass audiences by Mickey Mouse in the animated cartoon movie, *Fantasia*. The common theme was that fate would punish with wicked irony those who thoughtlessly sought to employ fearsome magic, whose original sober purpose was the collective defence, in the trivial pursuit of saving human labour.

The central problem with the golem was that as a man-made artefact it was inherently flawed because it lacked some essential characteristic that only God could impart to a being. Any conceit by man that he was adopting the position of God in creating new life was sure to backfire in a way that would be totally unanticipated by the human intellect. The story of the golem is generally thought to have inspired Mary Shelley's novel, *Frankenstein, or the Modern Prometheus*. In it, the youthful Frankenstein successfully brings to life a creature he had composed of parts of corpses, and then treats his creation with disdain. The creature, having no soul, cannot be loved, and in its anger and frustration at being created but unfulfilled, turns on his creator. The story is one of scientific man being punished for his impudence in usurping God's station in the cosmos.

Through all of these myths run the dual intuitions that man will for ever be incapable of creating an intellectual artefact with all the subtleties of the human mind, and the parallel notion that the very attempt is bound to lead to man's ruin. These intuitions were safe abstractions until the rush of innovations in computing in the 1940s, when the popular press began to anthropomorphize electronic computers as 'electronic brains'. The prospect was raised among some computer scientists that digital computers might be designed to mimic higher and higher elements of human cognition, and that perhaps the human mind was only one of many possible manifestations of true intelligence, and perhaps not the ideal among the possibilities. As theorists in what the public saw as a new brand of technological sorcery considered the possibilities of intelligence in artefacts, the recurring themes of the golem resurfaced in the form of a philosophical puzzle: could man create a machine that was truly a mind, or would any man-made artefact necessarily lack that very kernel of being that distinguished the human mind from all else in creation? And if man created such a machine, could he control it?

Alan Turing's paradigm for universal computability, as expressed in his notion of the Turing Machine, was only the first of his two monumental contributions to computer theory. The other came in 1950 in a philosophical paper in which he proposed a straightforward test for determining whether or not a machine could be said to be intelligent.[2] According to Turing, if a computer could enter into a dialogue with a person, and the person could not distinguish from the content of the responses whether or not they were composed by a machine or by another person, then the computer was thinking. The point was not that the machine would be mimicking intelligence, but that it would possess intelligence in every sense of the word, and as surely as humans do. Turing pointed out that this is essentially the same test we commonly apply to each other to gauge intelligence – in fact there is no other way for anyone to detect intelligence in anyone else – and that it was inherently arbitrary to balk at employing this test on machines. In an interview that same year, Turing coldly predicted a machine would exist by the year 2000 that would be capable of passing his test.

What became known as Turing's Test breathed the breath of life into a branch of computer science that was intent on producing intelligent behaviour in digital computers, an area of research that has come to be called artificial intelligence. To a future generation of AI researchers, the metaphysical truth embodied in Turing's Test was an article of faith, and to many its fulfilment has become their goal. The enduring status of the test is undoubtedly due to its simplicity, particularly when contrasted with the baffling edifice of psychology and philosophy built around definitions of intelligence. The test was tremendously liberating to researchers because it was a practical functional definition of what was expected of any intelligent entity. Because it refers only to manifestations of intelligence external to the system being examined, Turing's Test explicitly ignores any issues relating to *how* intelligent responses are produced: it is only concerned that they are produced, and in a form that is functionally equivalent to that produced by intelligent people.

With drastic declines in the cost of computational resources in the 1960s and an intense behind-the-scenes interest from the military, research in AI became an increasingly visible discipline in the new field of computer science and bright, creative computer scientists were drawn to it in increasing numbers. Reflecting Turing's initial dictum, most AI research tended to focus on results, rather than on the elegance or potential universality of concepts. The potential bonanza that awaited the researcher who broke new ground in artificial intelligence was apparent from the beginning, and competition for fetching concepts and eye-catching results could be pitched. The US federal government, adopting the viewpoint that the national security hinged on leadership in recondite AI concepts, poured money into projects that qualified as fundamental scientific research, principally through generous defence expenditures and secondly through educational institutions such as the National Science Foundation.

122

With the generous funding and prestige to be had, the field began to assume a characteristic that dogs it still. Artificial intelligence research was a science with a noticeable dearth of accepted scientific laws, a sort of conceptual anarchy with few shared paradigms. This is a common feature in the birth of any legitimate science, and a feature proto-science shares with pseudo-science: in fact, the ability to move beyond this point is the primary distinction between the two. Without these shared paradigms, concepts of artificial intelligence were judged primarily on their promise to solve the problem at hand or to demonstrate a specific hypothesis, and relatively little concern was shown for grand theories that could comprehensively explain the total workings of the mind. Two prominent AI researchers write poignantly of the attitude of 'ontological promiscuity' that runs through AI research. 'Conceptualizations are our inventions', they write, 'and their justification is based solely on their utility.'[3]

In this Wild West of research, the opportunity for schism presented itself at every inference. Even if researchers subscribed to the validity of the Turing test, the question of how one approaches the agreed-upon goal was inherently divisive. One school, the so-called 'cognitive modellers', held that the most promising stratagem was to discover the underlying biological mechanisms of the brain that were responsible for intelligence with an eye to reproducing them in hardware and software. A competing group, the 'intelligent artefact' school, held that one should focus on results and employ established computational techniques toward reproducing them, consciously disregarding the particular example of the human brain. To the proponents of intelligent artefacts, the only practical approach to creating artificial intelligence is an engineering one, to work incrementally toward interim artefacts that display aspects of intelligent behaviour, and to build from these systems artefacts capable of more comprehensive thought.

Even within the intelligent artefact school, there were no universal paradigms. It was easy to agree that universal principles of intelligence, biological or otherwise might emerge from this approach as its techniques matured, but *must* universal cognitive principles emerge from this tinkering? To the so-called 'weak AI' branch, it was absurd to think that research would identify universal principles: there were infinitely many ways to skin a cat, and there is no reason to suppose that the method of one's choosing (specific intelligent artefacts) has any bearing on any other (the human mind). But from the opposite perspective, since there were universal laws of computation, there might also be universal laws of thought – a sort of 'Turing's Mind' that defined the bounds of thought just as the Turing Machine defined the bounds of computation. From this perspective, tinkering with intelligent artefacts was bound to lead to insights that would lead to the fundamental laws of 'mind'. If this were true, then the intelligent artefact and cognitive modelling approaches were like two teams of tunnellers burrowing through the same mountain: if each side steered their discipline correctly, they should meet at some point with a definitive understanding of the human mind and of minds in general. To these researchers, the 'strong AI' school, tinkering with intelligent artefacts was a sort of experimental cognitive science, and whenever these researchers were able to reproduce an intelligent-seeming response in a computer, it was in their terms fair to term the event a discovery in the nature of intelligence itself.

The new religion of AI had spawned, within only four decades, a number of contentious sects in a manner that recalled the history of the more established faiths of psychology and philosophy, the very faiths the more vociferous AI evangelists claimed AI would come to displace. But internecine debates of dogma within the realm of AI were trivial compared to the clash of attitudes between the faithful and heretics: to many outside the field, the basic precepts of artificial intelligence were impudent, repugnant, or just silly.

The subject of mind, and the relation between mind and the universe, has always been at the core of philosophical discourse and has remained a fertile topic of debate among philosophers in the modern era. Rather than circumventing the very complicated philosophical argumentation that had characterized these subjects before, the cavalier new notions expounded by some AI researchers about machinery and mind precipitated a whole new round of philosophical debate, bits of which found their way into the public's awareness through occasional media attention. The esoteric objections of some philosophers to Turing's approach mirrored some common-sense notions among laypeople: even if the machine responded with apparent intelligence, how could it ever 'understand' what it was doing? Wouldn't any essentially mechanical contraption always be missing some key ingredient, that man was incapable of giving it, that made the machine something less than a mind?

As scepticism festered in some quarters regarding the metaphysical claims of some AI experimenters, the field was saddled with the perception that its practical potential was suspect as well. The trend was for a researcher to announce flashy results from a computer system that mimicked some narrow region of intelligent-seeming activity – such as discovering a new mathematical proof or cleverly manipulating abstract representations of physical building blocks – and based on these results propose a new paradigm of mind. But attempts to broaden the system to include the richness of meaning and ambiguity that even the most simple-minded human handles with ease were manifestly difficult. For many years, true utility from artificial intelligence systems seemed always to be just beyond the researchers' grasp.

The debate whether machines were on the verge of true intelligence has simmered since Turing's original challenge, but has more recently been revived by John Searle's collision with those AI researchers who believed that thinking computers were imminent. In a series of events that recalled

Mandeville's challenge to moral philosophy, this latest tiff started in 1984 when Searle, a professor of philosophy at the University of California at Berkeley, purported to demonstrate conclusively that it is impossible for a computer to think.[4] His rationale brought an immediate and, in some cases, passionate response from the most prominent among the artificial intelligentsia. Though derision for Searle's argument is the norm among the strong AI elite, he clearly touched a nerve, and to the amazement of both Searle and his critics this debate has largely defined the discussion of intelligence in computers since then.

Searle, who coined the terms 'strong-' and 'weak AI', was shocked at the sweeping claims that ran rampant through the strong AI school that significant discoveries were being made into how people think, based on results from computer programs that seemed to reproduce the workings of the human mind, and fumed at the suggestion that results of AI tests necessarily pointed to verities about the actual operation of the mind. But Searle did more than argue that certain computer operations did not necessarily reproduce intelligence, he sought to prove that no computer, however advanced, will ever be able to think. According to Searle, because computers fall into a special mathematical category of *formal systems*, they can reliably manipulate symbols, but can never apprehend their meaning.

The concept of a formal system is a basic one in mathematics, and has been at the centre of particularly fruitful speculation in this century. A formal system is one in which tokens, or symbols, are manipulated according to a finite set of rules. The manner of manipulation must be digital, so that the results from any particular operation are discrete, precise and predictable. The salient characteristic of formal systems is that they are 'formal': it is the form of the system, and not its physical manifestation, that lends it its distinctive character. It does not matter in a formal system how the tokens are represented or the type of physical processes employed to manipulate the tokens. All that matters is that the inherent relationships between the symbols and operations is maintained.

The game of chess is a common example of a formal system. It is digital, in the sense that it exists as a series of discrete steps: it is illegal for a token partially to occupy two squares. The physical expression of the tokens and the operations allowed on them is irrelevant to the characteristic form of the game. If the squares alternated red and green instead of light and dark or if we referred to the king as the 'president' or 'Ralph', we would still be playing chess. The tokens could be made of wood or ivory or plastic, or we could dispense with physical tokens entirely and play by marking up successive sheets of paper with the new arrangement of pieces, and we would still be playing chess, because the intrinsic form of the game had remained unchanged. But if we decided that a pawn can move sideways we are not playing chess, we are playing another game.

There is nothing wrong with a formal system that is a meaningless game like chess, but formal systems take on a unique power when *meanings* are attached to the tokens and operations. Then the formal system becomes subject to any *interpretation* that is consistent with the original definitions. A certain equivalence can be crafted between the elements of the system and other phenomena, so that 'mechanical' operations within the formal system yield results with useful interpretations. These interpretations must be expressed in a *metalanguage*, or a mode of representation that exists 'above' and outside the rules that govern the formal system. The principle is that of an abacus: once you accept that the tokens and rules of an abacus mirror in some important way the operations of quantities, you can concentrate on correctly manipulating the abacus and be confident that the results can be reliably interpreted as a quantity. Like an abacus, formal systems can be employed as tools of abstraction, so that one can manipulate symbols without being mindful of their meanings, and still have confidence in the interpretation of the results.

The original object of mathematicians' interest in formal systems was not so much to open whole new areas of mathematics as it was to truly understand the nature of mathematics itself, for the branches of mathematics are nothing but related formal systems. Arithmetic is a formal system: numerals are tokens which are interpreted as numbers according to specified rules and subject to operations such as addition and multiplication. Similarly, algebra and geometry can be employed to render worldly problems in abstract terms, and to provide reliable solutions to these problems by slavishly observing the appropriate rules of operation.

Babbage's notation for the operation of the analytical engine was a formal system, one of his own creation that was a tremendous aid in abstracting the machine's operations. Of course, the machine itself was a formal system, and the utility of the notation lay in its special relationship to his machine. For every state in one system – the configuration of the wheels in the engine or the arrangement of symbols in the notation – there was a unique corresponding state in the other system, and each permissible operation in one corresponded exactly to one permissible operation in the other that yielded an analogous result. The two systems were *formally equivalent*, and the operations of one could be said to *map* to the operations of the other. The practical benefit of formal equivalence is that it is possible to reproduce the results from an operation within one system in another system, perhaps one that is more convenient or comprehensible. This formal equivalence is what made the notation so valuable, because it could be used to predict with certainty the actions of the proposed machine, without necessitating the expensive task of actually building the contraption, and it was because of this that Babbage was able to abandon the actual construction of the engines and set out to develop its features entirely on paper. Boole's algebra bore the same formal equivalence to the operation of electronic circuits.

The fact that formally equivalent systems map to each other illuminates the mathematical significance of the Turing Machine. Turing demonstrated that this hypothetical machine is formally equivalent to all digital, mechanical computers, and so was able to prove that at one level of abstraction the operations of all computers map to each other. Theoretically, any home computer can solve any problem that the most massive mainframe can solve, as long as it has enough 'scratch paper' for recording interim results and enough time to perform the sequence of operations.

With this foundation in terminology, the point of contention between John Searle and the strong AI proponents becomes explicit. Simply stated, the strong AI advocates consider that the mind is a formal system, and that what is required to pass the Turing Test is nothing more or less than a computer system that is formally equivalent to the human mind. From this perspective, there is no real distinction between the two forms of intelligence, just as there is no real distinction between chess played with wooden tokens as opposed to chess played with brass tokens. Searle, on the other hand, purports to prove that a mind necessarily cannot be a formal system, and that what the AI researchers are unwittingly doing is reducing certain aspects of intelligent behaviour to formal description, and mapping this description to a computer system. This strategy, according to Searle, can *simulate* some aspects of intelligence in computers but can never in any real sense *reproduce* it whole in a mechanical artefact.

Searle formulated a model for demonstrating his contention. Imagine, he said, that you participate in an experiment calling for you to sit alone in a room with a digital computer. A series of written Chinese characters are passed to you through a slot in the door that – since you presumably have no understanding of Chinese – are meaningless to you. Now suppose you take this apparent gibberish and feed it to the computer sitting next to you in the room. The computer is running a program that takes the symbols as input and produces other Chinese symbols as output, which you then pass back out through the slot to the outside world. Obviously, you still have no understanding of Chinese and are incapable of intelligent discussion in that language.

But, Searle says, what if the people outside the door have no knowledge of what is going on inside the room? To paraphrase his argument, what if they are in the midst of a Turing Test, being conducted in Chinese, and you are unwittingly participating? What if they call the gibberish they pass into the slot 'questions' and the gibberish you pass back out 'answers'? What if they are declaring at this very moment that they have discovered intelligence within this room? After you got over the implied insult that you were suspected of not being intelligent at all, you might feel a twinge of guilt that you had passed the test without understanding what was being said, what you were answering, or even that you were being tested in the first place.

Searle claims that his example, the so-called 'Chinese room thought experiment', makes a profound point about the limitations of formal systems: formal systems that rely on rules can ultimately only be concerned with *syntax* (the form of the message that is the domain of formal systems) and can never apprehend *semantics* (the meaning of the message). As it was with the golem, something in a formal system will always be missing. According to Searle, though the syntactical capacity of computer systems is potentially unlimited, semantic meanings can never arise from mechanical operations. This is consistent with the mathematical concept of the formal system, where the meanings of the symbols are imposed from outside the system, and can be expressed only in a metalanguage that is outside the language of the tokens.

Searle's example is essentially a negative one, in that his description of what does constitute intelligence is not definitive. In the absence of a positive proposal for what (other than a brain) is capable of demonstrating semantic understanding, what Searle has really done is to muddy the crystalline waters of the strong AI approach, much as Mandeville frustrated the claims of moral philosophers in his era. Searle has introduced into strong AI belief a family of nagging inconsistencies about the mind that has pestered modern philosophy since its inception.

If one accepted the intuitively appealing notion that the realm of meaning must necessarily lie outside the realm of any formal, 'mechanical' system, and also accepted the notion that mechanical artefacts can be made to think, then one had some explaining to do. To accept both ideas simultaneously, one was led inevitably to what John Haugeland calls *the paradox of mechanical reason*.[5] For a machine to understand, it must be engaging in operations above and beyond those that are purely mechanical, because its understanding must have some bearing on the results. But if non-mechanical operations have some bearing on the results, then the system is not purely mechanical. Simply put, if it thinks, it can't be a machine; if it is a machine, it isn't thinking. This, of course, is not really a paradox unless one thinks, as strong AI proponents do, that machines can think.

It is generally conceded, however, that humans think, and the instinct through the ages has been that there is something more than material in the make-up of humans that endows them with a cognitive spirit that transcends the material. This is the instinct underlying, among many others, the story of the golem of Prague. Some alchemists deduced that this essential character must be an entity of some kind, and that, perhaps reasonably from a male-chauvinist standpoint, he must be passed from generation to generation via semen.[6] One of the first uses of the microscope was to observe this entity, and sure enough, there he was (or rather, there *they* were, millions of them) swimming around like anxious microscopic tadpoles. For a brief while it was assumed that within the body of each spermatozoa there was a tiny but whole man, a *homunculus*, which is Latin for 'little man'.

The term homunculus was first associated with a medieval Swiss physician and alchemist named Paracelsus. Though actually quite progressive in many of his notions, Paracelsus maintained a weakness for mysticism that was typical of his time. He travelled widely in Europe in the sixteenth century, learning the folk magic of the various peoples. Among the magical traditions that influenced him strongly was the kabbalah, and it is thought that the procedure for the creation of golem was particularly influential on him. Paracelsus, however, modified significantly the procedure for fashioning artificial men and came up with very different results.

The procedure attributed to Paracelsus was that semen should be put in a glass phial and buried in dung for forty days. At the end of that time, it will have a somewhat human form, and by feeding it human blood, within forty weeks the careful alchemist will have at his disposal a tiny child as perfect in form as any borne of a woman. This homunculus could continue to mature, but could never exceed a foot in stature. The homunculus would always be frail and perhaps even a bit ethereal in appearance, but it would possess keen instinctive insight into the mysteries of the world. To alchemists, who were obsessed with obtaining transcendental knowledge, these little men were tremendously desirable possessions, though some Christian mystics who felt that the mysteries of the world should be apprehended through a righteous and spiritual life denounced the practice as cheating. Paracelsus, renowned for his mystical wisdom in his day, was reputed to carry a homunculus about on the hilt of his sword, and a later alchemist, who was awed by Paracelsus' procedure, thought that by creating more and more of these creatures, a wise race of supramental homunculi would be the inevitable result.

Though they shared the same origins, the contrast between the creatures Rabbi Loew and Paracelsus were said to have created could not have been more stark. The yearnings of the two men were evidently different – Rabbi Loew desired physical protection for his people, Paracelsus was looking for a quick route to mystical insight – and the creatures that resulted from their magic reflected their yearnings. The golem was a giant material brute who lacked the essence of human insight, the homunculus was a wispy embodiment of insight itself that had only a tenuous hold on the material world. Each creature was patently incomplete, and in essence each lacked what the other possessed.

The discovery of spermatozoa only seemed to reinforce the notion that the homunculus – the essence of thinking man – did indeed exist in semen as Paracelsus had described. But in a rational material world, the apparent discovery of the homunculi only raised a disturbing question: if one's essential child can be observed only under a microscope, how small are one's still unborn grandchildren? or one's grandchildren's great-grandchildren? Obviously, the notion that there were physical homunculi who were fully formed versions of their adult selves was untenable.

This difficulty reasserted itself in the issue of the paradox of mechanical reason as it related to humans, for in order to maintain that the human mind was not mechanical and was truly possessed of intellectual insight, philosophers were forced to concede that there must be some agent of essential insight within the mind that was not bound by the physical laws that determined the actions of machines. This could be a particularly thorny assertion in a modern world philosophically attuned to materialism and averse to holding a place in the universe for anything that did not have a material basis. In fact, long before John Searle posed the question, 'how can a machine understand Chinese?' philosophy had become thoroughly entangled in the question of how a *person* can understand Chinese. If your mind is a feature of your brain, and your brain conforms to the mechanical laws of physics, where is the little man in your brain that can (potentially) understand Chinese and is exempt from physical law? By what magic does that little man's thoughts become manifest in the larger individual's actions? In other words, how does this little man intervene over physical processes? If one protested that there certainly was no homunculus rattling about in his head, then how did one claim that he had any power to intervene over his thoughts or actions? The choice seemed to be: either there is a homunculus in your mind, or free will is an illusion.

If a philosopher of mind were backed into the position of stating that there must be some essential non-mechanical entity within the mind that imbues it with semantic understanding, he is tempting critics to pounce on his theory by pointing out that there is, philosophically speaking, a homunculus in his system, and face the same withering *reductio ad absurdum* that those who saw homunculi in spermatozoa faced. Though the particulars vary, the essential difficulty is the same: if a system is truly thinking, then some component (its 'homunculus') must understand the meaning of the symbols being manipulated by the system and must exert some influence over the physical processes of the brain. If some components of the system can be shown to be working mechanically, then the homunculus must lie in some aspect of the remainder of the system. This remainder will have components that can be formally described, so the little man must obviously be littler still. As the scientific understanding of the brain proceeds, this little man will become inordinately tiny. Where will he be discovered? Where would one expect to discover a physical process in the brain that absolutely defies physical law, a signal that represents the intentions of the homunculus? Believing in homunculi of the mind could be a very messy view of nature, and one out of touch with modernity.

130

But Searle is putting a new twist on things: rather than using the necessity of a homunculus to confuse discussion of what makes a physical brain a mind, Searle is in effect saying that physical machines cannot be minds by demonstrating that there is no little man within them.[7] The physical processes of every bit of a machine are formally understood by someone – where will there ever be room in any machine for a homunculus? The problem with the Chinese room is that there is no homunculus in it, or at least not one that understands Chinese.

Searle's Chinese room example elicited a flood of critical response, and characteristically there was a diversity of opinion among his critics over what the correct refutation would be. Most typical among the responses were those who insisted, along the lines suggested by Turing, that certainly the person in the Chinese room did not understand Chinese, but that the system within the walls of the room – the person, the computer and the computer program – did in fact exhibit intelligence and did in fact understand Chinese as well as any person could. Searle tried to anticipate this line of reasoning, by pre-emptively stating, in effect, 'forget the computer, say the person writes down all the instructions in the computer program and then follows them in order to manipulate the symbols, then is he thinking in Chinese?'

Here is the requirement for a homunculus again, in a thinly veiled disguise: if there is not a little man in this system somewhere who understands Chinese, the system is merely simulating an understanding of Chinese, but not really duplicating the intelligence that we associate with humans who speak Chinese.

If philosophy had struggled with this issue with no clear resolution, Searle was at least successful in tangling strong AI in an equally monstrous problem. Far from being free from philosophical conundrum, the field of artificial intelligence found that at its core was the same intricate metaphysical knot that had long confounded philosophy: the place of mind in the universe.

Alexander the Great entered the city of Gordium, the capital of Phrygia in what is now Turkey, in 333 BC at the very beginning of what would become a previously unimaginable conquest of the known civilized world. The citizens of the city anxiously led him to the chariot that had belonged to Gordius, the ancient founder of the city. For many years the yoke of the chariot had been firmly lashed to a pole with an intricate knot, tied so that the ends of the rope were concealed. The chariot and the knot were the seat of a powerful myth to these people, that whoever could untie the knot and free Gordius' chariot was destined to conquer Asia. According to the popular account, when Alexander saw the knot, he unsheathed his sword and sliced the knot in two.[8] He went on, of course, to conquer Asia and to leave us with a potent metaphor.

The phrase 'to cut the Gordian knot' now commonly refers to an instance when drastic action is required to solve a problem, but the larger context of the event displays a more subtle meaning. The people of Gordium had a fundamentally flawed and myopic concept of what was required to topple their society. They saw their destiny as linked to the recondite reasoning required to unravel that which they considered the secret of dominion over them, and one can even imagine that perhaps the Gordians were not as diligent as they could have been in addressing the other threats to their society that did not fit their preconceived model. Alexander's shattering of this cosy notion, elegantly symbolized by the swift stroke of his sword, was shocking to them because it came so unexpectedly from outside the bounds of the problem as posed, and left the myth of the Gordian knot as humiliating testimony to their naiveté.

Perhaps the story of the Gordian knot says something about the profound anxiety that has always been produced by our numerous recurring myths about human-like intelligence being embodied outside the human brain. This same anxiety is at the core of popular attention to the latest claim to artificial intelligence – the chess programme that beat a master, the new mathematical theorem discovered by a machine, the computer that talks just like a psychologist, or like a paranoid psychotic. Can a machine think, just as a human can? Will this shake our secure claim to dominion over the universe? The hand-wringing in some circles over each announcement that some other aspect of human intelligence has been observed in a computer is the same anxiety that must have swept over the Gordians each time a pretender tugged confidently at some strand of the Gordian knot, the gasp that would have rushed through the crowd whenever they felt the knot had yielded in some discernible way, the hush that followed as each wondered if the unravelling of the knot was about to accelerate before his eyes.

As in the story of the Gordian knot, the locus of popular anxiety over the philosophical debate on whether machines can think is sadly misplaced. There is no real social reason for computational machinery to converge on the human mind as a goal, and if they happen to do so, it will only be as a side-effect of machinery's true social function, which is not to emulate humanity but to displace human labour.

There will be no prize to unravelling the philosophical tangle of whether a machine can think like a human. Philosophers may always disagree over whether computer programs are duplicating or merely simulating intelligence, but there is no debating that the potential capacity of computers to simulate any aspect of human thought is unlimited. It is naive to think that computer technology would converge on the human mind as a goal, for the same reason that it was naive to think that any real conqueror of Asia would feel constrained to pause and untangle a knot. The trajectory of modern history makes clear that technology assumes the form that is most economically compelling, despite the preconceived notions for how it will, or should, develop.

Of the varied sects that artificial intelligence has come to encompass, some have chosen submission to this ritual of economic determinism and are allowing their research to be consciously guided by economic considerations. No branch of AI more purely reflects the approach that is most consistent with the historical pattern of mechanization than the field of expert systems. Expert systems refer to computer systems that can reproduce to a greater or lesser extent the conclusions that human experts would derive from the same set of data. The related discipline of 'knowledge engineering', an umbrella term for how expert systems software is developed, betrays the practical engineering frame of mind behind these systems. Developers of expert systems explicitly recognize the cost and value of human expertise and seek to replicate that expertise in computer systems. The shared strategy in all expert systems is to reduce expertise to formal operations so that it can be computerized, a straightforward approach within the time-honoured technique of mechanizing human labour that skirts entirely the philosophical muddle involved with minds and machines.

An expert system is expected to determine a probable cause for an observed phenomenon, and perhaps to select a productive course of action given the data that is available to it: in short, to seek the solutions to problems presented to it. This is a much more open-ended problem than the straightforward algorithmic processes that dominate computer applications today. An algorithmic process proceeds from specified inputs to specified outputs according to a rigidly defined sequence of operations, and carries with it a certainty that the outputs will be produced in a finite number of steps. Using established algorithmic approaches, for example, a computer program can read information on the mass, shape, direction and muzzle velocity of a projectile and combine it with data on atmospheric conditions to plot the trajectory of the shell, and it can perform this task in a predetermined sequence of operations that produces certain results – or, more correctly, results that are certain given the input data and the presumed rules for manipulating it. An expert system, however, might be posed an entirely different type of question: rather than calculating the range of a gun, it might be asked where to aim it. These types of questions, those which require 'judgement', cannot be arrived at through a cookbook approach. They call for interim judgements, such as determining which enemy target is most important, or most vulnerable, or poses the most immediate threat. Solving problems of this type frequently requires more information than is initially presented, and an expert system must know to request more data, or alternatively to suggest an experimental course of action calculated to illuminate some unknown aspect of the problem.

The central problem that any expert system must face is the unmanageable number of possible solutions there are to any problem calling for judgement. The problem was apparent from the very beginning of electronic calculation, when the first of what would fall into the category of expert systems were being developed to play chess. Chess is, in many important ways, a much simpler problem for a computer program to approach than almost any real-life situation, and it has therefore been a model for AI research from the beginning. The game is conveniently digital rather than the analogue processes that most real-life situations present, and the tokens, their possible moves, and the desired goal (checkmate) are not difficult to formally define. Even with these considerable advantages, chess presented the computer pioneers with the problem of *combinatorial explosion*: there are simply too many possible combinations of moves and countermoves to predict with certainty the ramifications of each move.

There is, in fact, an algorithm for precisely determining each player's move in a chess game, an algorithm that is so exhaustive in its analyzing the initial scenario that it could assure the white player (the one who moves first) could literally never lose. The algorithm would proceed to play out every potential move arising from a proposed move, and simply select the combination of white moves that cannot result in a loss. The successful implementation of such an approach would of course destroy the game of chess, but fortunately for chess lovers, a problem lies in the time that it would take for this algorithm to arrive at a solution. It has been estimated that there are 10^{100} possible chess scenarios that can unfold from the initial position of the tokens. To examine exhaustively every possible game that might result from any position in chess is a practical impossibility for any computer, and in fact for any computational device that can be imagined.

Because of the combinatorial explosion associated with solving any significant real-world problem of judgement with certainty, expert systems must employ some strategy for managing the infinite (or for practical purposes infinite) possible ramifications of an action. In the game of chess, for example, rather than exhaustively searching ahead for a situation where one player has won, it is more practical to search only a few moves ahead for a situation where one player is 'ahead'. Any expert chess player can glance at a chess board and quickly determine which player is in the stronger position, based on the number and strength of the tokens available to him, their position on the board and the squares they influence. He might use 'rules of thumb' for sizing up the relative strengths of the two players at any point, such as by 'scoring' each player according to the relative values of the tokens each possesses and of the squares each controls. Based on these rules for playing, an expert system can approach a chess game in a more practical manner, because it relieves the programme of the responsibility of seeing ahead to total victory at any time, and allows it to search ahead for situations that are merely advantageous.

Though AI research has made some impressive inroads into expert systems that play chess, actual warfare – the activity chess itself was originally intended to simulate – presents difficulties several orders of magnitude more complex than a simple digital game but also presumably rewards that are infinitely more desirable than winning a game. Despite the truly dismal record expert systems hold in military projects, the military continues to be the primary push behind research and development in artificial intelligence in the United States. The persistent problem is that true total warfare is vastly complex with unpredictably shifting norms of rational behaviour, and it consistently strains the bounds of formal description that can be developed in a laboratory.

In many commercial applications, however, the domain of the problem can be sufficiently, almost arbitrarily delimited so that an expert system can function quite serviceably, as economic organization shields the technology from confounding data. The medical profession is the target of much development along these lines. The milestone medical expert system was undoubtedly MYCIN, the first of a stream of medical diagnostic systems developed at Stanford University in the mid-1970s. MYCIN was designed to aid physicians in diagnosing blood infections and suggesting therapy for them. Through prompts and typed responses at a terminal, the system enters into a dialogue with an attending physician in which the system leads the physician through a series of relevant questions about the patient, lab tests, symptoms observed, etc. MYCIN keeps asking questions until it is satisfied that it is appropriate to suggest treatment. If a physician desires an explanation of its reasoning, the system can provide it.

In principle, expert systems can work this way with any professional to aid in, and potentially to perform autonomously, critical analytical functions. Researchers at SRI International, in co-operation with the United States Geological Service, have developed another expert system named Prospector. Designed for geological analysis, Prospector enters into a similar dialogue with a geologist, asking questions related to minerals found in various strata and their condition, and from these responses and generalized data about the region deduces the locations of geological formations and mineral deposits.

Though the technical details of these two systems were certainly influential within the field, the profound significance of these systems was their practical results. MYCIN's ability to manage both considerable medical detail and routine clinical uncertainty allowed it to suggest safe interim treatments while further tests were being conducted, and its potential to reproduce expertise that was valuable and scarce was immediately apparent. Prospector's utility was spectacularly demonstrated by its discovering two major mineral deposits, copper in British Columbia and molybdenum in the state of Washington. Each of these deposits had been overlooked by human experts, and both proved to be worth several million dollars to the discoverer.

It is significant that in the areas of application cited – in chess, war, medical diagnosis and geology – the expert system is being programmed to simulate the judgement of experts in these fields: the chess master, pilot, tactician, physician, geologist. The judgement might be simulated in any one of several programming techniques in these and the myriad other applications that are attracting work in expert systems, but, in contrast to many other directions in AI, there is no pretence that this approach actually mechanically reproduces the workings of these experts' brains – any more than one would presume that a robot's arm is moved by the same chemical reactions that propel human arms – but only simulates the final results, and only within a very narrow field of expertise that it is cost-effective to mechanize. There are two critical components to an expert system that enable it to simulate this expertise.

First, the subject of the expertise – the game of chess, the biochemistry of the human body, the geology of the earth – must be formally represented in the computer. In other words, the chess pieces or the earth strata must have computer tokens that correspond to them, and for each computer token there must be a set of operations that logically correspond to their analogues in the outside world. As an example, a chess-playing program must have a symbol that corresponds to each chess piece, and must be able to identify its type (king, queen, bishop, etc.) and its position on the board. By referring to the rules it is given for the ability of a certain type to move to new positions, and examining each piece's current position, the system will be able to determine new positions that piece can assume.

A second critical component to any expert system is a formal representation of a method for manipulating the tokens in such a way as to proceed towards a desired resolution. The steps that a physician might describe for going from a set of facts to a diagnosis might be formally programmed into the system. What do you ask first, how do you proceed to list tentative diagnoses, how do you ask the proper questions to eliminate some tentative diagnoses and strengthen your suspicions regarding others? This is the method that needs to be extracted from the experts and embedded into code.

The significance of these two features is their formal description, the reduction of real-world objects, actions and inter-reactions into formal symbols and allowable operations. There is no pretence that experts actually reason in this manner, and the expert system cannot take advantage of the hunches or prejudices that populate actual human judgement. The system only unwittingly repeats the reasoning process that has been formally described to it. The trick is to render both the system being simulated and the rules for inference in formal terms, and from there a formal system can perform the reasoning so described.

A key event in the development of an expert system is the messy process of transmitting the skills of the expert to the system. Within the expert system industry, the prevailing technique for this process is called 'mining', a revealing metaphor for describing how the ore of expertise must be extracted from the earth of experts' brains, and how the precious nuggets of formalized

136

reason can be gleaned through rigorously analyzing the raw ore. Typically, a mind is mined by knowledge engineers painstakingly interviewing the expert, and from the expert's fuzzy self-appraisal are derived nomenclature and rules. Nomenclature can be abstracted as symbols, and rules can be abstracted as allowable operations, and so expertise is committed to formal representation in a computer program. Mining is merely a recent and naked example of how a productive function being performed by a person is rationalized and formalized so that it can be performed by a machine.

Even learning and innovation, areas that are frequently and erroneously declared to be beyond the bounds of mechanization, lend themselves to the relentless process of formalization. The rules of thumb, or *heuristics*, that expert systems employ were at first programmed into the system by human knowledge engineers, but as researchers considered the process of developing heuristics they inevitably began to formalize the procedure so that an expert system might become skilled in innovation. In the early 1980s, Douglas B. Lenat of Stanford developed a pioneering expert system with this capability that he named Eurisko – an amalgam of 'eureka' and 'heuristic'.

Eurisko was designed to play one specific game, a naval battle simulation game called Traveller. In essence, each player in Traveller concocts a fleet of fighting vessels using a predetermined amount of resources. Desirable features in the ships cost valuable resources to build, and the trick is to find the optimum allocation of resources toward producing the most survivable fleet. The variables regarding how best to use the resources are complex – how many ships to make, how fast they should be, specifics about armour, firepower, control, etc. – and the number of possible fleets is practically infinite. Eurisko was designed to determine the fleet configuration that would prevail in any battle, and to achieve this goal Eurisko had to employ the heuristics presented to it by the programmer as well as develop its own new heuristics. Proposed fleets would be set against each other in battle, and Eurisko would tirelessly set about analysing the wreckage of these abstract struggles in an effort to correlate trial approaches with success or failure. From these correlations, Eurisko would develop new interim heuristics to test in conjunction with previously proven heuristics. Just as military scientists do in peacetime, Eurisko poured through one hypothetical scenario after another, testing its hypothetical fleets against hypothetical enemy fleets. Its success relied on how accurately it could simulate battle, and on how well it could build rules of thumb for faring better in the next mock battle.

Eurisko proved unbeatable in Traveller to the point that Lenat gracefully withdrew from competition with humans. A hallmark of the system was the totally unexpected results it would occasionally produce, some absurd, and some eerie. At one point Lenat discovered that Eurisko had discovered how to cheat. On another occasion Lenat noticed that the system had developed a provocative heuristic, based on its empirical assessment that the man-made heuristics presented to it were consistently more reliable than the machine-made ones it was supposed to develop. In response, Eurisko developed a heuristic that stated, in effect, 'whenever Eurisko encounters a heuristic that it created, delete it'. The heuristic immediately deleted itself. It was struggling, in its own way, with the liar's paradox, a problem upon which human intellectual giants have foundered and whose ultimate resolution in this century proved the existence of a sort of intellectual seam in all logical systems. On a more practical level, the fundamental approach behind Eurisko was used with great effect in other applications, including the design of a radical new three-dimensional AND gate that is now used in advanced integrated circuits.

Even to those who have become somewhat jaded by the parade of technological marvels that confront the contemporary observer, the capabilities shown by expert systems are consistently amazing. But we should keep in mind that it is not scientific curiosity that is producing these wonders, or philosophical thought experiments, but rational self-interest. The sheer number of expert systems applications that are being developed, the massive amounts of venture capital that companies involved in AI attract, and the pressing demand for researchers skilled in AI techniques speaks eloquently of the intrinsically economic motivation behind all this development.

The attraction of expert systems to contemporary enterprise is similar to that of machinery since the inception of the industrial revolution: it represents the latest example of a familiar process of formalizing and mechanizing a productive process that had formerly been performed by humans. When a knowledge engineer 'mines' the expertise of a geologist, he is attempting to render formally the process by which a geologist goes about aspects of his work. The engineer then formalizes the rational process into tokens and rules that can be coded into a computerized process. Capturing the judgement of a geologist in the software and hardware that comprise Prospector is just a more recent manifestation of the same economic event that lead to capturing the craft of draw loom weavers in the punched cards and wooden rods of the Jacquard device.

It is a commonplace among those in the market-oriented private companies involved with expert systems that the applications to seek are the ones where the profit to be gleaned from replacing the human expert is greatest. While traditional computer applications displace the work of lower-level employees such as clerks, typists and bookkeepers, expert systems offer labour savings in higher-level employment categories. In addressing the question of how to gauge activities for their applicability to AI, a prominent expert systems researcher counsels the businessperson to consider areas where human expertise is scarce, rather than 'two-a-penny', and where a high degree of knowledge is required. Such an area is easily recognizable 'by the telltale symptoms of high salaries, job hopping and queues for vocational training courses'.[9] As a rule, expert systems will be employed to replace doctors before orderlies, geologists before roughnecks, generals before foot soldiers, computer programmers before computer operators. Simply put, if an occupation is attractive to an individual because it pays well, is intellectually challenging, and calls for freedom of judgement, it is necessarily also an attractive application for artificial intelligence.

Predictably, the craft of knowledge engineering itself is a hotbed of innovation for streamlining the process of mechanizing intelligence. Special programming languages such as LISP and PROLOG have been developed specifically for developing AI applications, and new computer architectures have been developed to handle more efficiently the processes coded by these languages. Intense research is under way to eliminate what is viewed as the obvious bottleneck in the knowledge acquisition process: the knowledge engineer himself, the person who crafts the process of extracting knowledge from experts. Ironically, it is the rare and expensive skills of the 'miners' that have attracted the impulse to be 'mined' themselves. Through natural language processing and expert systems that can mimic the judgement of the knowledge engineer, the goal is to have experts interviewed in a spoken language by an expert system skilled in knowledge engineering, so that expert systems can create expert systems without resorting to human interpretation.

Through the process of knowledge engineering, knowledge is being systematically extracted from the realm of human craft and placed instead in the realm of machinery, and so promises in the future to be an industrially produced commodity. The passage from craft to industrial production has historically been accompanied by a precipitous increase in the scale of production, since mechanization opens up new capacities for economies of scale that are not practical by individual craft labour. It is easy for us to see how this was so with familiar past examples of industrialization, but more difficult to imagine when considering the same process when applied to knowledge because it is intuitively difficult in our age to conceive of knowledge as a disembodied commodity. Before the introduction of mechanisms such as the Jacquard device, it would have been difficult to impress upon the weavers of Lyons that a machine could replicate their craft – or that machines could be made for mass producing the machines that replicated their craft – and much more difficult still to make them imagine the level of cloth production and the changes in their society that would follow. Do we really apprehend the ramifications of knowledge being produced on an industrial scale?

Unit costs tend to drop when commodities are repetitively produced, and as knowledge becomes a commodity, it exhibits what may at first seem peculiar economies of scale. The successes of MYCIN, Prospector, and Eurisko spurred the re-use of the inference procedures endemic to each in entirely different realms of knowledge. The development of MYCIN, for example, required about 50 man-years of effort before it was a passable implement for diagnosing blood samples, but the original 'shell' of the programme was re-used to create other medical diagnosing packages as well as expert systems in entirely unrelated fields such as structural engineering. The re-use of the 'inference engines' cut the development time for new packages to a fraction of that required for the parent package.[10] Similarly, a team of researchers working on an expert system for diagnosing failures and recommending remedies for malfunctioning satellites discovered that the knowledge base they were developing was in many ways identical to that being developed by a cancer researcher who was embarking on his own expert system project, and the two were able to share much of their work thereafter.[11] Because knowledge models can be proposed that can be employed in a variety of applications, a number of software companies now specialize in purveying expert system shells, so that the purchaser can more economically develop individual expert systems for a variety of activities.

Before becoming indignant at the larger share that will doubtless be claimed by machinery in our future knowledge base, or tremble at the prospect that disembodied intelligence may be a significant component of our future lives, we should pause to reflect on the admitted difficulty humans are having in keeping up with the knowledge that they are expected to maintain in many recondite fields of endeavour. The difficulty of simply keeping track of current research findings in fields such as medicine and the sciences threatens to become unmanageable. Research indicates that the information base of the typical scientific field, as measured by the number of scholarly papers published, consistently doubles every ten to fifteen years.[12] It is reasonable to suggest that sophisticated knowledge tools will be required to manage the technical information base of the future, so that the mass of information that is being produced can be assimilated at the scale and speed with which it is being produced and comprehended into the larger whole of knowledge. Edward Fredkin has offered the image of knowledge processing machines stepping into the void, communicating with each other with a rapidity that is quite literally mind-boggling to humans, developing the scientific and technological concepts for future society with blazing speed and precision. The temptation in this vision is to communicate with these intellectual beasts, to cast about for some intellectual crumbs from their feast. But what, he asks, could these electronic minds possibly have to say to a human?[13]

In the present day, the issue of international competition enters into all discussions of industrial output, and in particular the striking success the Japanese have had in gearing industrial production in key areas of technology relative to the other Western industrialized countries. In October 1981, the Japanese government announced a major ten-year development effort that is designed to push back dramatically the frontiers of knowledge engineering, and the response in the United States and Europe, largely precipitated by accounts from Fredkin and McCorduck's book, was anxious and, by some accounts, frenzied. While 'strong AI' research had been generously underwritten for years by the United States government, the market-driven stepchild of knowledge engineering had taken a back seat. But whereas before AI research was generously funded out of a conviction that it might be critical in wartime technologies of the future, the new panic was that a healthy commercial AI industry was critical to economic survival. The fact that the Japanese focused on market-driven approaches within AI was enough to precipitate generous government funding for national efforts in knowledge engineering in the United States, England and France, and to engender a begrudging co-operation between computer giants who had previously been maniacally secretive about their work.

There are apparent ironies that surround the fact that computer systems have come to exhibit such a subtle capacity to reason through an unrelenting process of analysing thinking behaviour into simpler and simpler tasks. Through the process of rationalizing, formalizing and mechanizing productive thought – essentially by removing all notions of meaning and judgement from it – we have begun to produce artefacts that exhibit an apparent facility with meaning and judgement, and have opened the door to machines that can far outstrip human capacity for intricate reason and problem solving. And as these machines seem on the threshold of conceptualizing, they test their creators' capacity to conceptualize them.

Since the earliest days of computing, the sheer complexity of even the simplest computing system has made it impossible to imagine the entire logical system of a computer as a comprehensive whole, and made it practically necessary to think of the computer as a hierarchy of logical sub-systems. As early as the 1830s, Babbage had implicitly recognized this fact in his notation by allowing major assemblies of mechanical components to be represented with simple symbols representing the function of the entire assembly. The notation facilitated an understanding of the relations between higher-level assemblies by obscuring the lower-level components that comprised them. Being able to abstract some established set of functions has been a key conceptual aid in building higher-level functions from lower-level ones, as in the realm of software production when assembly language was developed in order better to manage machine-level instructions and higher-level languages were developed in order better to manage assembly-level instructions.

A common technique among computer literati for abstracting any aspect of computation whose internal mechanics are not being considered is to think of the mechanism as a conceptual 'black box'. In other words, it is sufficient at one level of abstraction to conceive of lower-level functions as being performed as if by magic within this black box and not be distracted by what goes on inside it. A black box is a sort of Chinese room, defined only by what output it produces in response to given inputs. Of course, were we to peer into this black box, the outlines of its operations would become apparent, but we would also discover more black boxes within it.

The conception of computation in terms of systems, sub-systems, and super-systems is in fact a vestigial reflection of the economic forces that incrementally brought computer systems into being. On the one hand, electronic computation was invented through an unremitting analysis of higher-level logical functions into progressively lower-level logical functions, until finally the entire complex relies on electronic gates that do nothing more than respond in a most rote manner to 'bits' (binary digits) of information, while on the other hand vast economies of scale could be acquired by building complex logical systems from less complex systems, which in turn formed the basis for still more complex logical systems.

Today, it is a practical necessity to anthropomorphize these functions and sub-functions in computers, to speak of sub-routines as 'sensing' events or 'talking' to one another. Enter into an extended conversation with an *aficionado* of any aspect of computers, and these human-like descriptions of the interaction between sub-systems will emerge; ask him to describe the operations without using anthropomorphic terms, and the explanation is likely to become strained. Similarly, by doggedly pursuing a series of childlike inquiries into the operation of computer systems ('But how does it know to do that? Yes, but then how does it know to do *that?*'), as one approaches the boundaries of the harried expert's understanding, one is likely to encounter an explanation equivalent to 'it just *knows!*' Most who are facile with computer technology find that they must specialize within some range of abstraction, so that at some point they must concede that there is a black box basic to the operations they understand that they cannot, in an intellectual sense, open. They have discovered – from the standpoint of their own necessarily limited comprehension – a homunculus in the computer.

A psychologist, Daniel C. Dennett, has suggested that there are indeed true homunculi in computer systems, and that research into artificial intelligence, for all its other disappointments, may have provided a keen insight into the nagging philosophical problem of the homunculus. According to Dennett, computer systems have for the first time demonstrated how intelligent-seeming behaviour can be created in a formal system built out of a vast edifice of logical computation, of systems within systems, each of which is capable of some semblance of intelligent activity. One might start with an intelligent-seeming entity that can diagnose blood samples, for example, and through a process of analysis discover within it a black box that can only add two numbers, and within that box more black boxes that can only compare two values, until finally one discovers homunculi in the binary electronic gates that are 'so stupid ... that they can be, as one says, "replaced by a machine" '.[14] In our search for the homunculus, we have found 'armies of such idiots' in the binary digits of electronic computation that perform intelligent-seeming work as an organized whole.

If it is the division of labour that leads to specialization, and if the definition of a specialist is one who knows more and more about less and less, then the armies of little men in computer systems are the ultimate specialists. Each knows nothing of the context of the question posed to him and is blissfully unaware of the vast legion of specialists working at his side. Each has no concern for whether his answer is interpreted as yes or no, true or false, universe or nothing, eternity or never. But he can deliver his answer with unwavering certainty and absolute precision, and with a speed that is inconceivable to those who were moved to create him.

Like the golem of legend, these armies have inevitably grown more massive and powerful, so that they represent productive rivals to increasingly sophisticated human functions. Unlike the humans who fashioned them, however, there is no real constraint to how massive and powerful in an intellectual sense these armies can become. To reflect on whether these machines will ever possess an understanding that rivals that of the wizards who created them is sadly misplaced anxiety, for the social force that pushes these creations to greater and greater power is not concerned with their being human, but only with their being productive. Like the golem, these creatures are neither inherently good nor evil, but the wisdom of myth suggests that when these awesome instruments are employed to displace human labour, something unpleasant and unforeseen is bound to happen.

7

Systems of Belief, Systems of Production

If one equates industrial capitalism with Christianity and casts Adam Smith as its Messiah, then surely its Saint Paul would have to be Frederick Winslow Taylor. Smith laid out a vision of God's design for the social universe and wrote of the general rules of proper conduct within this plan, but it was Taylor who brought the message home in prescribing the details of industrial life and in his unquestioning faith in his vision of capitalism. Frederick Taylor was an eloquent apostle of capitalist rationalization and 'Taylorism' became a universal symbol for the path industrial capitalism had taken. No one came to exemplify the capitalist perspective of the rationalization and formalization of work – and its excesses – more than he.

Taylor was the first of the fabled efficiency experts, the inventor of time-and-motion studies applied to labour and the progenitor of what he called 'scientific management'. Born in 1856 in Philadelphia, the son of a lawyer of comfortable means, Taylor was, as a youth, bright, disciplined and somewhat idiosyncratic. Even as a boy he displayed the characteristic tendency to analyse in detail his every motion in order to perform even the most routine tasks with optimal efficiency. As an adult and guru to large-scale industry, Taylor was obsessed with efficient motion and his unshakeable belief that management should formalize the actions of workers down to the most minute detail. His adherents – and Taylor's work was of huge influence in all the industrializing world – considered him an eccentric genius; his detractors thought him a compulsive neurotic.

Taylor originally set out to be an attorney but, ironically in the eyes of his future detractors and fortuitously to his future adherents, he had to abandon the road to the legal profession after being temporarily blinded from studying too hard. After regaining his vision in 1875, he became apprenticed as a patternmaker and machinist in a Philadelphia machine shop, an unusual vocational choice for someone of his background. After learning the craft, he took a job as a machinist-labourer at another Philadelphia firm, where he rose rapidly through the ranks to become foreman, and then chief engineer. It was here that Taylor first began to develop the techniques of scientific management. Taylor insisted that the motion of workers be studied and plotted in minute detail, so that all motion that was 'wasted' could be systematically identified and eliminated. Taylor would use his stopwatch (which became his trademark), to time the most detailed tasks and rigorously compared the relative speed with which alternative techniques could perform them. Through such an analysis he would develop formal regulations for the most minute aspects of labour: how full coal tenders' shovels should be with each scoop, how many steps a labourer should take between stations, how many minutes a machinist should spend on a part. His outlook was that of total management control over every detail of work.

Though Taylor understandably came to be an immensely unpopular symbol to American labour, many of his innovations in technique were actually quite helpful and in hindsight seem little more than common sense. It would shock many today to realize how chaotic industrial practice was as recently as Taylor's time, and how little control management exercised over workers' practice. Taylor considered himself a reformer and, though he personally confronted an endless stream of angry workers in the course of his career, was strangely deluded into thinking that he was on very good terms with the workingmen when in fact his philosophy was anathema to them. Labourers' enmity arose not only because he was adamant in his resolve to boost their output, but also because there was an unmistakable tendency in his work to consider them as machines. His very name still rankles.

Taylor's compulsion to an extreme formalization of labour is his enduring legacy. The unmistakable message in Taylorism is that there is no practical limit to formalization and that it would continue until human labour was devoid of any real decision-making. Managers have had to disavow his extremes and avoid using his name and terminology, but his influence on management techniques endures. To the capitalist perspective, Taylor was a clever hero; to the Marxist perspective, he symbolized the oblique evil inherent in the capitalist system of production. In fact, he did little more than dramatically spur and focus attention on what was bound to happen anyway. Frederick Taylor's life and work could not have served better to represent the logical extension of rationalization in capitalist enterprise.

Taylorism was undeniably effective and resonated with the timber of capitalism, but it was also deeply disturbing to consider. Not only was labour uniformly opposed to it, but thoughtful people who were not directly affected by it often found it disconcerting because it indicated that there was no limit to how far the capitalist system would go in the pursuit of the rationalization of work. The relentlessness with which Taylor's techniques could be applied sent ripples through the social sciences. As long as scientific management squeezed more and more productivity from labour and returned money to those who controlled production, there was no apparent reason why scientific management should ever stop or even slow, and that was a disturbing thought to many social scientists, who simply could not see this as a welcome development for workers of all categories in future societies. Taylorism seemed bent on devouring and digesting more and more jobs, eliminating some but making the remainder dreary and routine.

Taylorism was all the more foreboding because it could not be discounted as an aberration. It seemed immanently consistent with a broad social dynamic that, from a modern perspective, could be observed throughout human history. The dynamic might loosely be termed with the familiar euphemism that with a single word encompasses an exceedingly complex meaning, Progress. Though Progress was generally viewed positively, it was also considered to be a social process that was uniformly linear, a process that could apparently only accelerate and advance, and the idea that Progress might hold undesirable features was a nasty thing to hear from social science. Taylorism seemed finely attuned to the current of Progress, and so obviously was not going to fade with time.

The phenomena of social 'progress' had been a central concern of social science from its birth in the death throes of the Enlightenment. Examining the world in the nineteenth century, and reviewing what was known of world history at the time, social scientists sought a scientific model of society that would encompass the 'progress' of mankind and explain its obvious recent acceleration. The issue loomed large because it seemed that a common thread of evolution pervaded all of human activity, from religious institutions to legal systems to science to technology to commerce to government. How, social scientists asked, might one explain the apparent progression from prehistoric sorcery to the prophetic religions of antiquity, to the rise of mighty religious institutions and their inevitable schisms? Why did some articles of religious faith seem inexorably to drift towards rigid dogma, which left them vulnerable to metaphysical speculation and forced them ultimately to yield to cold scientific law? Why, after centuries of calm increase, had mankind turned so maniacally inventive, so that new machines appeared at a pace never before seen? Why was the divine right of kings, after centuries of unchallenged dominance, suddenly such an outdated anachronism? What explained the persistent increase in the complexity of law and government regulations, of instruments of credit and methods of exchange?

There did seem to be a universal social principle at work and it was given its definitive term in the early twentieth century by the German sociologist and historian Max Weber, who borrowed it from the common German term then in use for scientific management: rationalization. Rationalization is a broad and evocative term, and its use to describe the social dynamic of human society was particularly enlightening in the way it married human reason to social 'progress'. In its broadest sense, rationalization is the uniquely human process of making observed phenomena conform to reason for the purpose of making it more intelligible and predictable. In order to render any phenomenon in rational terms, it is necessary to relate that phenomenon in a consistent way with a system of belief, or paradigm, that adequately accounts for not only that particular phenomenon, but all other phenomena that would be expected to be related to that phenomenon as part of a larger system. Rationalization allows logical inferences to be made about any event that is thought to be subject to an accepted system of beliefs, based on the component's supposed relationship with the larger system.

It is this process of rationalization that spawned and continues to drive rational science. According to the common conjecture, first elucidated by Auguste Comte in the nineteenth century, prehistoric peoples observed natural forces – the weather, fire, gravity, the movements of the heavens, etc. – and developed systems of gods and magic to explain them. With the gradual rejection of old paradigms for new, advanced societies progressively ascribed to world views based on superstition, then theology, then metaphysics and finally on science. Each world view was a system of belief, wherein the observed phenomena of one's age could be understood as components of the system. Speculation on future phenomena could centre on extrapolations on the workings of the system as then proposed, and each paradigm was assured general acceptance as long as it served as an accurate predictor of events.

That there was presumed to be a rational basis for 'social science' merely reflected the belief that human society itself operated according to discoverable paradigms, and the paradigm that society in all its various aspects was becoming more rational lent a distinctively linear and deterministic flavour to social science's assessment of social evolution. Rationalization did not seem to be a reversible process: rationality could do nothing other than advance. It might lead to conditions of injustice or provoke upheaval, but the process itself could not be reversed. It was observed that, just as physical systems inevitably progress to advanced states of entropy, human systems are destined to greater degrees of rationalization.

The obverse face of rationalization is that, as more of the environment becomes amenable to reason, less of it is irrational or mysterious. Like civilization encroaching on retreating wilderness, rationalization systematically captures within its domain aspects of those things which had previously transcended comprehension. As with the loss of wilderness, the retreat of the transcendent is tinged with melancholy, and with it the resulting world seems to have irrevocably lost some of its intrinsic beauty and meaning. This can be stressful and lead to a sense that there is an inherent baseness or evil about contemporary human society. There are numerous examples in history of societies spasmodically rejecting the ways of the world, and it is interesting to note how frequently this reaction is associated with a religion (either a new religious movement or a fundamentalist movement within an established religion) when that system of belief collides with developments which more rational, secular societies are tempted to term 'progressive'. Thus the medieval monastic movement arose during a period of general anxiety in Europe over the reordering of secular society, and contemporary Iran has been convulsed by a fundamentalist Islamic movement following an obsessive programme by the former shah to rush that nation into the modern technological age. Perhaps this type of reaction explains why mysticism seems ever present today even as the basis of modern society is becoming so overwhelmingly rational.

The process of rationalizing a phenomenon is the process of accommo-dating its characteristics within some cohesive system of belief, so that these characteristics come to draw their significance from their relationship to other elements in the system. The phenomenon then becomes subject to reason because it conforms to the rules that guide it and all the other elements of the system. This bears a striking resemblance to the mathematical concept of a formal system, which is comprised of symbols and a set of rules for defining the allowable operations upon the symbols. Viewed in this way, the concept of 'force' within the science of physics is analogous to the concept of 'king' in the formal system of chess: neither is of any ultimate importance, other than the relationship each has with other elements of the system, physical science in one case and the game of chess in the other. One might say that the rationalization of natural phenomena is the search for a formal system of belief that 'maps' to reality in some useful way.

The rationalization of scientific concepts is a helpful paradigm for under-standing mankind's historical progression from sorcery to science, but is obviously insufficient for explaining the broader sweep of rationalization in all human affairs. The human urge to purge the irrational from one's environment is not limited to questions of nature, but applies to the social environment as well, and particularly it applies to the production of goods and services. If there is a central insight behind Adam Smith's *Wealth of Nations*, it is the cohesive vision of the role played in modern society by the rationalization of systems of production: the division of labour and the related processes of specialization and mechanization. Smith did not call this process rationalization, but his keen sense that it was the underpinning of all social relations seems to leap from every page of the book. What he called the division of labour was the source of all advances in the production of society, and the excitement one senses in his text was doubtless a result of the universality he saw in the principle. The root motive behind the process was undoubtedly self-interest, but Smith confessed that he was unable to elucidate why humans are the only species who engage in this activity. He vaguely suggested that it must have something to do with humans' capacity to reason, and left it at that.

Rationalization, then, is a process applied both to systems of belief and systems of production, and in a rational world systems of belief are the realm of science and systems of production are the realm of technology. Seen in these terms, both the distinction and affinity between science and technology become explicit. Their obvious affinity is that they are both the subject of constant rationalization and that in both cases the rationalization springs from someone's 'rational' sense of self-interest. Their distinction lies in the ultimate utility of the rationalization: the ultimate utility of science is to comprehend and predict the phenomena that comprise one's environment, the ultimate utility of technology is to boost productivity.

When Smith declared that mechanization was the ultimate manifestation of the division of labour, he was describing the process of rationalization when it had advanced to such a state that all aspects of the task had been made so much by rote and so formal that it was economical to replace this component of the productive process with a machine. In order to reach that point, all judgement that relied on human competence and expertise would have to have been removed entirely from this portion of the productive process, so that there were 'mechanical' rules for the appropriate action that should be applied in any anticipated circumstance. This is just another way of saying that, through the process of rationalization, this portion of the task had been completely formalized: any opportunity for human (i.e. non-formal) intervention in the process has been systematically rooted out, so that the process can proceed in a rational, deterministic, 'mechanical' manner.

For the fact of the matter is that any process that can be formally described – reduced to formal rules and operations – can be mechanized, and will be mechanized if it is in the rational self-interest of a decision-maker. Jacquard's device was predicated on the assumption that there was a formal, mechanical process by which the draw boy selected sets of strings to correspond to a line of fabric, and that there was in theory a machine that could make the same correct decisions in all respects that a human draw boy could make. Babbage's difference engine was explicitly based on Prony's formal procedure for solving mathematical problems, wherein the larger task of computing certain mathematical values had been rationalized and formalized to such an extent that much of the work was relegated to rote addition and subtraction, which could be done by a machine. Babbage's next step, the design of the analytical engine, rested on his discovery that still higher human functions could be formally described, so that the machine could perform even more complex algorithms without human intervention. Expert systems rely on a formal description of the actions of human experts in a defined set of circumstances. Even the process of innovation itself seems amenable to formal description and mechanization.

149

From this perspective, the bold descriptions of the present information age and the precipitous break it represents with the world of the past seem a bit overblown, for there is a very strong continuity between the rationalization of the past and the present, and no indication that this primal operation is likely to change fundamentally. The process by which hand weaving is rationalized into huge industrial looms is not intrinsically different from the process by which hand-operated draw looms were replaced with Jacquard looms, or for that matter by the process by which clerks are replaced by computers or physicians by expert systems.

Smith was correct in associating the division of labour with self-interest, and in accounting for its pervasiveness in these terms, but he did not probe the issue of self-interest deeply (which may account for his impatience with Mandeville, who pursued the issue ruthlessly). To Smith the process of rationalization seemed objective and absolute, and there was no reason to suppose that there were alternative methods or modes of realizing it. The reality, however, is that the impulse to rationalization is born of human desires and shaped by human goals. There is no objectively 'optimal' manner of rationalization, there are only possible methods that satisfy different goals with varying degrees of success.

In contrast, Max Weber had a clear and sophisticated understanding of the underlying forces behind rationalization, and with his encyclopaedic knowledge of social and economic organizations through modern and ancient history he was able to focus attention on the variety of ways that this process could manifest itself in social relations of many types. The unifying concept to Weber that maintained the universality of rationalization while allowing for almost infinite variations in its manner of expression was that the process of rationalization is inextricably associated with the goals of the person who is rationalizing.

Weber delved deeply into different types of self-interest and how they might manifest themselves in different incidents of rationalization. He distinguished between what he termed 'instrumentally' rational (*zweckrational*) and 'value-rational' (*wertrational*) social acts. *Zweckrational* acts are calculated to produce a practical result, such as organizing correspondence chronologically in a file so that letters can be found more readily. Value-rational acts, on the other hand, arise from a conscious belief in an ideal for its own sake and without caring for its practical prospects, as when in the Bible story the Christian is urged to present the other cheek to one who has slapped him. Weber's division is perceptive, for it demonstrates how different perspectives can affect rational actions.

Ultimately, Weber leaves no room for actions that are entirely irrational – much as Mandeville left no room for acts that are entirely virtuous – only for acts that are irrational from certain points of view and with certain goals in mind. From the *zweckrational* perspective, value-rational acts are bound to appear irrational, but practical actions may also seem irrational even to practical observers if there is a divergence of goals among practically minded people. When Western nations denounce the government of Iran's actions as irrational, this may be the result of *zweckrational* observers being unmindful of the goals of individuals who are pursuing supremely value-rational goals, a turn of events that would be particularly ironic when one recalls the role Western-style rationalization played in triggering the fundamentalist backlash in Iran in the first place. But the fact that the government's actions appear irrational from a *zweckrational* view of the nation's self-interest does not mean that the purveyors of these acts are necessarily being value-rational and ignoring the pragmatic aspects of the material world: a group within the nation may well have its own immanently *zweckrational* goals, but their selfish interests simply diverge from that of the nation as a whole.

In Weber's view, one might engage in social actions for several reasons, as in order to be fashionable or to follow established tradition. But the obvious historical current of rationalization in mankind was away from unthinking observation of conventions and towards a more practical, 'scientific' appraisal of cause and effect, accompanied by a more deliberate impulse to self-interest. Weber describes the modern man as a being of predominantly selfish, *zweckrational* behaviour. Predictably, these rational economic individuals that arose in the modern era after centuries of rationalization in human relations are themselves remarkably predictable. A mass of individuals unselfconsciously pursuing their own self-interest display a consistency in their behaviour that far surpasses any that could be imposed on them by the most ruthlessly enforced edict or the most intuitively compelling metaphysic. The emergence of rational economic man and the apprehension of the laws that guide his actions are, as Weber observed, the central paradigm behind the rational science of economics, which explains why the discipline of economics is most comfortable with those human actions that are most nakedly selfish and *zu eckrational* – those that reduce themselves to formal mathematical description – and conversely is ineffectual when dealing with vestigial, 'irrational' aspects of human nature – like the love for the land or the sadness evoked by a despoiled wilderness.

Just as rationalization grows out of perceptions of self-interest, shifting perceptions of self-interest cause concomitant shifts in the course of rationalization. The present era has been characterized by such processes, an example of which are the subtle but profound shifts in economic organization at the national and international level that have resulted from the new international economy. A new and keen awareness of international economic competition has made many polities increasingly aware that their self-interest is served by new forms of co-operation that would have seemed irrational just a decade or two before. Hence, in the United States and Europe are found industry consortiums in electronics and aerospace between companies that were recently bitter, suspicious rivals. The European Economic Community, after years of fractious rivalry and economic irrelevance, has suddenly become the centre of a unified European economy, and the citizens of Europe are fairly breathless in their anticipation of the withdrawal of all trade restrictions between member nations scheduled for 1992. Even the closed communist societies of the world have been forced to modify their view of self-interest, and the Western world has been stunned to observe the *perestroika* of the Soviet Union and a similar trend in China (though temporarily retarded), as evidenced by a decided shift away from central planning and gunboat diplomacy to more liberal entrepreneurial production. These new developments are not attributable to less selfishness among citizens of various nations, just to a shift in their conceptions of how their self-interests are best served.

It is frequently presumed that, in Western economies, the perspective of self-interest that guides the rationalization of work is that of some creature called a capitalist. This creature really existed and was a prominent player in nineteenth-century capitalism, but today, though the term persists, rigorous rationalization has made the ownership of capital and the management of productive processes much more complex and diffuse. Except for a relatively small and insignificant number of individuals for whom the traditional meaning of 'capitalist' still applies, the name has lost its utility as a category of individuals. What has persisted to this day is the capitalists' perspective of self-interest, and it is this perspective, in fact, that most accurately defines both the modern and antiquated capitalist: that productive processes should be rationalized so as to increase the profitability of firms, and that this type of rationalization serves the self-interest of the believer. This is the philosophy enumerated by Adam Smith. Smith's 'invisible hand' was nothing more or less than economic rationalization viewed from the capitalist perspective.

Of course, there are dissenting perspectives, such as that of the Luddites, of Robert Owen, of Karl Marx and Friedrich Engels. Viewed from a worker's traditional appraisal of his or her self-interest, rationalization would proceed in an entirely different manner and toward different ends. According to the Marxist system of belief, capitalist rationalization was a systematic process of extracting from workers the value produced by their labour. Marx did not disdain rationalization or mechanization in the abstract, in fact he cheered the processes as labour-saving and potentially enriching to society. What Marx railed against was the employment of rationalization and mechanization in a capitalist frame of mind. Though the particulars will always change, the opposing perspectives of capitalism and Marxism are remarkably persistent and robust. Either will accuse the other of being fatally flawed or even irrational, but objectively these accusations are rooted in each system's premises. It is even difficult to discuss the relative successes or failures of the various implementations of the two systems, since each invariably defines success and failure in different terms.

152

Systems of Belief, Systems of Production

From the capitalist perspective, rationalization of economic systems should proceed without abatement. All aspects of economic activity are inevitably headed for successive states of greater rationalization, and so eventually to formalization and mechanization. Those distinctive human qualities that can aid in productive processes – judgement, reason, skill, and creativity – are inevitably bound to be made rational and absorbed into rational systems of production, while those distinctive human qualities that do not contribute to productive processes – emotion and feelings such as fatigue or jealousy – are bound to be extracted from them. The outline of this process is unmistakably discernible from history, only the state of technology and the set of human functions that potentially fall prey to this process has changed. The tendency of advanced societies to become more formal and specialized became a near obsession with economists and sociologists in the first half of the twentieth century, when the twin figures of bureaucrat and technocrat tended to dominate academic assessments of the future of society. It was difficult to avoid rather depressing prognostications about how the individual psyche would suffer in the coming world. Emile Durkheim felt that the age of meaningful employment for the masses had disappeared, and hoped wanly for the emergence of a new ethic in which individuals might labour anonymously in dreary employment, guided by an undefined new ethic of social responsibility. Durkheim's rather feeble theory was that fraternal trade organizations would arise to replace the lost sense of belonging that he saw naturally engulfing the individuals in this lifeless world.

Among some sociologists and economists there was a vague optimism that formalization and specialization would lead to more rational (if less dynamic) government, since armies of technically oriented bureaucrats were bound to displace the crass politicians and political hangers-on that pervaded politics. Among most mainstream social theorists, however, the salient issue in modern economies was the stifling effect of bureaucracies on business firms. The recurring theme that ran through a diverse stream of social critique, through among others Marx, Sombart and Schumpeter down to John Kenneth Galbraith, was that there was an incipient threat of stagnation lurking behind bureaucratic firms and governments. Surely the rationalization that made organizations so large and unwieldy would smother innovation and make change increasingly difficult.

These reservations about the future of capitalism are part of a curious trend in economics to descend into melancholy when current economic science is not able to accommodate adequately the effects of dramatic shifts in technology. Intermittently since the publication of the *Wealth of Nations*, a recurring pessimism has surfaced in both Marxist and neoclassical political economy that the path of rationalization was a dreary road to ruin. From the Marxist perspective, taken as it was from the outlook of the workers who were confronted with the passage of this boundary, the sequence of rationalization, formalization and mechanization was a cruel evil inherent in capitalism. The worker was said to assume a particular skill early in life because that skill commanded relatively good wages and allowed freedom of judgement and control – the work was fulfilling and meaningful because it was vital and respected. But the most enriching skills were the best targets of rationalization, and they were constantly and systematically devalued by the capitalist system. As time passed and technology proceeded, the worker would inevitably find that both his purchasing power and social standing have dwindled. Economic law seems bent to extract from his control all elements of his personal judgement. Rather than meaningful, the worker's job becomes mechanical in nature, and perhaps the job is lost altogether to machinery. Taken as a whole, such a system from a Marxist perspective was inherently corrupt and would inevitably collapse. Machines might replace workers, but their introduction brought only fleeting profits in the face of competition. Consumption would be choked by rising unemployment, and widespread bankruptcies would lead to social revolution. Neoclassical economists were more accepting of rationalization, but were still prone to fits of doubt about its eventual effects. Malthus had society tripping up on finite resources and declining productivity, Ricardo on the shift of social products away from the workers due to mechanization. Other commentators drew pessimistic prophecy from the rational course of capitalism, having it foundering in imperialism and war, or stifled by bureaucracy and regulation, or derailed by the anomy of the proletariat. The destructive character of change in capitalism was the basis for economics as the dismal science.

Though the theorizing that accompanied these gloomy scenarios was, and still is, illuminating and valuable as social critique, and though many of the secondary effects of capitalism that were predicted have come to pass, the truth of the matter is that capitalism has never been in any real danger of structural collapse, and today capitalism seems to be surging ahead while competing philosophies that ignore market forces are in retreat. Relative to the world of the neoclassical economists, most would agree that the industrialized world is far better placed today, and even among those who most vociferously argue that the changes wrought by capitalism are not an unqualified benefit, it is obvious that rationalism breeds more than mere misery and petty profits. Though each of these doom scenarios for capitalist economies accurately captured some aspect of the fallout from rationalization, each missed its larger mark.

The reason that these dismal critiques fell short was that each shared a flawed premise that was reminiscent of Malthus' dark prognosis for the food supply. When Malthus predicted that the food supply could not expand enough to support the burgeoning population, he based his argument on the diminishing returns to labour that would ultimately limit the amount of food that could be wrested from agricultural land. There was an element of truth in this appraisal, but the reason things did not pan out as Malthus predicted was that there were tremendous gains in the productivity of agricultural land due to mechanization and scientific methods. Malthus' view was limited by his not being able to see the tremendous productivity that could result from mechanizing agriculture, just as twentieth-century economists were slow to acknowledge that intellectual activities could be mechanized. The fears that social rationalization and formalization would irrevocably lead to a bureaucratic stagnation or a technocratic oligarchy were mistaken in the presumption that intelligence is inherently different from other aspects of human activity. If productive intelligence could not have been mechanized, then surely the doom-sayers of yesterday would have had a point, and it would be plausible to presume that today, in the absence of computers, massive and unmanageable bureaucracies would have developed in order to cope with the burgeoning complexity of society. But what has happened instead is that, as the limitations of human intelligence presented a more formidable constraint to economic rationalization, different aspects of the mysteries of mentation found themselves on the borders of advancing rationality, lent themselves to formal description, and lay prone to mechanization, or more precisely to computerization.

Though organizations such as government and business firms have indeed become increasingly large and bureaucratic since Marx's time and have exhibited some of the tendencies of petrification that social science has feared, the mechanization of intellectual functions has caused some trends that would have surprised critics from previous eras. In recent years, there has been a decided shift away from middle managers in many large companies, a trend towards reduced numbers of management layers in firms that has been explicitly aided by computer technology. In the absence of computers, middle-level managers abounded in major corporations, making routine decisions and enforcing the formal standards of the corporation. But with the advent of computers, formal decision-making and conformance to standards becomes the subject of algorithms engineered or purchased by the companies in the form of software. The function of the middle-level manager is eliminated as the control of higher-level managers is extended.

Bureaucratization is not simply an inevitable outgrowth of formalization, but is more precisely the result of formalization in the absence of any economical method of mechanizing intellectual functions. A large bureaucracy, like any other large labour pool, does not speak *per se* to the level of rationalization in an organization, but only to the relative economies of formalizing human labour with machinery as opposed to other means. Prony had developed a perfectly serviceable bureaucracy in rationalizing the production of logarithms, and in the absence of mechanical means to do the same task this bureaucracy had a perfectly legitimate social function. But with economical mechanical alternatives, such a bureaucracy was eminently inefficient.

From this perspective, the role of humans in capitalist enterprise is clear: humans fill the roles in productive processes that are uneconomical to mechanize. This should not be a shocking statement, for if any of our jobs could be done at a lower cost by a machine there is no doubt that this would come to pass. Similarly, there is no doubt that each day technology closes in on new intellectual tasks that previously required human intelligence, which is just another way of saying that the task is being rationalized to the point that it can be reduced to formal description and performed by an algorithm. If there is not at this very moment someone formulating a plan for displacing all or part of your labour with machinery, then the sad fact is that you make too little money to make it worthwhile.

All of us who labour occupy a place in society that lies somewhere close to the boundary between what is so routine as to be already mechanized and that which is so rare and incomprehensible that the present state of technique cannot economically rationalize it. As technology advances, so does this boundary between what a machine can economically do and what requires human intervention, with the result that technological advance is constantly flushing workers from their sanctuary of skills, forcing them to readapt to newly created tasks that lie along the shifting boundary between mystery and machine.

8

Technology and Employment

Modern economies are networks of production. They are complex economic systems that arise out of the interplay of the innumerable production processes of which they are comprised. These production processes encompass the entire range of economic activity that shapes the modern world: processes varying from the assembly of automobiles to food preparation and service, from software design to mineral extraction, from clerical work to medical diagnosis. Individuals engage in productive activity because they consider it valuable, and in modern societies production dominates the social allocation of time and resources. Production consumes our labour and remunerates us for our efforts, it demands our skills and experience and assigns us our social status largely in exchange for them, and it produces the goods and services that we consume ravenously. The issue of how advances in computer technology will affect the value of human labour is the issue of how labour is employed in production processes, how production processes work in isolation and in tandem with each other, and how shifts in technology cause shifts in production functions.

Every production process employs a specific balance of technique, tools and materials that is calculated to produce the product in a desired manner. It is not at all glib to refer to this balance as a recipe, for indeed it is exactly that. Every productive process expresses a recipe for performing a task in a particular way: how many people will be employed and what they will be doing, what materials are required and when they will be needed, what tools are required and how they should be used. The purpose of selecting a particular recipe is consistently to produce a specified product with the application of the components of the recipe, a specific output that necessarily flows from specific inputs. That recipe, which promises to produce a product from specific inputs, is what economists refer to as the *production function* for that product.

Just as systems of belief serve as scientific paradigms, a production function may be thought of as a technological paradigm: a sort of model for how to employ certain inputs in the production of certa'˜ outputs. Like scientific paradigms, production functions do not spontane ˛usly occur and do not change without human intent – they are devised and revised for a reason. Generally in market economies, production functions are devised by those who control them in order to produce a profit. According to neoclassical common wisdom, for a productive process to yield a profit mandates that the marketplace accept what it produces, which is another way of saying the product of the activity must sell. The value it delivers to buyers must be perceived to be higher than its cost, and higher than the value of competing products of similar price. The producer attempts to identify the product that is most desired by buyers, and produce the most valuable product possible at the least cost. In doing this, the producer is doing nothing more mysterious than attempting to maximize the money to be made from engaging in this productive activity.

The invention of a new product wedges a new production function into the existing network of production functions. If the product is accepted by the marketplace, the revenues from its sales pay for the capital goods and labour employed in the new product's production, and increase demand for these inputs. The demand for the product indicates a fundamental value as a consumption good (used by consumers for its own sake) or as a capital good (used in other production functions to produce other products). This is the type of innovation that is universally admired in a capitalist system, the type of innovation involved in a clever capitalist literally inventing a better mousetrap. The capitalist makes a windfall on his invention, of course, but he also is responsible for the creation of new jobs that had not existed before, and the purchase of other capital and service inputs that benefit the general business environment in which he operates. This type of technical change, in which a new production function is formulated in order to produce a new product, is referred to as a *product innovation*.

A mountain may be the creation of a most dramatic geological event, but once created it immediately falls prey to the humbling and incessant forces of erosion. Though the force of wind and water pale before the explosive power of geological upheaval that created the mountain, their real power lies in their persistence and ubiquity, and the more salient the outcropping the more it attracts erosion. Such is the pattern of the forces of innovation in modern society, for, once created, production processes are immediately subject to a mundane and persistent process of petty rationalization. Rather than representing a revolutionary new production process, these more common and persistent innovations represent the more evolutionary process of streamlining existing production functions, cutting production costs or boosting the quality of the output and thereby making

158

its production process more efficient. This type of innovation, as opposed to the more dramatic product innovation that precedes it, is referred to as *process innovation*.

Like product innovations, process innovations are born of the perceptions of self-interest of those who control production. Given any particular state of technological development, there has to be, from the production manager's perspective, an optimum manner in which to organize any particular production process: a magic mix of tools, technique and materials that will produce the most saleable product at the least cost to the producer. It is the burden of all production managers to modify constantly their production functions to fit their evolving notions of what this ideal function is, even as advancing technology is modifying the ideal. The modifications that are made in the various production functions we recognize as innovations, and if the innovations reflect an accurate appraisal of a costly difference between the ideal and actual production functions, there is profit to be made in introducing them.

Reduced to a cold mathematical description (which is just the way economists like to view the world), a production function becomes a mathematical abstraction that does no more than describe the proportional amounts of inputs that are required to produce a given output. Unlike a cooking recipe, though, 'inputs' include everything that is necessary for the economic spectacle of production: not only raw materials, but capital goods (factories and tools), energy, land, and human skill and labour. These inputs that are sufficient and necessary to the production function are called *factors* of production.

The current state of technology is defined by the ideal production functions that manifest it. Changes in the state of technology cause changes in the ideal production functions for different products, so that a different combination of inputs is required to produce the same output. For a process innovation to be economically rational (that is, for it to benefit those who control production), it should increase the profits that accrue to the producer, by either decreasing the total cost of the inputs or increasing the total value of the outputs. As economies become more complex and their production functions more rational, competing enterprises necessarily respond to common trends in production processes, so that the production function for any particular product tends to converge towards an ideal.

For a production process to become more profitable, the marginal productivity of its inputs, considered as a whole, must increase in some way. If one thinks of all the factors of production as falling into one of the two general categories of capital and labour, then for the marginal productivity of the inputs as a whole to increase, then either both capital and labour must become more productive, or either capital or labour must become so much more productive that the boost in efficiency makes the innovation worthwhile, even to the extent that a drop in the productiveness of the other category of input is offset. A process innovation, by changing the way inputs are used in production, modifies the mix of capital and labour desired for optimum production. If a process innovation encourages a change in the mix between capital and labour that has proportionally more capital than before, that technological change is said to be *labour-saving* (or *capital augmenting*) as opposed to an innovation that encourages less capital for a given share of labour, which is *capital-saving* (or *labour-augmenting*). Introducing rickshaws in crowded automobile traffic is an example of a capital-saving device, since it encourages increased human labour in the transportation process and less use of automobiles or motorcycles. It is no coincidence that rickshaws are found in regions of the world where labour is inexpensive and machines are prohibitively expensive, where any shift in the capital/labour ratio towards more labour would be expected to lower costs. It is also no coincidence that the vast majority of technological advance introduced into Western industrialized countries has traditionally been labour-saving. The Jacquard device, the difference engine, computers and automation in general are intensely labour-saving, since they tend to displace human operations with mechanical, capital-intensive ones. Labour-saving technical innovation is the hallmark of economies in the modern age, and is the process that is bound to dominate the economies of the foreseeable future.

Process innovation is the type of change that workers most commonly confront and, since it is so frequently intended to be a labour-saving shift, it tends to highlight some rather distasteful aspects of capitalism. Process innovation, from the perspective of the worker, may seem to be almost obsessive in its concern for restricting and formalizing the worker's actions to the most trivial detail, or quickening the pace of work to unnatural and debilitating extremes, or eliminating workers entirely when mechanical substitutes are available. Process innovation is the supposed evil that the Luddites rioted against, that Robert Owen wanted to block at New Lanark, and that socialist critics have assailed in this century. Marxist economists to this day have tended to become preoccupied with this type of change in production, as did the classical economists who preceded them, and this preoccupation has contributed to the dreariness of their descriptions of modern economies.

To early economists, the immediate effects of process innovation were already plain, and though the terminology has changed, their descriptions of these immediate effects are still valid. Since production functions reflect the particular mix of production factors that is most efficient to produce at a given capacity with a given state of technology, common sense dictated that a probable impact of technological advance on the production function is to modify the optimum mix of factors of production. With labour-saving innovation, more of the capitalist's costs would be oriented to capital goods at the relative expense of wages to labour. Except in the absence of greatly expanded demand for the product or service being produced, labour-saving process innovation would have the effect of reducing employment in the industry, or lowering the prevailing rates for workers in the industry, or both. Though the introduction of new capital-intensive processes quite naturally necessitates a new demand for a new class of labourers with new skills oriented to working with the new machines, the pattern familiar even in Ricardo's time was that the total employment in the industry would tend to drop, even as a few new highly skilled positions were created. The old pattern of skills that had been well remunerated in the old production function was obsolete, resulting in what later economists would refer to as a systematic 'de-skilling' of the labour force, leaving the baleful term of 'technological unemployment' to describe the mass of workers whose skills had been incorporated into the workings of the machines which had replaced them.

The Jacquard device represented a particularly bold process innovation that illuminates the shifts in production functions that can occur with mechanization. The device eliminated the lower-skilled position of the assistant and allowed a single weaver to produce a brocade by himself. It also expanded dramatically the capacity of the region to produce fine woven silks, with the result that these silks became more affordable. From a very simplistic standpoint, one could say that the process innovation represented by the device had the effect of displacing some unskilled labour, boosted productivity and lowered consumer prices, as it obviously had done.

But the situation was more complex than that. For centuries, the parties involved in silk weaving – the merchants, the master weavers and the workers – had been embroiled in a contentious social process through which the weaving of fine silks had been rationalized. Many years before, it had been the master weavers who largely controlled the process, hiring workers and selling their wares to merchants, but with the passage of time the merchants came to intrude more and more into different aspects of the production process. Eventually, the merchants were able to get the master weavers to work for them, providing the weavers with raw materials for production and paying a fee for fabric produced in the master weavers' small family shops. From an original position of controlling the process, the master weavers were reduced to a lower social position that was subservient to the merchants, who by then were more capitalists than merchants. Understandably, the rise of the merchant-capitalist was not a process that the weavers accepted gladly, and the region was fraught with conflict and occasional open rioting in the nineteenth century.

The Jacquard device played a contributing role in this social transformation, and its introduction was only one of a stream of developments, both techno-logical and organizational, that served to enhance the merchant-capitalist's control over the production process. The process of designing fabric and

161

punching the cards was controlled by the merchant, and with the widespread use of the device the skills involved in producing designs and punched cards became more highly prized, though the numbers employed in these relatively prestigious fields would never approach those that had been employed weaving. It was the merchants, then, who owned the cards, and they would leave the cards with the master weaver in his shop along with the order for fabric. The weaver would set up the loom to produce the fabric and return the fabric and the cards to the merchant upon completion. The effect of the device was to hasten the decline of the social status of the master weavers and to blur the distinction between weavers and wage labourers, while placing incrementally more creativity and control over the process in the hands of the merchant and his staff. From their original station as powerful possessors of the skills upon which the industry depended, the master weavers were forced to cede to the merchants another bit of intellectual suzerainty over the production process. A merchants' newspaper summed up the shift in relations between merchants and weavers in stating that 'the merchants compose the intellectual portion of the industry. The difference between a master weaver and a merchant is that between a construction worker and an architect.'[1] This comment appeared less than a year before riots racked the silk-weaving industry in Lyons once again.

The tumultuous social changes in textiles due to technical innovation were issues of great importance to economists of the nineteenth century. It was difficult for these economists to escape entirely the common-sense notion that the primary impact of process innovation is on labour, while the primary impact of product innovation is on the consumers of the products that compete in some way with the new product being introduced. These are indeed the immediate areas of effect, but the true social impact of these two processes is much more subtle than common sense alone would indicate. With each type of innovation certain effects are indeed immediately apparent, but the complicating consideration is in the interconnectedness of all processes of production, so that a realignment of costs in one production function forces a slightly less severe realignment of costs in related production functions, which in turn causes shifts in the employment of resources that can in theory (and in many cases in fact) be demonstrated to ripple through an entire economy. Individual sectors of an economy may be cast into a state of instability due to a major innovation, and then after a period of unrest assume a new state of relative equilibrium that reflects a new pattern of employment among factors of production. But this apparent equilibrium belies unrest that the innovations have brought about in the rest of the economy.

Using a hypothetical example, consider the impact that the introduction of word-processing equipment has made in the modern economy. Word-processing was hungrily adopted by modern business, causing an expansion in employment in the companies that produce word-processing software and systems and increasing cost competition between them. Companies in competing areas such as the manufacture of electric typewriters would see sales slump as managers adopted word-processing in their various production processes, since word-processing offers obvious productive advantages over typing at a competitive price. Word-processing, being much more efficient than typing, requires fewer operators to produce the same amount of product, and so many typists find themselves out of work, and the remaining typists find that their real wages have declined since the competition for open typing positions becomes more heated. Not only do wages for typists decline, but so do the wages for related types of relatively low-skilled labour such as secretarial and clerical work, as the glut of unemployed typists drives down wages in other areas as well. Word-processing skills become more highly valued for a time, but unless there is a huge expansion in the need for keyed documents, the number employed as word-processors will never approach the previous number of typists. But through it all, the price of producing a letter has fallen dramatically, and the quality and consistency of the letters has improved. Businesses find their operations slightly more efficient, and due to the relative drop in the cost of producing keyed documents tend to use letters more than they did before the introduction of word-processing. Telephone usage declines, while profits to the public and private services that deliver correspondence and other written documents would be expected to rise. There is literally no limit to how far one can trace the effects in the wider economy of a single, significant innovation, whether organizational or technological in character. And when viewed as its ultimate impact on the economy as a whole, is the eventual result of a technological innovation helpful to workers as a group or harmful? Smith believed that it necessarily was helpful and was the key to social progress; Marx was fervent in asserting that it was harmful and would lead to the collapse of social institutions. Ricardo couldn't say, though he had suspicions that it could be harmful under some circumstances, and economists still ponder the matter.

Economists consider it fundamental that, though analysing the changes in production functions of a single industry is useful, it is ultimately necessary to consider the eventual result in the larger economy in order to gauge comprehensively the effects on labour and prices. When the entire economy is thought to be relatively stable in its various balancing of supply and demand for labour, capital and commodities, when it successfully co-ordinates its myriad constituent production functions, it is said to be in a state of *general equilibrium*. When only one sector of the economy is thought to balance its demands and desires, without considering its effects on the larger economy, it is said to be in a state of *partial equilibrium*.

There is no serious debate about how a labour-saving technological shift in a production function affects a sector of an economy (its 'partial equilibrium effect'): costs drop, labour input requirements decline, workers are displaced

163

and many of the remaining workers require less extensive skills than the workers they replaced. Some sparks will fly when economists debate the wider general equilibrium effects of labour-saving technological advance, the same argument that so enlivened Ricardo's dinner party, but even here some sort of consensus has emerged. Lower costs in one sector undoubtedly increase profits and capital accumulation in that sector and others, and the stimulative effect of the technological advance reverberates, and actually increases, as it ripples through the economy. The stimulated economy, expanding under the prodding of technological advance, demands labour in its growth sectors, and theoretically the increased demand would generally be greater than that supplied by displacement in the declining, newly mechanized sectors. From a somewhat impersonal and removed perspective, then, the effects of technological innovation are generally conceded to be helpful to the economy as a whole, since it boosts productivity and increases the net wealth of society.

Net wealth, however, can be a glib and irresponsible concept to bandy about when discussing a drastic social transformation. Though many consumers and business owners indubitably benefit from technological innovation, the general equilibrium effects of technology on many workers is continually and insistently to flush them from tasks that can be economically mechanized. How one prospers or suffers due to technology depends on how far from the boundary of rationalization one's job tasks fall and, when nudged or displaced by technology, how quickly and effectively one can scramble to a new job task further from the boundary of rationalization.

The uprooting of workers from their job tasks is a characteristic of all technological change, a reflection of the factor substitution that occurs in production functions when the cost of a capital input drops in a significant way relative to the cost of labour inputs. This is the process that transformed farming from an activity that employed 74 per cent of the US population in 1800 to less than 4 per cent in 1970, even as the product per farmer (expressed in terms of the number of people fed by his labour) increased by a factor of almost twelve.[2] It is also the fundamental process behind the dramatic increase in service jobs relative to blue-collar jobs in the current era. Each of these transformations were stressful on the segments of the labour force that were being displaced and serves as an example of what an era of rapidly decreasing costs in computational technology is likely to bring to the fabric of society.

In past episodes in industrialization, the set of tasks that had gravitated towards being mechanical in nature were those involving physical work, from shovelling coal into furnaces to plucking weft threads in draw looms. It is by now almost trite to state that the general trend since proto-industrialization has been towards mechanization of increasingly sophisticated skills and intellectual endeavours. But one facet of industrialization has remained constant even as the faces of industrialization change with increasing rapidity: the prime target of mechanization has always been what society has considered 'unskilled' labour. What is changing is the set of tasks that society considers unskilled, for the basis of defining unskilled labour has always been the intelligence or knowledge required to perform the task. As machines have taken on intellectual tasks, knowledge workers – middle class professionals – have begun to feel the heat.

Of course, in order for one's social standing to be damaged by mechanization, it is not necessary for a machine overtly to arrogate the task. Far more frequently, machinery presents itself either as a partial alternative, offering to perform some aspects of the task and reducing only some of the human labour involved, or as an alternative factor of production, bidding down the wage to be gained in that field of employment. In free market industrial economies, workers are not replaced by machines from out of the blue, but by a step-wise migration in job descriptions towards tasks that are each more rational, more certain and more accessible to the jaws of machinery. The jobs which are most adversely affected by mechanization are those that have already become mechanical in nature.

Intellectual mechanization is ripping through the economic landscape in search of that labour which it is most economical to replace, and whenever it encounters unskilled labour, it finds a treasure that is pre-digested and ready to be consumed. The net effect on a society where it is economical to mechanize intellectual labour, like past societies where physical work was being mechanized, is for the impact of mechanization to ripple throughout the economy. Those who are closest to the border, who fit the current profile of unskilled labour, are hardest hit, and every task in the general vicinity of the event is made at least a little less valuable. But the society as a whole is becoming more efficient, more productive and potentially richer, if its citizens can make an orderly enough retreat from the boundaries of mechanization, assume new valuable tasks further away from the border, and be prepared to move again when it becomes necessary, as it invariably will.

The metaphor of workers retreating from the skill transformations resulting from advancing technology echoes a salient observation that has been made about the nature of social change brought about by technology: that technological change can occur too rapidly, that societies have a sort of technological absorption rate above which they are likely to be overwhelmed and harmed by innovation. This would metaphorically correspond to an orderly retreat breaking down because it could not maintain the pace of swiftly advancing technology, and would shed light on why the subject of technological displacement has become so much more pressing in an era when technological innovation is obviously accelerating. It would also point to the subtle danger involved when a society embraces a pace of technological innovation that is out of step with its endemic market forces, such as when a Third World country indiscriminately adopts technologies from more advanced countries, or when any nation allows its technological innovation to be guided by military or other nationalist motives that have no foundation in markets.

We in Western industrial society may consider ourselves generally competent to handle these metaphorically couched difficulties, but there is one other difficulty that may speak more to our weakness in market-driven economies. According to our metaphor, it is the same troops that are constantly being uprooted and forced to retreat, and in many respects it is those troops least equipped to re-establish economic positions elsewhere. The process of mechanizing intelligence, like the physical mechanization before it, is aimed by economic considerations at the less educated and least knowledgeable about their job opportunities. Society endangers itself when its leaders do not understand the true nature of the battle and when its front-line troops do not have the basic education with which to retreat.

That the same workers are incessantly uprooted from their social roles has been noted by economists, many of whom subscribe to the notion that there are in fact two fundamental markets for labour. In the upper tier are those whose jobs involve a generalized body of intellectual activity, far from the boundary of being subject to economical mechanization, and who can expect good wages, equitable treatment in the workplace and relatively stable employment. In the lower tier are the long-suffering front-line troops, whose skills are normally acquired through brief on-the-job or vocational training, and whose positions are subject to high turnover and rapid transformation or even outright elimination.

How fluidly we respond to the shifts in labour demands arising from the impact of technology is a critical item on the social agenda. Workers who find themselves unemployable either from the direct or indirect impacts of technology hold the key to our future. When workers are overwhelmed by their loss of jobs and are not equipped even to investigate alternatives, they can become discouraged and even more difficult to employ. Ultimately society finds ways to communicate its sense that these people are useless and burdensome, exacerbating their uselessness and the burden they have become. This class of people are the structurally unemployed, an unintentionally evocative term in that it describes people who have been expelled from the fundamental structure of productive society, even to the point that they do not appear in official government counts of the unemployed. To qualify as unemployed according to the US Bureau of Labor Statistics one must be seeking employment but have not found it. Because of this specific definition of unemployment, those who have given up hope of finding a job are not included, and so it is universally acknowledged that the BLS figures for unemployment do not give the full picture of the number or characteristics of the unemployed and underemployed in the United States. It is left to concerned and thoughtful citizens to discern among the underclass the unmistakable visages of those stripped of any opportunity to participate in society, and to ponder whether breathless announcements of smarter machinery is good news to them.

The metaphor of technology as an advancing army, with lower-skilled labour being on the front line of its advance, touches on the adversarial nature that pervades labour–management relations, but may connote a malicious motivation on behalf of those who employ technology to substitute capital for labour in production processes. Not even Marx at his most curmudgeonly could bring himself to claim that this general trend was a manifestation of overt malice on the part of capitalists toward workers, only of a more petty selfishness. To Adam Smith, of course, this rational, human selfishness was the magic behind the whole process of wealth-creation and social betterment. But the dynamic of self-interest is more complex than a simple consideration of whether a course of action benefits one's position or not, there is the more complex issue of when benefits will be realized. One may pursue a course of action, such as mechanizing a portion of a productive process, in order to receive an immediate benefit or in order to position oneself for long-term benefits, and the difference in goals will have a profound effect on the manner in which technology will be introduced.

What capitalists expect back from the employment of physical capital (the so-called rate of return on capital, reflected in financial markets as interest rates) reflects, essentially, their greed, their uncertainty of success and their preference for short-term over long-term gain. As with any investment, the decision to substitute physical equipment for labour in a production process is shaped by the capitalists' expectations for return. With the highly competitive international economy, cultural differentials in expectations for return come into direct competition with each other, and distinctive cultural patterns of technological innovation and factor substitution become apparent. We in the West had always enjoyed these comparisons until the precipitous emergence of the Japanese as an industrial and technological power.

Eileen Applebaum quotes a hypothetical case that, though vastly simplified, is thought to correspond closely to the truth.[3] Suppose that a US firm substitutes a number of robots for factory workers, releasing those skilled workers to the ranks of the unemployed and replacing them with far fewer programmers and unskilled robot attendants. This is a classical example of technical substitution through de-skilling labour. Simultaneously, a competing Japanese firm of equivalent size and wherewithal invests in the same equipment, but organizes its production in such a way that the skilled workers learn programming skills. The Japanese firm is left with many more novice programmers, but the programmers have a much better sense of the operations of the robots and their place in production. Though the US firm realizes the immediate profit advantage, it is left in a weaker long-term productive position: its work force is much more limited in its area of competence, its man-machine organization is less flexible to shifts in production requirements and likely to become obsolescent faster than the Japanese manifestation. This scenario hardly needs to be played out any further, in view of how Japan has come to dominate the production of so many key consumer items in Western markets.

Professor Applebaum's example has the moral flavour and theme of any of a dozen parables whose message is that patience and moderation will eventually be rewarded and profligacy is a path to ruin. It is the American business manager's greed that leads him to disaster, his insistence for the quick pay-off that prohibits him from choosing the long-term path that is not only more profitable, but also less disruptive of his firm and his nation's labour resources. The truth that is sensed in the example has been manifested in any one of the stream of criticisms that has descended on American managers along with American industry's decline in competitiveness with the Japanese. Americans are said to be obsessed with short-term gains while the Japanese are concerned with long-term progress. Americans focus on profits, the Japanese on market share. Faced with expanding demand, Americans prefer to invest in physical capital over human capital; faced with declining demand, Americans cut costs and lay off workers while Japanese cut prices. Though crude generalizations, these familiar charges are really restatements of the same thing: that inflated expectations distort the beneficial impacts of advancing technology in industry.

Wassily Leontieff, the Nobel prize-winning economist who pioneered computer simulations of production functions in the American economy, and whose study of technology's impact on employment is a landmark among economists and government planners,[4] arrived at a similar conclusion based on his definitive study. Comparing the production and employment profile of the United States in 1979 to that which he predicted would exist in the year 2000 given current plausible projections of new technology, Leontieff was able to characterize the shifting relationship between the rate of return expected of innovation and its ultimate effect on real wages.[5] He noted that, at current expected rates of return on capital, the expected technological shifts in production could possibly benefit both labour wage rates and profitability, but that at lower expectations of return on capital, the benefits to both wages and profits would be even more pronounced. Noting the lowered expectations for short-term returns on capital from Japanese investors, reflected in the traditionally low rates of interest in Japanese capital markets, he suggests that this might explain the higher propensity of the Japanese to shift to new technologies.

The Wealth of Nations was not a call for surrendering to the marketplace all aspects of social behaviour, but was instead a comprehensive social model that could be used to judge which social activities should be left to the marketplace and which are the proper domain of governments. The book was conceived in a milieu of widespread, partisan and ignorant government meddling into the economic affairs of firms and individuals, and was in general a polemic for expanding the domain of markets at the expense of government. The ultimate issue in deciding whether responsibility for managing a social function should fall to markets or the government was whether the greater public interest would be best served in either case, subject to fundamental and immutable tenets of justice. Since the point of the book was to elucidate the many ways that unbridled market behaviour contributed to social progress, notions that were counter-intuitive to many at the time – the book argued persuasively that in many ways the interests of the nation would be best served by expanding the domain of market behaviour. Unfortunately, for many today the only memorable aspect of the book is this polemical slant – so appropriate to its own times but frequently not to our own. Smith's legacy is that in many conservative polities his 'invisible hand' has become an integral part of the political mythology, and where this myth reigns it can be very difficult to confess that market forces are betraying the best interests of the public.

Environmental pollution is an example of an economic activity that carries with it a social impact that markets do not handle fairly and efficiently, and where government intervention is necessary. In the absence of prohibitions to the contrary, firms have demonstrated that they will release the physical by-products of their production processes into the environment to the detriment of the public. From a strictly economic standpoint, this is a perfectly rational thing to do: the cost of simply releasing an agent into the environment is infinitely less expensive than treating it before it is released or modifying production so that harmful agents are not produced. Before industrialism, in fact frequently until very recent times, the apparent impact of this activity was negligible, since the natural environment was capable of diffusing the relatively small amounts of released agents. With industrialism, however, pollution became more and more voluminous and the chemical characteristics of the released pollutants became more foreign to the natural environment, prompting public outrage and government action.

Environmental pollution is an example of the actions of private interests incurring a cost to the public that cannot be reimbursed efficiently through market forces, and where government intervention is necessary to assure that the real costs of releasing industrial by-products into the environment are borne by the consumers of the product. Like widespread environmental pollution, rampant and unbridled job displacement is not only repugnant, but in the long run counter-productive, because it allows private interests to adulterate a social resource for their own short-term gain.

Releasing de-skilled workers into the labour market in response to technological innovation can be analogous to environmental pollution. From the
firm's point of view, the action is perfectly rational, but it saddles the public
as well as the displaced individual with social costs that the firm is not likely
to bear in total, such as the cost of extended unemployment or underemployment, the ripple effects of the worker's reduced income in the local economy,
and the cost of retraining the worker for other skills. As with pollution, in
the past the social costs of technological displacement were negligible, or at
least easy for the firm to shirk, but with the industrialization of intelligence
the quantity of displaced labour resources will grow precipitously and the
social stakes will grow proportionately. Today, as technological advance and
international competitive pressures grow, so does the social strain from shifts
in production functions that can de-skill and displace labour.

The challenge to society that is obviously coming is made even more
pressing by the manner in which innovations in computer technology are
being spurred by national governments in order to enhance military and
economic competitiveness. The result is a pace of innovation far in excess
of what traditional market forces would have set, and of what has been more
than sufficient in the past to shake the social order violently. Technology has
in the past chased workers off farms to urban areas, and flushed them from
manual labour to intellectual labour. These displaced workers have always
been reabsorbed into the economy, assuming productive activity in other
burgeoning sectors that required new human skills. From our perspective
these past episodes may seem clean and precise, but the dim light of history
tends to obscure how tumultuous they really were. Though admittedly it has
always been difficult to imagine the new types of labour that would rescue
society from the technological displacement of the age, does anyone really
have any reassuring concept of what meaningful role in production hundreds
of millions of labourers can serve if the very pace and capacity of their thought
is obsolete?

9
Human Capital and the Wealth of Nations

On a bright, warm June afternoon in 1947, a general addressed the elite of learned American society, his figure framed by the colonial-revival portico of a Christian church named for the dead sons of Allied nations in the First World War. Harvard's first completely normal graduation exercises since the beginning of the Second World War were the occasion. As he spoke, he gazed out over a sea of two thousand white male faces, seated in tidy ranks and columns and uniformed in crisp black robes and square cardboard hats, neat packages eagerly awaiting their release to industry, government and academia.

Though the general had just received an honorary degree, he wore neither cap nor gown, an apparent gaffe that elicited sufficient comment from reporters to warrant an express exoneration for his dress from the university president. The nation would learn to be tolerant of college graduates informally dressed, for there would be a shortage of cap and gown for the next few years, as veterans swelled the ranks of colleges under the GI Bill.

General George C. Marshall wore a plain grey business suit and a blue tie that befitted his position as Harry Truman's Secretary of State. His ten-minute address was remarkably commonsensical for a speech that was literally to alter history. His focus was Europe, home of the audience's ancestors and the stage for an accelerating competition between the Western allies and an ambitious Soviet regime. The European theatre of the Second World War had been fought in the very cradle of industrialism between the most educated and technically skilled peoples in history. In addition to destroying substantial

171

portions of Europe's industrial base, Marshall pointed out, the complex web of socio-economic relations that characterized European civilization had been disrupted for a decade, and without an infusion of American capital the economies of Europe might well unravel. He proposed a bold programme for the United States to support financially Europe's recovery, in which the United States would not prescribe how development funds would be spent as long as the nations of Europe worked and planned as a group, demonstrating initiative and expertise in charting their own course to recovery. Marshall could not say that a primary goal of the plan was to thwart Soviet exploitation of the unsettled European societies – the Soviet Union and its European satellites were pointedly invited to participate – but his perceptive audience understood Marshall's agenda, interrupting him with applause as he pronounced, in veiled tones, the United States' resolve to oppose those 'who seek to perpetuate human misery in order to profit ... politically'.

Western Europe seized upon Marshall's proposal, arranging a Paris planning conference with a promptness that would spin the heads of Eurocrats today. Joseph Stalin, however, viewed the offer of funds to any decimated country that would participate in international planning as a veiled capitalist bribe, designed to lure battered Eastern European states away from Soviet Marxism. At Stalin's instruction, the Soviet delegate to the Paris conference feigned initial interest in the proposal while setting out to undermine the talks; the Western delegates made it plain that they would not allow Soviet obfuscation to interfere with their potential windfall and announced their intention to participate in the plan regardless of any other nation's choice in the matter; the Soviets forbade Eastern Europe's participation in the scheme. Within weeks Europe was divided along the now-familiar lines of whether or not it was participating in the Marshall Plan.

Western Europe's economies responded brilliantly to the programme: it was administered wisely, precipitating the postwar era of economic co-operation and robustness in the Western European community. Communist participation in the governments of France, Belgium, Italy and West Germany evaporated as those national economies recovered, and the funds served as a valuable enticement to anti-communist forces during the Greek civil war. The Soviets' rival economic programme for Eastern Europe, by contrast, could not escape the bullying and exploitative nature of its commandant, and Eastern Europe's economies descended into listlessness. For the remainder of the decade and into the next, a rapt audience of world nations watched as the opening act of an economic drama was played, in which a capitalist suitor and his Marxist rival vied for the loyalty of European nations. The generous and compassionate Americans had clearly upstaged their brutish and domineering rivals.

As the scene shifted away from the European theatre in the 1950s, America sought to reprise the role that had won it such acclaim. The emergence of the term 'Third World' signalled a new awareness in America of the nations outside Europe that were neither within the Western nor the Soviet sphere of influence, and of the potential in these nations to establish new economic bulwarks to contain communism. The United States eagerly extended offers of economic assistance – Western technology, Western technicians, and Western values – to the Third World, and the offers were just as eagerly accepted. A new partnership born of the cold war and buoyed by the example of the Marshall Plan strode confidently into the future.

But in trying to replicate the European miracle in the undeveloped expanse of the non-European world the United States underwent a bitter and befuddling experience. Direct capital investment in Third World countries seemed damned by fate: for most undeveloped countries it seemed that the harder they tried to employ foreign assistance wisely, the more dependent on foreign interests they became. Following the example of the Marshall Plan, development assistance to undeveloped countries was oriented towards industrialization and targeted for the urban centres, precipitating massive migrations from agricultural hinterlands to poor cities ill-prepared to receive the increased population and altogether incapable of providing work for them. As agricultural land was abandoned or landowners ejected tenant farmers in order to grow cash crops for foreign markets, nation after nation trod the demoralizing path from agricultural self-sufficiency to importing basic foodstuffs from more developed countries, a development that strained an already fragile balance of trade. Development subsidies were taxed by waste and corruption, and even when they bore fruit in gleaming production facilities the investments were frequently barren, frustrated by lack of supporting markets or infrastructure.

Strangely, even when capital investment did take hold, it seemed attuned to reinforce feudal social relations rather than lift the poor from poverty. Industrial development, the same agent that had more evenly distributed income across the population of Western Europe, frequently made the distribution of income even more extreme in the Third World. There were nagging difficulties in establishing a middle class where none had existed before: Third World professionals (many of whom were educated abroad at public expense) were loath to labour in frustration at home and migrated to countries where their skills were more handsomely compensated, while small-scale entrepreneurs were hamstrung by a dearth in domestic demand. The established power elites – landowners, military leaders and religious figures – possessed the traditional offices of authority and were predominantly the members of society who were highly educated, and so were in a position to bend economic assistance to perpetuate their authority, reinforcing class divisions and breeding contempt for Western ways among the lower classes.

In many cases, foreign assistance to the Third World was less than merely inadequate, it was disastrous. The economic fortunes of many of the poorest countries in the world – measured by percentage of world gross national product, by exports and by comparison to US per capita income – actually worsened in the years between 1955 and 1980.[1] The United States found itself with a rowdy, indignant list of client states. Characteristically, the ruling classes were frequently quite content with the relationship with America, but among the masses who had experienced hunger and a jarring shift from traditional to Western market society, resentment was often intense. New theoretical models surfaced positing that any relationship between technologically advanced capitalist countries and undeveloped countries was necessarily exploitative. Terms such as 'neo-colonialism', 'unequal exchange' and 'imperialist exploitation' became current, indicating a new sympathy in the Third World for Marxist ideology. The United States sensed that it was suffering in the propaganda war. The American people began to perceive the Third World as fickle, incompetent and ungrateful; foreign aid became increasingly controversial in domestic politics; and on many fronts US foreign assistance retreated. The Marshall Plan technique, so effective a tool for spurring industrial development and dampening the appeal of Marxism in Western Europe, had brought misery to millions in the Third World and fanned the flames of Marxism in developing nations.

If there was a lesson for the Western world to derive from the Marshall Plan and the Third World fiascos that followed in its wake, it was that human skills and knowledge play a fundamental role in the health of national economies. Operating a factory without the proper inventory of human skills is no more productive than operating it without power, or raw materials, or any other necessary factor of production; inserting an engineer into a society that cannot fully utilize his expertise is no more productive than handing a slide rule to a baby. Like an undeveloped society, the Europe that received funds from the United States had a deficient physical capital base, but in contrast to undeveloped societies possessed an intact, advanced base of skills and learning that were appropriate to advanced industrial society. What Europe possessed that the Third World lacked was a wealth of human capital. Human capital, strictly defined, is the productive potential that can be developed in people, encompassing the abstract knowledge, skills and physical health of a population. Like physical capital, human capital is accumulated through investment that in some way requires the postponement of immediate utility or pleasure in anticipation of an enhanced productive capacity in the future. The worker who learns how to use a new tool, the athlete who labours at lifting weights, the graduate student who researches a thesis, and the child who endures the consumption of manifestly odious vegetables are each making human capital investments in anticipation of a future return. But unlike physical capital, the human variety of capital cannot exist independent of its human vessel, so that anyone who desires to employ the human animal for its skills must reimburse the human spirit for its disutility. Human capital accumulation in market economies, then, is unique in that it implies a contract, present or anticipated, between the person accumulating the capital and the enterprise that will employ it.

Enterprise employs human capital as a factor of production and, as with any factor, if the economy finds it in types and amounts appropriate to the demands of its industries, society will be efficient and productive. As the scale and complexity of modern industrial economies increase, their requirements for inputs become more pressing and precise, and the supply of appropriate human capital to enterprise – like the supply of any critical input – becomes an ever-increasing social imperative.

America and Europe share a legacy in the manner in which human capital has been developed for social needs, a legacy that was shaped by historical circumstances and religious attitudes and has in turn shaped our current institutions and beliefs. In preindustrial Europe, training in recondite skills, along with the actual production that accompanied these skills, fell to the medieval craft guilds. Reaching their height of influence from the twelfth to the fifteenth centuries, the craft guilds were jealous repositories of craft techniques. Guild members promoted an aura of mystique about their work in order to embellish the apparent impenetrability of their skills and to enhance the monopoly they held over a particular craft, as evidenced by the common English term of 'mystery' for craft guilds. The guild's policy was typically administered by a small group of ministers and perhaps a council of advisers, with the actual performance of the work being performed by masters, each of whom were allowed a restricted number of journeymen and apprentices. Master status was conferred upon journeymen who exhibited sufficient skill (as evidenced in their 'masterpiece') and social standing, so that technology was developed and transmitted exclusively within the guild.

The guilds that controlled the most difficult skills or those that were most critical to the local economy came to possess considerable political power, and with time the social and political standing of the guilds became rigidly hierarchical. Which crafts fell within the purview of which guild was serious politics and imprecise science. The need to specialize and the urge to monopolize led to some interesting configurations: there were reported to be several dozen specialized metalworking guilds in Nuremberg, where metal-lurgy was an established art, while painters and surgeons' apothecaries found themselves in the same guild in Florence, where political pragmatism was the established art. Petty boundary disputes were common and rancorous, particularly between guilds of related trades.

The guilds' political power in the urban areas grew to the point where by the fifteenth century many European cities were completely under their direct jurisdiction. The trajectory of their rise brought them into a

175

collision course with the merchant class, who had also risen propitiously in status with the commercial boom in Europe. Wealthy, entrepreneurial and unselfconsciously rational, the merchants' sympathies and ambitions were patrician, and their economic interests ran completely contrary to the monopolistic and cloistered craftsmen. Military skirmishes erupted between guild and merchant groups throughout Europe, but were inconclusive.

What warfare could not decide was resolved in a more oblique manner by economic reorganization. Though the craft masters controlled aspects, sometimes broad aspects, of production, finished goods required the sequential processing of many craft guilds who may or may not have been on speaking terms with each other. The merchants were in a unique position merely to spirit intermediate goods between crafts, playing rival guilds against each other and leveraging the powerful urban guilds against the more docile rural cottage workers. Initially, the new arrangement seemed to represent little change from the established pattern, since the craft masters were merely dealing with intermediaries rather than assuming entrepreneurial chores themselves, but in fact a new manner of production had arisen: the *Verlagssystem* or 'putting out' system, in which a merchant *Verleger* controlled production by moving incomplete goods between guild components until the productive process was complete. With time, the elite craft guilds, so obstinate in political and military confrontations, were lulled by the merchant *Verlegers* into economic subordination. The *Verlagssystem* was the historical bridge between medieval craft production and modern industrial capitalism in Europe, and the circumstances surrounding its formulation still colour Western assumptions regarding the development of human capital for industry. The *Verleger* – who was ridiculously under-capitalized by today's standards – operated in an environment in which human labour and skills had seemingly always been abundant, but in which the demand for final products was maddeningly inconsistent due to the fledgling nature of market-oriented society. The *Verlagssystem* allowed the *Verleger* access to human capital when the demand for goods was strong without committing him to employ it when demand was slack. The *Verleger* was not responsible for developing the human capital he employed, and would only pay for it when he needed it. That attitude is still apparent in Western capitalism today.

While European crafts were being subordinated to protocapitalists, European culture began philosophically to embrace individualism, to emphasize the rights and responsibilities of the individual in society. Philosophical speculation on all matters was dominated by the Christian church, which was itself a radical off-shoot of Judaism that had arrived in Europe after being filtered through the rigorous rationalism of Greek philosophy. Christianity drew from Judaism many of its basic assumptions about the individual, God and society, and transmitted them to contemporary Western culture.

The Jewish cosmology is so familiar to Westerners and so ingrained in Western thought that it is instructive to re-examine the incipient break it represented relative to other religions. Beyond the central Jewish innovation of monotheism was its peculiar rendering of God as an individual, a supreme being of indisputable free will and power, a god of action. The Jewish Yahweh revealed his will to mankind by actively intervening in the affairs of his chosen people. Though fundamentally a loving and protective god, Yahweh's actions showed a remarkable range of activities: God could teach, intervene in battles, exact angry retribution, even enter into contracts. God was the model for man, who had been shaped in God's image, and under Judaism man's actions assumed sweeping significance. Man was empowered to affect God, to offend him or please him by his words and deeds. The Jewish ideal for a person was to do good works: Judaism was a singularly action-oriented religion. Christianity, though it differed in details, retained the fundamental Jewish belief that an individual's actions were the key to his or her salvation.

The opportunity to do righteous works carried with it the option to sin, so that discrimination between good and evil acts was a central issue in Judaism. God's direct assessment of the actions of men was historically rare, so that the Jew was in need of a rational mechanism for guiding his day-to-day dealings with God and other people. That mechanism was thoughtful reflection on and obedience to the Law as revealed in the holy books of the Torah. The Law allowed individuals to exhibit a degree of self-interest, but expected them to confine their selfish activities to what was consistent with living in harmony with God and society. Implicit in this injunction was that the person who abided by the Law and was righteous in other respects was allowed some latitude to pursue selfish interests, which might include material possessions.

The Jewish evaluation of the material world that was passed down to Christianity differed fundamentally from other religions, particularly those of the East. The material world was far from base or illusion: it was the product of God's conscious labour, created to suit His purposes, and had been explicitly characterized by Him as good. If man's ultimate salvation was gained through his labours on earth, it was not such a huge leap to suggest that material possessions were a temporal blessing gained through one's labour. By medieval times, Thomas Aquinas, the Catholic academic, would write of a man's right to enjoy the fruits of his labour and would even naively explore the moral foundations of setting wages, a cast of mind that foreshadowed concepts of economic science. By the early seventeenth century, the practice would become common for working men and women to gather by trade in various locations in towns to offer their labour to employers, prompting Thomas Hobbes to note that '[a] man's labour is a commodity exchangeable for benefit as well as any other thing'.[2] Adam Smith was able to combine a deistic view of individual industry as the process that propels God's plan for man on earth, and at the turn of the present century,

Max Weber would provocatively pronounce that the spirit of capitalism had arisen as a result of the Protestant 'work ethic'.

With the advent of industrialism, European society had come to possess through its religious legacy a cultural emphasis on the rights and codified social responsibility of the individual along with a moral acceptance of private appropriation of material possessions through labour. On a parallel track, through the institution of the *Verlagssystem*, European industry had come to expect that it could employ human skills whenever they were required, and that the development of these skills would naturally occur outside of the firm. These features, in the presence of a heightened demand and capacity for production, spawned the concept that there was a market for labour, in many ways similar to the established markets for other commodities.

As industrial capitalism took hold in Europe in the eighteenth and nineteenth centuries, production came to occur within facilities and processes that were increasingly controlled by the centralized management of the firm. In the United States and much of the Western world, the system that came to be was that firms would buy only the labour and skills they needed in the cultural milieu of a 'free' labour market, relying on exogenous forces to provide most of the human capital they would eventually need. Western capitalism saw the labour pool as being composed of millions of spiritual atoms, each of whom entrepreneurially purveys its skills to capitalist enterprise. A social contract developed that called for the capitalist firm to employ the skills of workers at their mutual pleasure: the firm was expected to employ only the amounts and types of human capital that conformed to its immediate needs, and the worker was expected to sell his skills without prejudice to the highest bidder. It is the natural course of things under this arrangement that firms immediately released surplus labour to the labour pool with the factor substitution that came of process innovation, just as it was the responsibility of the individual to cultivate the most marketable skills possible and to develop human capital of a more marketable type when former skills became obsolete. Western industrial capitalism still demands what the *Verlagssystem* demanded: that labour and human capital be provided by institutions external to the productive enterprise, and be available and expendable in conformance with the productive enterprise's needs. In the United States and Britain today, labour as a factor of production is referred to by economists as a 'variable input' (as opposed to 'fixed inputs' such as machinery and equipment) because it can so expediently be drawn from or released into the labour market.

In this venue, where skilled labour is perceived to be abundant and readily available, where straightforward issues of self-interest are expected to dominate indeterminate considerations of loyalty between worker and employer, it is irrational for firms to invest in human capital development beyond the most rudimentary level necessary to bend the employee's interchangeable skills to the particular demands and idiosyncrasies of the organization. It is irrational for a firm to invest in capital it cannot subsequently control, to create or enhance an economic entity that is rationally expected to offer only the slightest loyalty to its benefactor. The motivational force behind human capital development lies with the worker, the one who will peddle skills on the market, rather than the buyer, who passively rents what is readily available.[3]

The individual is expected to conduct or to have previously undergone a personal human capital investment programme, directed, as with any investment programme, by the desire for the greatest ultimate gain that can be obtained by postponing immediate satisfaction in preference for capital investment. For the young, investing time, effort and money in one's personal skills is an overbearing cultural imperative. To a dyed-in-the-wool neoclassicist, a free-market arena for prospective workers selecting their career path according to what appears to be most ultimately rewarding, and independently undergoing a period of personal capital-skill development has the innate elegant self-regulation and objective allocation of resources inherent in the free-market approach for developing any capital good. According to neoclassical political economy, the pecuniary reward associated with any area of skill development accurately expresses society's need for skills in that discipline and sufficiently encourages individuals to modify their human capital programmes in response. In theory, it is precisely the skills most difficult to master and in shortest supply that command the highest wages and attract the most candidates.

While neoclassical economists were developing their view of the presumed societal benefits of a free labour market, Karl Marx was railing at the suggestion that such a system actually improves the human capital resources available to society. Their divergent conclusions sprang from divergent assumptions. Classical economists supposed that the presence of wealth in society revealed the diligence, shrewd planning and creativity of generations past; Marx said wealth was material evidence of past criminality. Classical economists viewed private property as just reward for man's labour and cleverness; Marx viewed it as a social licence for ruinous individualism. Classical economists saw the free labour market as a fertile field in which individuals could develop their skills to best suit society's needs; Marx saw it as a barren repository for an unwanted, inappropriately skilled army of labourers, used by the system of production only to bid down the wages of those with jobs.

Marx's description of the mechanics of introducing technology to industry was not fundamentally different from that proposed by neoclassical economists, nor from the prevailing wisdom today, but because his moral perspective diverged so radically from the prevailing view he continually saw evil where others saw benevolence. He saw technology as aiming to replace the skills of workers, to rearrange the means of production to

179

the benefit of the capitalist. As labour is displaced, it is released to what he termed the 'industrial reserve army' – we would say 'the ranks of the unemployed' – to join with the other dross of the industrial system whose skills are irrelevant to the current means of production. The introduction of technology presumably produces some surplus revenues to the enterprise, at least until competition drives down profits to the market rate, but the capitalist need not share the temporary windfall with the remaining workers. The 'free' labour market assures that workers constantly bid against the unemployed for their livelihood, so that even if workers' wages inch up with rampant industrialism, the distribution of income – Marx called it the 'relative immiseration of the proletariat' – would become even more skewed in favour of the rich. To Marx, the industrial reserve army was more than an unfortunate consequence of capitalism, it was a fundamental component of the capitalist system. To this day, Marxist critique continues to hammer away at the capitalist cosmology whenever it shirks responsibility for the unemployed.

What Marxist criticism sees acutely is that, just as the labour market responds to the demands of a society's production functions, so does a society's production respond to the human capital resources available to it. If there is a surplus of unskilled workers and a shortage of skilled technicians, society will assume the profile of an undeveloped country, with a mass of low-wage employees and an elite of wealthy owners and managers. Modifying the production of such a society along an uneven front by introducing technology out of step with the society's native human capital resources may result in the lifting of the *average* income of society while lowering the *median* income: the net societal product increases, but the benefits are disproportionately allocated to the wealthy. This is the classic description of a less-developed society being exploited by a technologically more advanced country, and the trap the Third World nations fell into in their dealings with the United States after being attracted by the success of the Marshall Plan, a trap whose signature is lackadaisical growth in productivity accompanied by an increasing disparity in the distribution of income.

It is a trap that America and Europe naively avoided in their own initial stages of industrial development, because industrial capitalism was born in Europe in the total absence of more advanced economies. Human capital had the opportunity to develop indigenously alongside technological dis-covery, so that it accumulated in small increments over a broad set of individuals over a long time. This indigenous growth in the absence of potential foreign exploitation may have contributed to the economic orthodoxy in England and America that the best results come from the least intervention, and may even have made the technological exploitation of the Third World more a crime of ignorance than of malice. In any event, until very recent times Europe and America had always enjoyed the luxury of discovering industrial capitalism rather than the trauma of being discovered by it.

When Commodore Perry sailed into Yokohama harbour in his fleet of black ships in 1854, he was challenging a society that possessed little more than a medieval state of technology. Perry had come to demand at gunpoint that the Japanese open their country to trade. The traditionally isolated island nation had witnessed the callous economic subordination of China and Southeast Asia by Western mercantile interests and was in no mood to allow Western influence into their country, but the persuasiveness of America's weaponry was irresistible. The concessions Perry extracted along with the prescient realization by the Japanese that cultural survival required mastering Western technology precipitated a political crisis in Japan, the Meiji Restoration. Superficially, the Meiji Restoration was an expulsion of the Tokugawa shogunate and the restoration of the emperor's power, but more significantly the restoration began an astounding self-introduction of industrial capitalism to a feudal society, a programme that relied upon a societal commitment to the systematic cultivation of human capital.

The intuitive recognition of the problem the Japanese faced and their triumphant response to it would not have been possible if they had shared the Judaeo-Christian tenets of individualism that characterized the Americans who had precipitated the crisis. The social ethic that has guided Japan since the seventh century emphasizes that the individual, rather than being free to pursue individualistic goals, should renounce selfish impulses in order to serve society, and that government, rather than passively prescribing the rules of fair play, should actively steer society towards greater good. Like Europe's, Japan's ideal of the individual in society had been born in an ancient and foreign country and modified to conform to contemporary social needs, but unlike those righteous Judaeo-Christian prophets and martyrs who stood alone before God and man in Palestine, inspiration for the Japanese social ethic came from the life of one frustrated, idealistic bureaucrat who had spent much of his life roaming northern China looking for a job.

Kong Qiu, whom Westerners know as Confucius, lived in China in the sixth century BC during a time of unusual turmoil, when society was brutally dominated by an overlord class that was devoid of social conscience. Capricious warfare between overlords, formerly a polite patrician sport involving a universally accepted code of honourable conduct, had disintegrated into an abominable and unmanageable slaughter as the rules of war were ignored. China tasted total war: prisoners and innocents were murdered in their thousands by occupying armies, in one incident more than 100,000 non-combatants were said to have been slain. Like war, oppressive taxation of the masses was a hereditary right of the overlords, who felt no duty to reciprocate their subjects' fealty.

181

Confucius was profoundly troubled by the inequity of the social contract. He saw unfettered, selfish individualism as a disease that was crippling the social order, and formulated a conservative philosophy that called for a return to traditional social relations, a presumed former state when individuals recognized the role they played in society and revered their responsibility to the group. Borrowing on the Chinese cultural imperative for respect for the family, Confucius came to regard mankind as a single family, the state as a co-operative enterprise between governors and governed. The privilege to govern, as with the privilege to serve society in any capacity, must be trusted only to individuals fit for the task, and for an individual to be fit to govern, he must possess both ability and virtue. Confucius would not deny the hereditary rights of ruling clans, but he did insist that they confide all administration to career ministers, and that these ministers be selected on the basis of their demonstrated ability and virtue.

Confucius believed that ability and virtue could only be developed through education, and so placed singular emphasis on the importance of education to society. His revolutionary belief was that the entire citizenry should undergo a common, basic education in order to have a truly enlightened and co-operative society. (This was a belief that was not to be generally accepted in the West for more than twenty centuries, when the demands of the Industrial Revolution forced the issue on to the public agenda.) Not only was a common education necessary to promote shared values and social cohesion, but it was critical to identifying the most innately talented individuals, who could then be comprehensively educated so that they could serve the public as bureaucrats. If Confucius agreed with later neoclassical economists that the best and the brightest will emerge from society if given an equal chance, he was certainly less confident that a society guided by the selfish interests of individuals would afford such an unbiased chance.

As a result of the Confucian legacy it adopted from China, Japan at the time of the Opening was highly literate and possessed a dedicated and forceful bureaucracy. Under Meiji rule, the government became more centralized, and dedicated itself to leading Japan into industrialism while avoiding economic exploitation. The Meiji reformers stirred the country to embrace *wakon yohsai*, 'Japanese spirit, Western technology', a call to preserve traditional values and find new expression for them in a new economic order. The reformers restricted the movements of foreigners as best they could considering their weak position and blunted foreign attempts to buy land or domestic capital stocks. The government established and operated model mills, shipyards and factories for producing tools and intermediate capital goods to serve as examples for entrepreneurs to emulate, and founded a national university in Tokyo to produce the learned leaders the new society would need. By the 1870s, the outline of a new type of capitalism had emerged in Japan, one in which the government felt a pressing responsibility to guide the nation into modernity.

The central challenge the Japanese government faced in modernizing the economy was a severe shortage of skilled labour. As a result of the shock from the Opening, the government perceived an urgent need to cultivate systematically the human resources of the nation. Unlike the Western experience of industrial capitalism in the presence of an abundance of indigenous skills, Japan's experience would be marked by a chronic shortage of skilled labour, resulting in a reverence for human capital that persists to this day in Japanese institutions.

The manner in which craft guilds were assimilated into industry in modern Japan demonstrates how an initial poverty of human capital contributed to the development of a uniquely Japanese version of industrial capitalism. Craft guilds held a similar social importance in pre-capitalist Japan as they did in Europe, but experienced a very different assimilation into the capitalist organization. While craft guilds in Europe were largely assimilated into proto-capitalist enterprise by the end of the Renaissance, in Japan they survived and maintained important social leverage right up to the nineteenth century, when the early Meiji reformers abolished them. As is frequently the case when edict attempts to contravene economics, the groups merely re-emerged as tightly knit groups of itinerant skilled labourers, called *kokata*, bound in the Confucian ethos to the paternal fealty of their patrons, or *oyakata*. When the government opened its model enterprises in the 1870s, the *oyakata* were retained to provide labour gangs to run them. The *oyakata* not only brought skilled labour to bear on industrial production, he was also responsible for managing the work, and so the *oyakata* began to master technical skills in a large-scale industrial setting. When many of the government plants were privatized in the late nineteenth century, the new owners inherited the *oyakata* and their manner of industrial management. Because of Japan's late introduction to capitalist production, craft guilds in essence survived into the modern era, actually directing the technology of large-scale industry for a time.

By the beginning of the twentieth century, the *oyakata* teams were central to Japanese industrial production, since they rigidly controlled the skilled labour that was in such chronic shortage in the newly industrialized country. As Japanese industry expanded rapidly with the Sino-Japanese war, the Russo-Japanese war and the First World War, a curious industrial organization arose: with the rising wages, the *oyakata* groups were becoming highly mobile, moving from factory to factory, offering their precious services to the highest bidder. This industrial organization that predated contemporary Japanese capitalism stood in curious contrast to the *Verlagssystem* that predated European capitalism: in Europe the proto-capitalists, sensing their economic power, moved goods between stationary and subordinate skilled labour; while in Japan it was skilled labour who sensed their economic leverage and transported their skills freely between fixed and subordinate proto-factories.

A few of the family-owned businesses that inherited the pilot industrial plants from the days of the Meiji reformers expanded rapidly with the wars, so that by the 1920s the Japanese economy was dominated by a handful of gargantuan industrial conglomerates, known as *zaibatsu*, or 'the wealthy clique'. The *zaibatsu* were administered by the sophisticated university and secondary school graduates streaming out of the national schools, who saw the *oyakata* as impeding the continued advance of Japanese industry. Rising wages and high turnover were dulling Japanese competitiveness, and the *oyakata*'s command of technical skills could not keep pace with the scientific capitalism of the West. The new managerial elite were anxious to control and rationalize the operations of the *zaibatsu*, so that Frederick Taylor's books on scientific management – considered by now inhuman and passé in America – became the bible of Japanese industry. The *zaibatsu* undertook to establish internal employment systems to stabilize the skilled workforce and to develop systematically the human capital resources that were so scarce. Though the *oyakata* form of production would persist in some industries through the Second World War, the *zaibatsu* approach was obviously ascendent.

In the period between the wars, the government guided the *zaibatsu* in their attempts to develop human capital resources internally, and encouraged the *zaibatsu* to retain these resources by instituting a lifetime commitment to employ the workers whom the firm had trained. The firms developed large personnel administration bureaucracies and placed great emphasis on selecting recruits and training workers, while assuring that the overall economic welfare of their employees was secure. Those who were accepted into this cradle-to-grave system of employment were known as *shain*, or lifetime members of the firm. White-collar workers were initially the prime candidates as *shain*, but as the Second World War approached and military involvement by the *zaibatsu* increased, more blue-collar workers were accepted as *shain*, leading to a reduced distinction between white-collar and blue-collar workers that characterizes Japanese industry today.

Japan's defeat in the Second World War rudely interrupted its precipitous climb from economic backwater to industrial power. The nation was shocked and spiritually shattered by defeat and the unprecedented humiliation of foreign occupation. It has been estimated that 25 per cent of its physical capital base had been destroyed, and almost half of its land empire had been seized. Disillusioned veterans and overseas nationals poured in, swelling the population by an estimated 8 per cent.[4] The economy was teetering, and the prospect of mass starvation was very real.

In the midst of what was probably Japan's darkest hour, the government bureaucracy resolutely set out to assume again its traditional role of leading its people back to industrial prosperity. Even before the war ended, some bureaucrats had outlined a strategy for a new industrial order, the development of physical and human capital-intensive, high-technology industry that would cater to world markets. The Ministry of International Trade and Industry and the Ministry of Finance were revived, and guided private industry along an economic plan by sponsoring research, underwriting capital investment, and licensing foreign technology for dissection and incorporation. The educational system spewed forth a new disciplined generation of engineers, technocrats and skilled workers once again to augment the skill resources of the nation. Large-scale industry instituted a new programme of human resource management, referred to by the Japanese as 'knowledge intensification'.

Western observers who were not mindful of Japan's original victory over industrialism thought they were witnessing an unprecedented economic miracle. Gross national product per capita increased an astounding 16.3 per cent per year over a twenty-five year period from 1952 to 1978 – more than three times that in the United States – and today is the highest in the world.[5] By 1968, Japan had already climbed from a defeated wreck to the third most productive nation in the world. Through it all, the Japanese have not strayed from their dedication to knowledge intensification in their citizenry, a national priority exhibited in schools, government and industry.

No Japanese institution exhibits this priority as obviously as the public school system. Viewed from a Western perspective, the Japanese educational system seems bizarrely mechanical and inhuman. In truth, it is an unsympathetic, industrialized approach to the development of human capital, a modern machine of the traditional Confucian social ethic that sorts the population by innate ability and shunts individuals toward the social role they are assigned. Entering public school to a Japanese child signals the beginning of an educational rat race, a kindergarten-to-college competition that results in prestigious job positions for the winners and lower social status for the losers.

But to focus on its competitiveness is to ignore the real strength of public education in Japan. The Japanese public school system is geared towards and is remarkably competent at educating the average student, providing Japanese society with citizens who have a uniformly high intellectual competence. Most four- and five-year-olds have already commenced formal schooling in public or private kindergartens, and older children attend school 240 days per year, compared to 180 days per year in the United States. Japan's best student scores on proficiency examinations are similar to those in other industrialized countries, but their average scores and the minimum standards for education are consistently higher.

The door to ultimate social status hinges on acceptance into one of the prestigious national universities, whose graduates are shunted towards employment in a specific field, and likely to enter the Japanese system of life-long employment. (Private universities carry little status with employers, largely precluding the alternative educational paths to social prestige that are available to the wealthy in the West.) To be accepted into a national university, a candidate must excel in his entrance exams, the taking of which is a necessary and traumatizing passage into adulthood for both student and family. Scores teenagers receive will indelibly mark their lives, but the tests are rigidly, objectively fair, so that, while a young man (though not a young woman) can stake out a road to the executive suite with an exemplary college career, he generally cannot be born to it. The consistent result of Japanese education is an intellectual meritocracy, albeit a meritocracy that seeks to reward a cultural ideal of competence and co-operativeness over originality. Paradoxically, the curriculum in the national universities is not particularly challenging: the role of the educational system is to select and screen candidates for industry possessed with stamina and discipline, not to develop individualistic intellects.

True to the Confucian ideal, the most socially prestigious employment to which a university graduate can aspire is with one of the prominent government ministries, which actively monitor and steer all aspects of Japanese society: business and labour, education, transportation, agriculture. Remuneration to ministry officials is low compared to private enterprise, but the respect one commands as a bureaucrat is a powerful inducement to the best and the brightest young candidates.

The most powerful ministries, the Ministry of Finance and the Ministry of International Trade and Industry (MITI), directly participate in industry not only in steering industry-wide policy, but by directly subsidizing key areas of research and development. Many Americans harbour a latent resentment of the Japanese industrial system, a resentment that certainly stems partly from Japanese competitive success in American markets, and is heightened by a neoclassical contempt for industry directed by government. If the disdain of Americans for government direction of enterprise was originally born of the conviction that the practice was counter-productive, it has hardly been mollified when faced with the empirical evidence of its effectiveness. In any event, it is a myth to view Japanese government involvement in industry as larger than American. Government spending as a percentage of GNP in Japan is currently only two-thirds that in the United States and about half that in European industrialized countries. Japanese government expenditures for research and development are only half those in the United States.[6] The difference between Japanese and American government subsidy is that the Japanese gear subsidies toward industrial applications likely to enhance the productivity of the Japanese workforce, while American subsidies are more oriented to military applications, basic science and high-visibility arenas such as manned space exploration, which incidentally benefit the economy but whose ultimate rationale must rest on non-economic goals.

When MITI provides funds to industry, the decision is explicitly based on the human capital rewards to be expected in encouraging industrial development in that sector. Industries are continually ranked by potential social benefit – star industries are actively promoted while undesirable industries are allowed to atrophy and emigrate. Whether an industry is to be spurred or neglected is largely based on the ministry's computation of the marginal product of labour to be expected from that industry. The government steers society towards sectors where human capital is most highly prized as a factor of production and neglects sectors where human labour is most routine. Since the Second World War, a familiar list of industries has been targeted, from steel production to shipbuilding to automobiles to consumer electronics to computers to biotechnology to materials science, and the more mature industries on the list are already starting to emigrate to nations such as Korea and Taiwan. Individual firms make similar assessments in negotiating foreign joint ventures, where almost unfailingly the work performed by the Japanese represent the intellectually more demanding tasks: the engine and chassis in automobiles or the electronic components and advanced materials in consumer items.

After a career with the ministries, the second most prestigious career to which a college student may aspire is employment with one of Japan's large corporations. This is the destination of the majority of graduates from the national universities. These graduates enjoy excellent prospects to become *shain*. The vaunted lifetime employment contract applies to only about 15 per cent of the work force, but significantly, the system is employed most often by companies on the leading edge of technology, those firms with the greatest and most sophisticated demand for human capital, where mobility in the labour force would be most debilitating.

The Japanese firm's predilection to assume responsibility for developing its own human capital, and its perceived self-interest in encouraging its immobility, has led to what Western observers may see as idiosyncrasies. Advancement within the firm is painfully slow and based on seniority and devotion rather than brilliance: it is quite impossible for a young man to leap-frog his seniors based on his talents and political know-how. There is a pronounced prejudice for firm-specific human capital, those skills and knowledge accumulated since joining the firm, over skills and knowledge imported from outside the firm. Firms do not expect college graduates to animate them with the latest techniques – the latest techniques are expected to have been developed in the firm – but instead are expected to demonstrate the loyalty, humility and discipline that came with the arduous study that got them into college in the first place. The ideal in Japanese industry is unity of purpose and consensus, which are strengthened by the firm's inward focus. An emphasis on group decisions, exemplified by quality control circles, contributes to the Japanese propensity for process innovations, as participants in production are encouraged to examine and discuss methods for streamlining the productive process. Devotion to the group and to the productive process is rewarded. The 'hot-shot' might get a desk by the window in both America and Japan, but in America the move represents a reward, a cultural signal assigning prestige to the meritorious individual, while in Japan the move may well be punishment that acknowledges the individual's non-participation with his comrades.

The Japanese flair for process innovation has quite predictably resulted in a vast number of robots in Japanese industry. There are more industrial robots in use in Japan today than in all the other industrialized democracies combined (even allowing for some excessive hyperbole in the Japanese government's definition of what constitutes a robot) and Japanese-produced industrial robots have become the technical standard for the rest of the world. The machines displace Japanese workers just as they would elsewhere, but in comparison with American unions Japanese unions have graciously welcomed automation. This is largely due to the differences in the social contract between business and labour in the two countries. In the United States, workers hire out their *skills*, which are largely expected to be developed outside the workplace, and both worker and employer are generally expected to get the best deal for what they have to offer. In Japan, workers offer *themselves* to the company, and both the worker and employer expect the company to cultivate the worker's skills to suit the company's needs, while the worker subordinates his selfish desires to the needs of the company. The Japanese worker displaced by labour-saving machinery is prone to view his job security as being enhanced by the innovation, since the increase in efficiency gives his company a competitive advantage and his company has an unwritten obligation to find something else for him to do. An American worker in the same situation senses that the skill he is peddling has been devalued and that his employer is generally responsible only to his own best interests, and quite sensibly he sees technology as a threat. While American firms park their displaced workers in the ranks of the unemployed, leaving them to their own efforts to rehabilitate their skills, Japanese firms reinvest in excess workers to their own eventual benefit, and if a declining industry cannot afford the investment, the government stimulates expanding sectors to take up the slack.

The competition between the United States and the Soviet Union has continued unabated in the four decades since the Marshall Plan was first enunciated, and today the Americans and the Soviets continue their debilitating military posturing in a world where warfare between them – as warfare was in the time of Confucius – is too horrendous to be practical. The two nations have consistently accounted for 60 per cent of annual world military expenditures for the past twenty years.[7] In the United States, frenzied military research and development absorbs increasing amounts of America's technical resources. From 1981 to 1986 military spending for research and development rose from a half to more than two-thirds of the total federal expenditure for research and development, so that direct military R & D grew from one-quarter to one-third the total research funds spent in the country.[8] During a similar period, real federal expenditures on non-military research fell at an average annual rate of 5.5 per cent per year.[9] Armaments dominate the manufacturing exports of both countries, so that each is becoming industrially irrelevant in non-military world markets.

But while the United States was striving diligently against military encroachment by the Soviets, the economic battle was lost to the Japanese. America's domestic markets are being flooded by less expensive, higher quality products from abroad, and for the first time since their own colonial revolution Americans are experiencing the burden of economic association with a technologically more advanced country.

In a twisted perspective, many in the United States see the competition with the Japanese as taking place exclusively on the frontiers of science and technique and ignore the qualitative investment the Japanese have cultivated across the entire range of their human capital resources. Americans should know from their bitter experience with Third World economies that investment in advanced technology alone can be disastrous in the absence of a rich and balanced human capital base. Calls in advanced nations to fund exotic industries while ignoring increasing structural deficiencies are folly at best, selfish and exploitative at worst.

As the United States is economically surpassed by Japan, its income and wealth profile is assuming the shape of an undeveloped country, where class distinctions are profound, distribution of income and wealth is extreme, and public debt is billowing. Since 1970, a greater percentage of Americans are wealthy, a greater percentage are poor, and a smaller percentage are neither wealthy nor poor.[10] There has been a surge in the concentration of wealth in the United States since 1960, and extreme wealth is now concentrated in fewer households in the United States than at any time since the Great Depression.

The tragedy of America's economic torpor is sealed by the unravelling of the single most important component to its future human capital resources: primary public education. State schools are ineffectual and physically dangerous to an extent Americans would never have imagined only a generation ago. Drug use, occasioned by the predominant ethic of immediate, individualistic gratification coupled with an alienation of children from busy adults, leads to increasing violent criminal behaviour among students. Teaching in state schools has become a frustrating, financially unrewarding and hazardous profession, so that the percentage of young people intending to enter

189

the field has dropped by one-third in little more than a decade.[12] Job dissatisfaction among teachers in the United States is at an all-time high and rises annually, and ominously the most dissatisfaction is voiced by the most highly qualified of the remaining teachers. The most experienced teachers also have the highest rate of attrition, and the younger teachers who are entering the profession are statistically less qualified academically than those they are replacing.[13] The wealthy, of course, want no part in state schools, precipitating a flight to private schools that accelerates social stratification.

A stratified society in a technologically advanced country indicates an unwise pattern of human capital investment and spells trouble for both the nation and its citizens. For a national economy to be robust and competitive in foreign markets, it must have a balanced, high-quality human capital base from which to draw skills and intelligence, not only so that skills will be present as they are demanded by industry, but more importantly so that workers have a broad base of skills and knowledge to draw upon as job requirements shift. From the individual's standpoint, an uneven opportunity to accumulate human capital deprives citizens of two critical capacities: the economic leverage one possesses when one acquires human capital, and the general capacity to understand and adapt to changing economic imperatives. When advanced training is held and maintained by a narrow segment of the population or when opportunities are denied other groups, the nation is arbitrarily deprived of the potential richness of human capacity available to it. A sense of despair in the poor and middle classes, and a lack of consensus between classes on national goals, would be expected.

Today, capitalism sees a new opportunity for circumventing the monopoly that human workers have always enjoyed over the skills enterprise requires, and it is an opportunity that offers a new threat to any society that ignores its responsibilities to cultivate a balanced human capital base in its population. Artificial intelligence has as its explicit goal the disassociation of judgement from humans, to equip machinery to perform sophisticated intellectual tasks that formerly required workers who possessed significant human capital. In short, artificial intelligence represents a naked effort to transform sophisticated human capital into physical capital, so that returns to investment in skills and knowledge will accrue progressively more to the owners of capital and less to workers: the social significance of intelligent machinery is not that it will exist but that it will be privately owned. Abstractly, the introduction of artificial intelligence to enterprise is no different than the introduction of any labour-saving technological improvement to a production function: one should still expect the pattern of sectoral discomfort with the potential of economy-wide benefits. But artificial intelligence differs from other labour-saving technology in that it is a flexible technique that can be applied to a broad range of productive activities, so that it should be expected to be applied over a wide range of productive functions and displace a large and varied segment of the work force in the coming years.

As artificial intelligence flushes workers from their sanctuaries of skills, the value of many specific skills will depreciate rapidly, but it is a mistake to think that this signals a decline in the social need for human capital. As many skills obsolesce, the ability of individuals to adapt to shifting job requirements will become more critical both to the individuals and society, as will the necessity of an adequate social machinery for continually reorienting and retraining workers. Human capital is the necessary lubricant against social friction in societies whose productive processes are perpetually shifting.

The economic reward to private companies for successfully developing artificial intelligence is immense, and the United States and Japan are engaged in a pitched rivalry to expand the boundaries of AI technique. It is fatuous to suggest that this rivalry is a race, that victory will go to the nation that makes the most significant discoveries first. In truth, the ultimate contest will be won or lost according to each country's ability to incorporate artificial intelligence as part of a broad, balanced economic advance. Japan is correctly poised to incorporate intelligent machinery into its economy to the benefit of its citizens: the Japanese industrial system recognizes that human capital must be diligently nurtured in the public at large, that government and industry are responsible for retraining workers to societal advantage, and that public investment should be oriented in a manner calculated to enhance the value of its human capital base. But America seems unwilling to re-examine its tired philosophy that neglects public education, rationalizes structural unemployment, and squanders public investment in unproductive technologies, and it is ill-prepared for the depositing of ever greater numbers of people into its labour market or the rapid depreciation of skills in its population.

If any nation continues to neglect human capital investment in the poor and middle class while indiscriminately stimulating physical capital accumulation in private industry, and if physical capital increasingly competes with human capital for a meaningful role in economic enterprise, the stratification of society can only accelerate, leaving more and more people with less and less marketable skills to bid for fewer and fewer mechanically performed intellectual tasks. One can almost hear Karl Marx screaming from his grave.

Epilogue:
On Leading the Leading Edge

Our era is one in which the social impulse to rationalization is given free and spirited expression, but also one in which governments have grown resolute in spurring this process towards their own ends. Science and technology have become key cogs in the political machinery of nations. The pressing moral issue of our day is not, as it was in Adam Smith's time, to come to grips with the process of rationalization, but instead to decide how best to lead it along.

In many persons' minds, the distinction between science and technology is a blurred one, and the two have obvious similarities. Science and technology obviously feed off each other. Both are essentially the social manifestation of a process of rationalization, and in both this process proceeds from a desire to serve the self-interest of some group of individuals, as when scientists seek to understand nature better or managers seek to streamline a production process.

Sociologists of science have developed models for the dynamic of scientific discovery, the most notable view of this process being elucidated by Thomas Kuhn in 1962.[1] According to Kuhn, scientific progress proceeds along a line that is at times evolutionary – that builds upon an established system of belief; and at other times is revolutionary – that overthrows an established paradigm and substitutes in its place a new system that better accommodates social demands. Kuhn used the term 'normal' science to describe the relatively calm evolutionary periods when scientific understanding is assumed to rest on the foundation of an established and secure system of scientific belief. In these times, research and scientific training proceed along familiar avenues, and the branches and techniques of science are relatively cleanly defined. New findings are comprehended and made to fit within the established paradigm, and areas that are not explained by the dominant paradigm are the subject of scientific speculation. Inevitably, according to Kuhn, the findings of science will uncover so many exceptions to established ways of thinking that revolutionary pressure will grow within the scientific community for a new regime of explanation, and the period of normal science will give way to a new era of 'revolutionary' science, one in which it is recognized on some level that a new system of understanding is required to explain the recent observations that have been made. Periods of revolutionary science are as intellectually tumultuous as periods of normal science are serene, being characterized by a cacophony of half-baked ideas that compete for intellectual prominence. Out of this anarchy, one paradigm finally emerges that explains the disparate phenomena that had eluded comprehension to that point, and with general acceptance this paradigm serves as the platform for a new period of normal science, until new discoveries inevitably make this new platform untenable as well.

It has been generally remarked that technological development mirrors in very interesting ways the process that Kuhn described in scientific revolutions. Just as in science, there are periods in technological development when rationalization proceeds within an established system of production, and times when there are economic opportunities for replacing established production functions with entirely new production functions. In this sense, normal science can be thought of as analogous to process innovation in production systems, and revolutionary science is analogous to product innovation. Just as normal science proceeds relatively calmly within an established system of belief, process innovation merely streamlines an existing system of production and does not call for any radically different patterns of production. But revolutionary science starkly calls into question the established system of belief and eventually replaces it with a new one, and this bears an interesting analogy to a product innovation which creates an entirely new system of production whose aim is partially or totally to displace the products of other existing production functions.

A new technological paradigm serves as a platform for a new stream of process innovations just as a new scientific paradigm serves as a platform for further scientific discovery, and in both this stream of enhancements is the test of the paradigm's robustness and the eventual source of its demise. The period since the Second World War has been dominated by the introduction of computers, a new technological paradigm that has proved to be incredibly robust in its potential to support process innovation, and even after four decades it is evident that the productivity of computer systems has not even begun to reach its potential. The platform for this evolution has been the von Neumann architecture for serial, electronic, digital computation, but as has been mentioned above the seeds of dissatisfaction with the von Neumann archetype were apparent from the very beginning and efforts to streamline its inefficiencies are leading unmistakably in the direction of entirely new designs for computer systems that break out of the serial and electronic shells. This evolutionary and revolutionary process is one in which Western governments today are intensely involved.

Obviously scientific and technological rationalization share many characteristics in their dynamics, but there is one critical difference between the two processes. The viability of technological change is ultimately adjudicated by markets, and the viability of scientific knowledge is ultimately adjudicated by a consensus within a community of scientists. Innovations in production succeed or fail according to whether or not the ultimate product sells, while innovations in science succeed or fail according to whether a consensus develops that the innovation is useful.[2] This is in fact the only meaningful distinction between science and technology.

This distinction is what characterizes the dynamics of change within the two realms. The self-interest that drives science is essentially the self-interest of the scientific community. Scientific innovation is inextricably involved in the bureaucracies and metaphysical beliefs of a community of individuals entrusted with the determination of scientific truth, and so scientific truth unavoidably reflects and conforms to the norms of this group. If these norms are worthy, as would be exemplified by an obedience to disciplined observation and experiment, intellectual openness and an allegiance to the pursuit of truth, the progress of science can be great. Conversely, if the norms of this group are cloistered and too protective of bureaucratic prerogatives, the product of scientific research can be dubious. In any event, scientific rationalization tends to be a function of a social group and generally proceeds only with the consensual blessing of this group.

Technological change, on the other hand, appeals directly to the self-interest of a much broader and diverse community of consumers. By appealing directly to the desires of this larger and more diverse group, technological innovation in effect bypasses the bureaucratic mechanism that guides pure science, and it is this independence from bureaucratic control that imbues technology with such a volatile nature in modern times. This is the element of technological change that gives it an aura of purity in a world sullied by small-minded human attempts at theory and organization, and is the element of the invisible hand that Adam Smith found so appealing. In fact, technological rationalization has repeatedly in the past shown an unmistakable impudence for scientific appraisals of how things should unfold in the future. Social science cannot seem to stay ahead of technology. Economics in particular has frequently retreated into a depressed funk whenever technological change outstrips scientific notions of how societies should be composed and how they will develop in the future.

In large measure, the economic success of the Japanese since the Second World War and in fact since the Meiji Restoration must be attributed to a skilful balance in the management of scientific and technological rationalization in modern society. The Japanese industrial system aggressively spurs technological development in a decidedly scientific way, by assessing promising new areas of growth and fearlessly employing public resources in scientifically designed plans to exploit the opportunities it recognizes. Sometimes these scientific appraisals and plans are on target, sometimes in retrospect they seem naive. But the saving grace of the scientific management of the Japanese economy is that it assiduously seeks the discipline of markets in directing

194

its goals. The Japanese system is not haunted by scientific notions of what consumers should have, but only by what they are likely to want.

If technological development is in any way shielded from the discipline of markets and is allowed to any extent to be controlled by a group, it begins to exhibit more and more the character of scientific revolutions and less and less the character of technological revolutions. The group entrusted with directing the technology and assessing its mission is destined to become an entrenched bureaucracy, and the technology it produces will reflect the needs and concerns of this bureaucracy. Such technology will to some extent diverge from what viable commercial markets would demand. This can make for a development path that may appear more orderly and rational than that exhibited in market-driven enterprise, but it also inevitably leads to a baroque implementation of technology and ultimately to an unjust allocation of social resources. This was the problem that afflicted technology in Ptolemaic Alexandria and the flaw that hamstrings contemporary centrally planned economies. It is the reason why the United States has been left with such a confused civilian space programme, and the rocks upon which a US government-directed industrial policy, if it is ever enacted, is likely to founder.

This trap, of technology directed by a bureaucracy that is not mindful of market demands, is what has snared the economy of the United States in the surrender to the military of so much of the task of stimulating technological development. As long as a military bureaucracy exerts considerable control over research and development funding, innovation will proceed in the service of military imperatives. The economic benefits of this research – the only benefits peaceful people hope to accrue from their investment – may only be rationalized as a side-effect and never as a primary goal. This is hardly a regime for scientifically seeking the best economic path for society, not to mention one that is mindful of the differential impacts the innovations may have on different segments of society.

So there are examples in the current world scene of both successful and unsuccessful attempts to direct technological development scientifically. While some governments' programmes are obviously more productive than others, the fact that all governments of all industrializing countries have active programmes for stimulating technology is eloquent testimony to the fact that, when given a choice, governments would far prefer to steer economic events their way rather than passively await what the invisible hand has for them. Governments can and do play a major role in the manner in which technological innovation is discovered and disseminated, and all advanced industrial nations today are moving unmistakably towards greater government involvement in innovation. The Japanese system will obviously be a prominent example to these efforts. A new age of nationalism, one with a definite mercantile spirit, is dawning.

The unthinking acceptance of pragmatic government support for spurring technology skips lightly past an issue that would seem to be of profound moral importance: what end is being served by channelling communal resources towards breaking new ground in technology? Even to ask the question in a comfortable Western country is to invite howls of indignant defences of the creature comforts that technology has visited upon us. But is this really why we accede to government programmes to spur high technology research and development? If we examine our motives closely, don't we cast our vote in defence of these programmes more out of an anxiety of being overrun by other more aggressive nations than out of any positive prospect new technology offers society? A thoughtful examination of these issues reveals the same base motives that fuel nationalism and racism, a desire to promote the interests of one's own class, however arbitrarily delineated, at the expense of other classes. In abstract terms, the problem with national programmes for stimulating technological development is not that they are ineffectual, because clearly they need not be, but that they serve frameworks of self-interest that are too narrowly drawn.

The best prospect for society is that technological and scientific rationalization in the future will respond to the rational and freely expressed self-interest of a broadly defined community of humanity, and that this appraisal of self-interest will be informed in the best tradition of scientific discovery. This is another way of saying that humanity's future, as it has always been, is hostage to our desires and beliefs, and so ultimately to our values.

Our values guide our rationalizations, and values arise from the meaning we sense in our existence. It is our values that ultimately guide the industrialization of intelligence, and it is in this sense of meaning that will for ever lie the distinction between mind and machine.

Notes and References

Notes for Introduction

1 Casson, Lionel (1985), 'Triumphs from the ancient world's first think tank', *Smithsonian*, June 1985, p. 160.
2 Claudius Ptolemy was not related to the Ptolemaic kings, but was probably named for them.

Notes for Chapter 1

1 Stephen, Leslie, and Lee, Sidney (eds) (1921), *Dictionary of National Biography* (London: Oxford University Press), p. 1046.
2 Smith, Adam (1976 reprint) *An Inquiry into the Nature and Causes of the Wealth of Nations* (Chicago: University of Chicago Press), p. 303.

Notes for Chapter 2

1 Erickson, Carolly (1986), *Our Tempestuous Day, A History of Regency England* (New York: William Morrow). I am indebted to Ms Erickson's fine characterizations of social custom and events of the period.
2 Griffith, G. Talboth (1926), *Population Problems of the Age of Malthus* (Cambridge: Cambridge University Press), pp. 1–26.
3 The 100 new Irish seats in the Commons after the Act of Union of 1800 included among them a fresh supply of 'rotten boroughs', safe seats that could be purchased or otherwise obtained by the powerful. The specific seat in question had been straightforwardly sold for most parliamentary elections since 1802, and had previously been purchased by a friend of Ricardo. At the time of Ricardo's filling the seat, his voting constituents numbered about a dozen, and the total population of the borough was less than 3,000.

   The specifics of the transaction spoke eloquently for the times, as traditional landowners in straitened circumstances sought to keep their fortunes afloat in an emerging era of capitalism. Lord Portarlington sold the seat to Ricardo in exchange for a £4,000 payment along with a £25,000 mortgage on the borough at 6 per cent interest. Though not uncommon, the manner of Ricardo's gaining a seat was a politically tender spot for the fledgling MP: on at least one occasion the affair was recalled by a rival for the obvious purpose of embarrassing him.

   See Ricardo, David (1951), *The Works and Correspondence of David Ricardo*, ed. P. Sraffa (Cambridge: Cambridge University Press), Vol. V, p. 289; Vol. VII, pp. 216–17, 232, 293, 306, 308, 346–8, 359, 382; Vol VIII, p. 327; Vol. X, p. 99.

Also Thorne, R. G. (1986), *The History of Parliament: the House of Commons 1790–1820* (London: Secker & Warburg), Vol. II, p. 682.

4   This according to Thorne (1986), *History of Parliament* (London: Secker & Warburg), Vol. V, pp. 11–13.

A more nearly contemporary account by one of Ricardo's close friends suggests the actual amount left to him may have been £800. See J. R. McCulloch's biography of Ricardo in *Political Economy Club. Volume I: Minutes of Proceedings, 1899–1920, Roll of Members and Questions Discussed, 1821–1920* (London: Macmillan, 1921), pp. 300–2.

5   Ricardo acknowledged that there was a bit more to the price of a commodity than this, having to do with scarcity, but he generally considered scarcity effects negligible.

6   Ricardo (1951), *Works and Correspondence*, based on an account in the MS diary of J. L. Mallet, Vol. VIII, p. 152, n. 2.

See also *Political Economy Club. Volume I* (1921), from the MS diary of J. L. Mallet, pp. 211, 212.

7   Ricardo (1951), *Works and Correspondence*, letter to H. Trower, 8 July 1819, in Vol. VIII, pp. 45–6.

8   Thorne (1986), *History of Parliament*, Vol. V, p. 12.

9   Ricardo (1951), *Works and Correspondence*, Vol. I, p. 386.

10   Ricardo (1951), *Works and Correspondence*, Vol. I, p. 392.

Notes for Chapter 3

1   Hyman, Anthony (1982), *Charles Babbage: Pioneer of the Computer* (Princeton NJ: Princeton University Press), p. 9. Hyman's book is the definitive current account of Babbage's life and work.

2   Babbage, Charles (1846), *On the Economy of Machinery and Manufactures* (London: John Murray), pp. 191–2.

3   Hyman (1982), *Charles Babbage*, p. 128.

4   Recent research of primary records by M. Jean Huchard, a scholar in Lyons on Jacquard and his machines, reveals that Jacquard's given name was 'Charles', and that he frequently signed his name that way.

5   It probably would have been painful to Babbage to have known the details under which Jacquard had his pension restored, since Babbage always felt that foreign interests were more appreciative of his work than were his own countrymen. Babbage did obliquely hint that he might take his abroad if he were not treated with more respect at home, but no one in England ever took the bait.

Notes to Chapter 4

1   MacHale, Desmond (1985), *George Boole: His Life and Work* (Dublin: Boole Press), p. 6.

2   The expression '$x + y$' may also be interpreted as 'the class of all things having the quality of x, *or* the quality of y'. Either interpretation works, as long as it is consistently employed.

3   The 'q' is a symbol Boole used to denote an undefined class, and for our purposes can be ignored.

4　British Library Additional Manuscripts, 37,198, folio 414.

Notes for Chapter 5

1　Hollerith's company, after merging with the Computing Scale Company, making weighing systems, and International Time Recording Company, makers of clocks, took on the ponderous name of Computing Tabulating Recording Company. Thomas J. Watson, Sr. became president in 1914, and in 1924 the company sensibly changed its name to that of its Canadian subsidiary, International Business Machines (IBM), now by far the largest computer company in the world. Powers's company was purchased by the Remington Typewriter Company, which later became Remington Rand, which merged in 1955 with the Sperry Corporation, a large defence contractor, to become Sperry Rand. Sperry was acquired by Burroughs in 1986 to become UNISYS Corporation, now the USA's third largest computer company. The British subsidiaries of Powers's and Hollerith's original companies merged in 1959 to form International Computers and Tabulators, a seminal British computer company that was forced by the Labour government in 1968 to merge with other ailing British manufacturers to form International Computers Limited. The French computer company Bull similarly owes its origin to punched card machinery.

　　See Moreau, R. (1984), *The Computer Comes of Age: the People, The Hardware and the Software* (Cambridge MA: MIT Press), pp. 24–5; and Flamm, Kenneth (1988), *Creating the Computer: Government, Industry and High Technology* (Washington DC: Brookings Institution), pp. 134–59.

2　Goldstine, Herman H. (1972), *The Computer: from Pascal to von Neumann* (Princeton NJ: Princeton University Press), p. 74.

3　By way of example, by interconnecting two NOT switches, three AND switches, and one OR switch in a certain combination, it is possible to construct a complex circuit that perfectly mimics the results of adding two binary digits. A more complex circuit can be composed of three NOT gates, seven AND gates, and two OR gates that will add three binary digits, which is useful because one of the three 'input' values from one of these circuits can be wired to one of the outputs from another identical circuit to mimic the action of carrying in addition, so that eight of these so-called 'full adder' circuits wired properly together can exhibit the sum of two eight-digit binary numbers.

4　Burks, A. W., 'Electronic computing circuits of the ENIAC', quoted from Goldstine (1972), *The Computer*, p. 153, n.

5　Moreau (1986), *The Computer Comes of Age*, p. 34.

6　Flamm (1988), *Creating the Computer*, pp. 116–19.

7　Nomenclature becomes difficult as one approaches the present, and the ultimate significance of technological developments becomes more controversial. The fourth generation has also been associated with distributed processing and processing using virtual storage, i.e. rapidly swapping RAM contents with high-speed direct access devices in order to run very large programs. The fifth generation has been announced by some researchers in artificial intelligence as being based on massively parallel architectures and softwares.

　　See Feigenbaum, Edward A., and McCorduck, Pamela (1983), *The Fifth Generation: Artificial Intelligence and Japan's Computer Challenge to the World* (Reading MA: Addison-Wesley), p. 15.

8 Meindl, James D. (1987), 'Chips for advanced computing', *Scientific American*, vol. 257, no. 4, Oct. 1987, pp. 78–88.

9 Information on the 80386 microprocessor provided by James Reilly of Intel Corp., November 1988.

10 Phillip Kraft (1979), 'The Industrialization of Computer Programming: from programming to "software production"', in Andrew Zimbalist (ed.), *Case Studies on the Labor Process* (New York: Monthly Review Press).

11 Lisp is the language of choice for US researchers, having enjoyed the continuing support of the military, while Prolog has been selected by the Japanese as the programming language for their fifth generation project.

12 Flamm (1988), *Creating the Computer*, p. 238.

13 ibid., p. 135.

14 Thomborson, Clark (1987), 'Role of military funding in academic computer science', in David Bellin and Gary Chapman (eds), *Computers in Battle – Will they Work?* (New York: Harcourt Brace Jovanovich), p. 283.

15 US Congress, Office of Technology Assessment (1985), *Information Technology R & D: Critical Trends and Issues* (Washington DC: US Government Printing Office), p. 3.

16 US Bureau of the Census (1986), *Statistical ASbstract of the United States: 1987* (Washington DC: US Government Printing Office), table 973, p. 564.

17 Flamm (1988), *Creating the Computer*, pp. 88–90.

18 US Bureau of the Census (1986), *Statistical Abstract of the United States: 1987*, tables 976, 978, p. 566.

19 Moreau (1986), *The Computer Comes of Age*, p. 188.

20 Flamm, Kenneth (1987), *Targeting the Computer: Govrnment Support and International Competition* (Washington DC: Brookings Institution), pp. 42, 62.

21 Athanasiou, Tom (1987), 'Artificial intelligence as military technology', in Bellin and Chapman (eds), *Computers in Battle*, p. 236.

22 *The Fifth Generation*, by Edward A. Feigenbaum and Pamela McCorduck, published by Addison-Wesley, Reading MA.

   Feigenbaum, a prominent member of what Louis Fein has called the artificial intelligentsia, is now on the faculty at Stanford University. He is a co-founder of both TeKnowledge, Inc. and IntelliCorp, Inc. of Palo Alto, Calafornia, and would be expected to be in favour of a strong public/private push in artificial intelligence research.

Notes for Chapter 6

1 There were many tales of golem in Jewish lore. Some Talmudic legends say that Jeremiah created one, and there is a fleeting reference to one in the Old Testament. The golem of Prague is the story that was most widely repeated and borrowed from, and is the seat of the current myths about golem.

2 Turing, Alan (1950), 'Computing machinery and intelligence', *Mind*, vol. 59, no. 236; more recently reprinted with an interesting commentary in *The Mind's I*; (1981), a collection by Douglas R. Hofstadter and Daniel C. Dennett (New York: Basic Books).

3 Genesereth, Michael R., and Nilson, Nils J. (1987), *Logical Foundations of Artificial Intelligence* (Los Altos CA: Morgan Kaufman), p. 13.

4 Searle delivered his objections in the 1984 Reith Lectures, presented annually by the BBC, subsequently published in book form in 1984, *Minds, Brains and Science* (Cambridge MA: Harvard University Press).

5   Haugeland, John (1985), *Artificial Intelligence: the Very Idea* (Cambridge MA: MIT Press), pp. 38–41.
6   To be fair, some thought that the entity might exist in the ovum.
7   This is necessarily a simplification. Searle calls his homunculi 'international states' and feels the infinite regression implicit in minds having homunculus-like elements is a false problem.
    See Searle, John (1983), *Intentionality: an Essay in the Philosophy of Mind* (Cambridge: Cambridge University Press), pp. 21–2.
8   Earlier accounts said that Alexander either hacked at the knot until he found the ends, or simply withdrew the pole from the knot.
9   Forsyth, Richard (1984), 'The architecture of expert systems', in Richard Forsyth (ed.), *Expert Systems: Principles and Case Studies* (London: Chapman & Hall), p. 15.
10 Feigenbaum and McCorduck (1983), *The Fifth Generation*, p. 79.
11 From an interview with Dennis Heher of Ford Aerospace, May 1988.
12 Price, Derek (1962), *Science since Babylon*, p. 102 n.; quoted from Bell, Daniel (1973), *The Coming of Post-Industrial Society* (New York: Basic Books), p. 180.
13 Quoted from McCorduck, Pamela (1979) *Machines Who Think* (San Francisco: W. H. Freeman), p. 347.
14 Dennett, Daniel C. (1981), *Brainstorms: Philosophical Essays on Mind and Psychology* (Cambridge MA: MIT Press), p. 124.

Notes for Chapter 8

1   *Le Courrier de Lyon*, 17 July 1833; quoted from Bezucha, Robert J. (1974), *The Lyon Uprising of 1834: Social and Political Conflict in the Early July Monarchy* (Cambridge MA: Harvard University Press), p. 39.
2   US Bureau of the Census (1975), *Historical Statistics of the United States, Colonial Times to 1970* (Washington DC: US Government Printing Office), pp. 127, 139, 498.
3   Applebaum, Eileen (1983), 'The economics of technical progress: labor issues arising from the spread of programmable autumation technologies', in US Congress Office of Technology Assessment, *Automation and the Workplace: Selected Labor, Education and Training Issues*, March 1983, p. 64. Ms Applebaum quotes an example originally phrased by Peter Albin of CUNY.
4   Leontieff, Wassily, and Duchin, Faye (1984), *The Impacts of Automation on Employment, 1963–2000* (New York: Institute of Economic Analysis, New York University).
5   Leontieff, Wassily (1986), 'Technological change, employment, the rate of return on capital and wages', in Daniel F. Burton *et al.* (eds), *The Jobs Challenge: Pressures and Possibilities* (Cambridge MA: Ballinger), pp. 47–53.

Notes for Chapter 9

1   Wood, Robert E. (1986), *From Marshall Plan to Debt Crisis: Foreign Aid and Development Choices in the World Economy* (Berkeley: University of California Press), p. 260.

2   Thomas Hobbes, *Leviathan*, Everyman edition (1924), p. 130; quoted from Braudel, Fernand (1979), *The Wheels of Commerce* (New York: Harper & Row), Vol. 2, p. 51.

3   This is not to imply that tenure within a firm does not increase an employee's value to that firm, or to competing firms, for it certainly does. Experiance with a firm represents an investment in human capital that yields returns in the valuation of the individual, both as educatuional investments similar to formal education and in familiarity with firm procedures, so-called 'firm specific' human capital. The point is that tenure is generally not morally valued in the abstract as much as it is economically valuated: the value of tenure is generally little more than a firm's calculation of a tenured individual's economic value versus a non-tenured individual's economic value.

4   Bronfenbrenner, Martin (1983), 'Economic history: occupation-period economy', in *Kodansha Encyclopaedia of Japan* (Tokyo: Kodansha), vol. 2, p. 154.

5   Patrick, Hugh (1983), 'Economic history: contemporary-period economy', in *Kodansha Encyclopaedia of Japan*, vol. 2, table 3, p. 154.

6   US Bureau of the Census (1986), *Statistical Abstract of the United States: 1987*, p. 568, table #983; p. 420, table #706.

7   ibid., p. 321, table #530.

8   ibid., p. 318, table #525; p. 568, table #983; p. 417, table #699.

9   US National Science Board (1985), *Science Indicators: the 1985 Report* (Washington DC), p. xiii.

10 Thurow, Lester C. (1987), 'A surge in inequality', *Scientific American*, May 1987, pp. 30–7.

11 Gordon, David (1987), 'The new class war: rich Americans get richer, while the rest of us pay their bills', *Washington Post*, vol. 109, 5 May 1987, p. B–1; Lawrence, John F. (1986), 'Society may pay as income gap widens', *Los Angeles Times*, vol. 105, 3 August 1986, p. IV–1.

12 US Bureau of the Census (1986), *Statistical Abstract of the United States: 1987*, table 235, p. 139.

13 Darling-Hammond, Linda (1984), *Beyond the Commission Report: the Coming Crisis in Education* (Santa Monica CA: Rand Corporation), pp. 2–14.

Notes for Epilogue

1   Kuhn, Thomas (1962), 'The structure of scientific revolutions', in *International Encyclopaedia of Unified Science*, vols 1 and 2; reprinted in 1970 as *The Structure of Scientific Revolutions* (Chicago: University of Chicago Press).

2   I am indebted to an excellent article by Norman Clark for making these distinctions so clear to me; see Clark, Norman (1987), 'Similarities and differences between scientific and technological paradigms', *Futures*, February 1987, pp. 27–42.

Selected Bibliography

Adelman, Irma, and Thorbecke, Erik (eds) (1966), *The Theory and Design of Economic Development* (Baltimore: Johns Hopkins Press).

Adelman, Irma, and Morris, Cynthia Taft (1973), *Economic Growth and Social Equity in Developing Countries* (Stanford CA: Stanford University Press).

Alexander, Jeffrey C. (1983), *Theoretical Logic in Sociology*, Vol. 3, The Classical Attempt at Theoretical Synthesis: Max Weber (Berkeley: University of California Press).

Applebaum, Herbert (ed.) (1984), *Work in Market and Industrial Societies* (Albany NY: State University of New York Press).

Armandi, Barry R. (1981), *Organizational Structure and Efficiency* (Washington DC: University Press of America).

Ashurst, Gareth (1983), *Pioneers of Computing* (London: Frederick Muller).

Austrian, Geoffrey D. (1982), *Herman Hollerith: Forgotten Giant of Information Processing* (New York: Columbia University Press).

Babbage, Charles (1830), *Reflections on the Decline of Science in England, and on Some of its Causes* (London: B. Fellows).

Babbage, Charles (1832), *On the Economy of Machinery and Manufactures* (London: Charles Knight).

Babbage, Charles (1864), *Passages from the Life of a Philosopher* (London: Longman, Green).

Babbage, Henry Prevost (1982), *Babbage's Calculating Engines* (London: Tomash).

Ballot, C. (1913), 'L'évolution du métier lyonnais au XVIIIe siècle et la genèse de la mécanique Jacquard', *Revue D'Histoire de Lyon*.

Barry, Patrick D. (1969), *George Boole: a miscellany* (Cork: Cork University Press).

Baum, Joan (1986), *The Calculating Passion of Ada Byron* (Camdem CT: Anchor Books).

Bell, Daniel (1973), *The Coming of Post-Industrial Society: a Venture in Social Forecasting* (New York: Basic Books).

Bell, Daniel (1976), *The Cultural Contradictions of Capitalism* (New York: Basic Books).

Bell, E. T. (1937), *Men of Mathematics* (London: Victor Gollancz).

Bellin, David, and Chapman, Gary (eds) (1987), *Computers in Battle – Will They Work?* (Boston: Harcourt Brace Jovanovich).

Bensan, Ian, and Lloyd, John (1983), *New Technology and Industrial Change: the Impact of the Scientific-Technical Revolution on Labour and Industry* (London: Kogan Page).

Berkeley, Edmund Callis (1959), *Symbolic Logic and Intelligent Machines* (New York: Reinhold).

Bezucha, Robert J. (1974), *The Lyon Uprising of 1834: Social and Political Conflict in the Early July Monarchy* (Cambridge MA: Harvard University Press).

Blaug, Mark (1978), *Economic Theory in Retrospect* (Cambridge: Cambridge University Press).

Bluestone, Barry, and Harrison, Bennett (1982), *The Deindustrialization of America* (New York: Basic Books).

Board of Education, South Kensington (1872), *Babbage's Calculating Machine; or Difference Engine* (London: Wyman).

Boisot, Max (1983), *Intangible Factors in Japanese Corporate Strategy* (Paris: Atlantic Institute for International Affairs).

Boole, George (1952), *Collected Logical Works*, Vol. I: Studies in Logic and Probability (Chicago: Open Court).

Boole, George (1916), *Collected Logical Works*, Vol. II: The Laws of Thought (Chicago: Open Court).

Boole, Mary Everest (1897), *The Mathematical Psychology of Gratry and Boole* (London: Swan Sonnenschein).

Boole, Mary Everest (1931), *Collected Works*, ed. E. M. Cobham (London: C. W. Daniel).

Braverman, Harry (1974), *Labor and Monopoly Capital: the Degradation of Work in the Twentieth Century* (New York: Monthly Review Press).

Burton, Daniel F., *et al.* (eds) (1986) *The Jobs Challenge: Pressures and Possibilities* (Cambridge MA: Ballinger).

Chirlian, Paul M. (1978), *Understanding Computers* (Portland OR: Dilithium Press).

Clapham, John (1952), *An Economic History of Modern Britain: Free Trade and Steel 1850–1886* (Cambridge: Cambridge University Press).

Clark, John Maurice, *et al.* (1928), *Adam Smith, 1776–1926: Lectures to Commemorate the Sesquicentennial of the Publication of 'The Wealth of Nations'* (Chicago: University of Chicago Press).

Cook, S. A., Adcock, F. E., and Charlesworth, M. P. (eds) (1928), *The Cambridge Ancient History*, Vol. 7: The Hellenistic monarchies and the rise of Rome (Cambridge: Cambridge University Press).

Cooper, C. M. and Clark, J. A. (1982), *Employment, Economics and Technology: the Impact of Technological Change on the Labour Market* (Brighton, Sussex: Wheatsheaf Books).

Darling-Hammond, Linda (1984), *Beyond the Commission Reports: the Coming Crisis in Education* (Santa Monica CA: Rand Corporation).

Dennett, Daniel C. (1981), *Brainstorms: Philosophical Essays on Mind and Psychology* (Cambridge MA: MIT Press).

Dubbey, J. M. (1978), *The Mathematical Work of Charles Babbage* (Cambridge: Cambridge University Press).

Durkheim, Emile (1973), *On Morality and Society*; selected writings, ed. Robert N. Bellah (Chicago: University of Chicago Press).

Edwards, Richard C., Reich, Michael, and Gordon, David M. (1975), *Labor Market Segmentation* (Lexington MA: D. C. Heath).

Ehrenhalt, Samuel M. (1986), 'Taking a Look at Job Quality', *New York Times*, 13 August 1986, p. D–2.

Fay, C. R. (1956), *Adam Smith and the Scotland of his Day* (Cambridge: Cambridge University Press).

Feigenbaum, Edward A., and McCorduck, Pamela (1983), *The Fifth Generation: Artificial Intelligence and Japan's Computer Challenge to the World* (Reading MA: Addison-Wesley).

Flamm, Kenneth (1987), *Targeting the Computer: Government Support and International Competition* (Washington DC: Brookings Institution).

Flamm, Kenneth (1988), *Creating the Computer: Government, Industry and High Technology* (Washington DC: Brookings Institution).

Forster, E. M. (1982), *Alexandria: a History and a Guide* (London: Michale Haag).

Forsyth, Richard (ed.) (1984), *Expert Systems: Principles and Case Studies* (London: Chapman & Hall).

Fox, Geoffrey C., and Messina, Paul C. (1988), 'Advanced Computer Architectures', *Scientific American*, vol. 257, no. 4, October 1987.

Gardner, Howard (1985), *The Mind's New Science: a History of the Cognitive Revolution* (New York: Basic Books).

Garrison, Fielding H. (1929), *An Introduction to the History of Medicine* (London: W. B. Saunders).

Gelernter, David (1988), 'Programming for Advanced Computing', *Scientific American*, vol. 257, no. 4, October 1987.

Giddens, Anthony (1971), *Capitalism and Modern Social Theory: an Analysis of the Writings of Marx, Durkheim and Max Weber* (Cambridge: Cambridge University Press).

Ginzberg, Eli (1934), *The House of Adam Smith* (New York: Columbia University Press).

Ginzberg, Eli (1985), *Understanding Human Resources* (Lanham MD: University Press of America).

Ginzberg, Eli (1982), 'The Mechanization of Work', *Scientific American*, vol. 247, no. 3, September 1982.

Glahe, Fred R. (ed.) (1978), *Adam Smith and the Wealth of Nations: 1776–1976 Bicentennial Essays* (Boulder CO: Colorado Associated University Press).

Goldsmith, M. M. (1985), *Private Vices, Public Benefits: Bernard Mandeville's Social and Political Thought* (Cambridge: Cambridge University Press).

Goldstine, Herman H. (1972), *The Computer from Pascal to von Neumann* (Princeton NJ: Princeton University Press).

Gordon, David M., and Edwards, Richard (1982), *Segmented Work, Divided Workers* (Cambridge: Cambridge University Press).

Haggarty, John (ed.) (1976), *The Wisdom of Adam Smith* (Indianapolis: Liberty Press).

Haugeland, John (1985), *Artificial Intelligence: the Very Idea* (Cambridge MA: MIT Press).

Heilbroner, Robert L. (1980), *The Worldly Philosophers* (New York: Touchstone).

Hillis, Daniel W. (1988), 'The Connection Machine', *Scientific American Trends in Computing*, vol. 1, p. 24.

Hirschhorn, Larry (1984), *Beyond Mechanization: Work and Technology in the Post-Industrial Age* (Cambridge MA: MIT Press).

Hodges, Andrew (1983), *Alan Turing: the Enigma of Intelligence* (London: Counterpoint).

Hofstadter, Douglas, and Dennett, Daniel C. (1981), *The Mind's I: Fantasies and Reflections on Self and Soul* (New York: Basic Books).

Hooper, Alfred (1948), *Makers of Mathematics* (New York: Random House).

Hyman, Anthony (1982), *Charles Babbage: Pioneer of the Computer* (Princeton NJ: Princeton University Press).

Inmon, William H. (1986), *Technomics: the Economics of Technology and the Computer Industry* (Homewood IL: Dow-Jones Irwin).

Johnson, George (1986), *Machinery of the Mind: Inside the New Science of Artificial Intelligence* (New York: Times Books).

Johnson, Paul (1987), *A History of the Jews* (New York: Harper & Row).

Katsoulascos, Y. S. (1986), *The Employment Impact of Technological Change* (Brighton, Sussex: Wheatsheaf Books).

Kaye, F. B. (1924), *Mandeville's Fable of the Bees: With a Commentary Critical, Historical, and Explanatory, by F. B. Kaye* (Oxford: Clarendon Press).

Kemp, Tom (1978), *Historical Patterns of Industrialization* (London: Longman).

Kemp, Tom (1983), *Industrialization in the Non-Western World* (London: Longman).

Kohl, Friedrich (1872), *Geschichte der Jacquard-Maschine* (Berlin: Nicholaische Verlags-Buchhandlung).

Kuznets, Simon (1978), 'Technological innovations and economic growth', in Patrick Kelly and Melvin Kranzberg (eds), *Technological Innovation: a critical review of current knowledge* (San Francisco: San Francisco Press).

Lamartine, Alphonse de (1866), *Jacquard* (New York: F. W. Christern).

Landes, David S. (1969), *The Unbound Prometheus: Technological Change and Industrial Development in Western Europe from 1750 to the Present* (Cambridge: Cambridge University Press).

Lenat, Douglas B. (1988), 'Computer Software for Intelligent Systems', *Scientific American Trends in Computing*, vol. 1, p. 68.

Leontieff, Wassily and Duchin, Faye (1986), *The Future Impact of Automation on Workers* (New York: Oxford University Press).

Lindgren, J. Ralph (ed.) (1967), *The Early Writings of Adam Smith* (New York: Augustus M. Kelley).

Löwith, Karl (1960), *Max Weber and Karl Marx*, edited and with an introduction by Tom Bottomore and William Outhwaite (London: Allen & Unwin).

Mabry, Bevars Dupre (1973), *Economics of Manpower and the Labor Market* (New York: Intext Educational).

MacHale, Desmond (1985), *George Boole: His Life and Work* (Dublin: Boole Press).

MacPherson, Hector C. (1899), *Adam Smith* (Edinburgh: Oliphant Anderson & Ferrier).

Machlup, Fritz (1984), *Knowledge: its Creation, Distribution and Economic Significance*, Vol. 3: The Economics of Information and Human Capital (Princeton NJ: Princeton University Press).

Mandeville, Bernard de (1934), *The Fable of the Bees; or Private Vices, Public Benefits*, edited and with an introduction by Douglas Garman (London: Wishart).

McCorduck, Pamela (1979), *Machines Who Think: a Personal Inquiry into the History and Prospects of Artificial Intelligence* (San Francisco: W. H. Freeman).

McMillan, Charles C. (1985), *The Japanese Industrial System* (New York: W. de Gruyter).

Metropolis, N., Howlett, J., and Roth, Gian-Carlo (eds) (1980), *A History of Computing in the Twentieth Century: a collection of essays* (New York: Academic Press).

Monro, Hector (1975), *The Ambivalence of Bernard Mandeville* (Oxford: Clarendon Press).

Montagna, Paul D. (1977), *Occupations and Society: Toward a Sociology of the Labor Market* (New York: Wiley).

Moreau, R. (1984), *The Computer Comes of Age: the People, the Hardware and the Software* (Cambridge MA: MIT Press).

Morrison, Philip and Emily (eds) (1961), *Charles Babbage and His Calculating Engines* (New York: Dover Publications).

Mossner, Ernest Campbell, and Ross, Ian Simpson (eds) (1987), *The Correspondence of Adam Smith* (Oxford: Clarendon Press).

Nihon tokei neukan (1986), *Japan Statistical Yearbook* (Tokyo: Sorifu, Tokeikyoku).

Noble, David F. (1984), *Forces of Production: a Social History of Industrial Automation* (New York: Alfred A. Knopf).

Peitchinis, Stephen G. (1983), *Computer Technology and Employment: Retrospect and Prospect* (London: Macmillan).

Rae, John (1895), *Life of Adam Smith* (New York: Augustus M. Kelley).

Rainer Born (1987), *Artificial Intelligence: the Case Against* (London: Croom Helm).

Reddy, William M. (1984), *The Rise of Market Culture: The Textile Trade and French Culture, 1750–1900* (Cambridge: Cambridge University Press).

Reid, T. R. (1984), *The Chip: How Two Americans Invented the Microchip and Launched a Revolution* (New York: Simon & Schuster).

Ricardo, David (1962), *The Works and Correspondence of David Ricardo*, ed. P. Sraffa (Cambridge: Cambridge University Press).

Roll, Eric (1974), *A History of Economic Thought* (Homewood IL: Richard D. Irwin).

Sabel, Charles F. (1982), *Work and Politics: the division of labour in industry* (Cambridge: Cambridge University Press).

Schultz, Theodore W. (1971), *Investment in Human Capital: the Role of Education and Research* (New York: Free Press).

Schumpeter, Joseph A. (1942), *Capitalism, Socialism and Democracy* (New York: Harper & Row).

Schumpeter, Joseph A. (1954), *History of Economic Analysis* (New York: Oxford University Press).

Schumpeter, Joseph A. (1965), *Ten Great Economists from Marx to Keynes* (New York: Oxford University Press).

Scott, W. R. (1937), *Adam Smith As Student and Professor* (Glasgow: Jackson).

Searle, John R. (1983), *Intentionality: an Essay in the Philosophy of Mind* (Cambridge: Cambridge University Press).

Searle, John (1984), *Minds, Brains and Science* (Cambridge MA: Harvard University Press).

Shannon, Claude E. (1938), 'A Symbolic Analysis of Relay and Switching Circuits', *AIEE Transactions*, vol. 57, pp. 713–22.

Sharpe, William F. (1969), *The Economics of Computers* (Santa Monica CA: RAND Corporation).

Sheets, Robert G., Nord, Stephen, and Phelps, John J. (1987), *The Impact of Service Industries on Underemployment in Metropolitan Areas* (Lexington MA: D. C. Heath).

Singer, Charles, *et al.* (eds) (1958), *A History of Technology* (Oxford: Clarendon Press).

Smith, Adam (1759; reprinted 1853), *The Theory of Moral Sentiments* (Indianapolis: Liberty Press).

Smith, Adam (1776; reprinted 1976), *An Inquiry into the Nature and Causes of the Wealth of Nations* (Chicago: University of Chicago Press).

Smith, Adam (1778), 'Thoughts on the State of the Contest With America', *American Historical Review*, vol. 38, no. 4, July 1933.

Smith, Adam (1880), *Essays Philosophical and Literary by Adam Smith* (London: Ward, Lock).

Stein, Dorothy (1985), *Ada: a Life and a Legacy* (Cambridge MA: MIT Press).

Stieber, Jack (ed) (1966), *Employment Problems of Automation and Advanced Technology: an International Perspective* (New York: St Martin's Press).

Struminger, Laura (1979), *Women and the Making of the Working Class: Lyon 1830–1870* (St Albans VT: Eden Press Women's Publications).

Swainson, W. P. (1939), 'Theophrastus Paracelsus', in *Three Famous Alchemists* (London: Rider).

Thorndike, Lynn (1958), *A History of Magic and Experimental Science*, Vols 7 and 8: *The Seventeenth Century* (New York: Columbia University Press).

Thurow, Lester C. (1987), 'A surge in inequality', *Scientific American*, vol. 256, no. 5, May 1987.

Turing, Sarah Stoner (1959), *Alan M. Turing* (Cambridge: Heffer).

US Congress, Office of Technology Assessment (1983), *Automation and the Workplace: Selected Labor, Education and Training Issues* (Washington DC: US Government Printing Office).

US Congress, Office of Technology Assessment (1985), *Information Technology R & D: Critical Trends and Issues* (Washington DC: US Government Printing Office).

US Congress, Office of Technology Assessment (1988), *Technology and the American Economic Transition: Choices for the Future* (Washington DC: US Government Printing Office).

US National Science Board, National Science Foundation (1982), *Today's Problems, Tomorrow's Crises: a Report of the National Science Board Commission on Precollege Education in Mathematics, Science and Technology*.

Walbank, F. W. (1980), *The Hellenistic World* (Atlantic Highlands NJ: Humanities Press).

Warner, Malcolm (ed.) (1984), *Microprocessors, Manpower and Society* (New York: St Martin's Press).

Weber, Max (1958), *The Protestant Ethic and the Spirit of Capitalism* (New York: Charles Scribner).

Weber, Max (1978), *Economy and Society* (Berkeley: University of California Press).

Williams, Michael R. (1985), *A History of Computing Technology* (Englewood Cliffs NJ: Prentice-Hall).

Wood, Robert E. (1986), *From Marshall Plan to Debt Crisis: Foreign Aid and Development Choices in the World Economy* (Berkeley: University of California Press).

Wykstra, Roland A. (1971), *Human Capital and Manpower Development* (New York: Free Press).

Zimbalist, Andrew (ed.) (1979), *Case Studies on the Labor Process* (New York: Monthly Review Press).

Index

Index

Index

Index

denies connection between mechanization and
   workers' misery 34–5
dinner parties 30, 34, 38, 164
discovers paradox re profitability of machinery
   33
divides humanity into classes 32, 36
doctrine of value 32–3, 35
family background 30–1
London house 30
makes fortune 31
marriage and renunciation of Judaism 31
Principles of Political Economy and Taxation 31,
   32, 35
purchases Parliamentary seat 30
revises opinion on relation between machinery
   and unemployment 35–7, 38
sudden death 37
Russell, Bertrand 65
Rousseau, Jean Jacques 13
Royal Astronomical Society 38
Royal Society 42, 47, 50

St Anselm 73
St Thomas Aquinas 177
Science
   dynamic of scientific discovery 192–3, 194
   viability adjudicated by consensus 193–4
Searle, John 124
   'Chinese room thought experiment' 127–8, 130,
      131
   point of contention with AI proponents 125,
      127–8, 131
Shannon, Claude: relates Boolean algebra to
   circuitry 87–9
Shelley, Mary: *Frankenstein* 121
Slide rule 84, 85
Smith, Adam 27, 29, 32, 35, 37, 43, 47, 50, 103, 107,
   144, 152, 163, 192
   callousness re human misery 23
   compares systems of government to machines 22
   concept of importance of division of labour 18–
      21, 23–4, 51, 148, 150, 153
   confusion re innovation in industry 24–5
   continental tour as tutor 15
   Deism 13, 17, 177
   fails to condemn slavery 23
   French influence on 15
   ignores faults in proposed system 25
   influenced by Mandeville 13
   notions of *laissez-faire* 16
   reverence for machines 21–2
   Theory of Moral Sentiments, The 13, 21
   view of mechanization as ultimate division of
      labour 149
   view of morality of self-interested behaviour 14,
      16–18, 22, 167
   views on government role in public interest 23,
      24
   Wealth of Nations, The 15, 16, 18, 19, 21, 23, 27,
      31, 44, 45, 148, 168–9
Soviet Union
   computer development 109–10
   economic difficulties 114
   military competition with US 188–9
   perestroika 152

prevents E. European participation in Marshall
   Plan 172
Sperry company 108
SRI International: Prospector geological analysis
   system 135, 138, 139
Stalin, Joseph 172
Stanford University 135, 137

Taylor, Frederick Winslow 144–5
   disturbing nature of Taylorism 145–6
   formalization of labour 145
   time and motion study 145
   unpopular with US labour 145
Technological development 193, 194, 195
   viability adjudicated by markets 193, 194
TeKnowledge company 117
Thinking Machines Corporation 117
Townshend, Charles 14
   chooses Adam Smith as stepson's tutor 15
   inflames American colonists 15
   influenced by Adam Smith 14
Traveller naval battle simulation game 137
Truman, Pres. Harry S. 171
Turgot, Anne Robert 15
Turing Alan 124, 127, 131
   Second World War work on breaking German codes
      89–90
   theorem of computability 86–7
   Turing Machine 86, 92, 97, 98, 121, 123, 127
   Turing's Test of intelligent machine 122, 127

United States of America
   Bureau of Labor Statistics 166
   Bureau of the Census 80, 81, 82
   census requirement, nineteenth c. 80;
      development of tabulating machine 80–2
   computer development 79
   development of clerical tabulating machinery 82–
      3
   DoD Arpanet network 109
   drug problems 189
   economic torpor today 189, 191
   educational decline 189–90
   Geological Service 135
   GI Bill 171
   ineffectiveness of aid to third world 173–4, 180
   loses economic battle with Japan 189
   military backing for computers, *see* Computers,
      post Second World War advances
   military competition with Soviet Union 188–9
   move from the land, 1800–1970 164
   problem of military control of R&D funding 195
   rise of computer companies 108–9, 110, 117
   SAGE air defense system 113
   Strategic Computing Program 116
   Strategic Defense Initiative 103, 112–13, 116
   success of Marshall Plan 171, 180
UNIVAC computer 91

Vaucanson, Jacques 58
Voltaire 15, 16
Von Neumann, John 90, 91
   computers associated with name of 91–3, 98, 103–4

Weber, Max 146

212

Index